Lectionary Worship Aids

Series VI, Cycle A

H. Burnham Kirkland

CSS Publishing Company, Inc., Lima, Ohio

LECTIONARY WORSHIP AIDS, SERIES VI, CYCLE A

Copyright © 2001 by
CSS Publishing Company, Inc.
Lima, Ohio

Some scripture quotations are from the *New Revised Standard Version of the Bible*, copyright 1989 by the Division of Christian Education of the National Council of the Churches of Christ in the USA. Used by permission.

Some scripture quotations are from the *Revised Standard Version of the Bible*, copyrighted 1946, 1952 ©, 1971, 1973, by the Division of Christian Education of the National Council of the Churches of Christ in the USA. Used by permission.

Some scripture quotations are from the *King James Version of the Bible*, in the public domain.

Library of Congress Cataloging-in-Publication Data

Kirkland, H. Burnham.
    Lectionary worship aids. Series VI. Cycle A / H. Burnham Kirkland.
        p.   cm.
    ISBN 0-7880-1814-0 (alk. paper)
    1. Worship programs. 2. Common lectionary (1992) I. Title.
BV198 .K57 2001
264—dc21   2001025081
                                                                             CIP

For more information about CSS Publishing Company resources, visit our website at www.csspub.com.

ISBN 0-7880-1814-0   PRINTED IN U.S.A.

To
Bishop James K. Mathews,
Friend and Former Colleague,
who has touched the lives of
countless pastors and congregations
by his leadership, example, and
devotion to our Lord, Jesus Christ,
I dedicate this volume.

H.B.K.

Table Of Contents

Foreword

Preparing to lead a congregation in worship Sunday after Sunday is an awesome responsibility. Since my last retirement I have found myself sitting in the congregation and have had an opportunity to observe many attempts to make worship more meaningful.

Experimentation can be helpful and sometimes leads to unusual worship opportunities that enable the congregation to be caught up in a great spiritual experience. Often, however, in my observation it leads to a disjointed worship service in which the congregation fails to be given an opportunity to experience all the elements of Praise, Confession, Thanksgiving, Prayer, Sacrifice, Proclamation and Responding to the Word, and Sending Forth. Something should happen in all our worship services that will send our people out more humble, more conscious of their own sin and unworthiness, more prayerful or more dedicated, more conscious of others. Something should happen!

It is my hope that these Worship Aids will be of help in your task of preparation. They are based on the Revised Common Lectionary — Cycle A. For each Sunday you will find the three suggested Scripture Lessons, a Theme, Call To Worship, Invocation (which may also be used as a Morning Collect), a Prayer of Confession, an Offertory Prayer, and suggested Hymns. After the Third Lesson you will find the Psalter for the day, Words of Assurance to be used after Prayers of Confession, a Pastoral Prayer, and Benediction or Sending Forth.

The hymns are all taken from the *United Methodist Hymnal*, 1989 edition, as are the suggested Psalter or Responsive Readings.

I have not attempted to colloquialize the language, but for the most part have used a traditional format and language that has stood the test of time.

Now it is in your hands. I humbly trust and pray that it will serve you, as with the help of the Holy Spirit you prepare and lead your people in what will, I hope, be for them the highest spiritual moment of the week.

H.B.K.

First Sunday Of Advent

First Lesson: Isaiah 2:1-5
Theme: Walk In The Light

Call To Worship

Today, as we begin our symbolic journey on the Advent Road, let us prepare for Christmas not as a day or a season, but as a condition of our hearts and minds; let us prepare not to *spend* Christmas, but to *keep* it; let us prepare to experience in the Christmas event the fullness of God's revelation of our life's meaning and purpose.

Invocation

O God, who did prepare of old the minds and hearts of people for the coming of your Son, and whose Spirit ever works to illumine our darkened lives with the light of the gospel: prepare now our minds and hearts that Christ may dwell in us, and ever reign in our thoughts and affections as the King of Love, and the very Prince of Peace. Amen.

Confession

Eternal God, we your Church, who should be instruments of your victory, confess that we have often put barriers in your way. Where we should be a light to the world, we participate in the sin around us. Forgive us, we pray, and free us to be a people prepared for your coming, through Jesus Christ our Lord. Amen.

Offertory Prayer

O Lord, as we offer to you our gifts in the spirit of joy, we also dedicate our lives so that we might be for you a light unto the world, in the name of Christ our Lord. Amen.

Hymns

"Come, Thou Long Expected Jesus"
"Christ Is The World's Light"
"Shalom To You"

First Sunday Of Advent

Second Lesson: Romans 13:11-14
Theme: Time To Wake Up

Call To Worship

Leader: Awake, awake put on your strength, O arm of the Lord.

People: Awake, as in days of old, the generations of long ago!

Leader: How beautiful upon the mountains are the feet of the messenger who announces peace,

People: who brings good news, who says to Zion, "Your God reigns."

Invocation

Great God of Power; we praise you for Jesus Christ who came as a light to this dark world to save us from our sins. We thank you for the prophets' hope, the angels' song, for the birth in Bethlehem. We thank you that in Jesus you joined us, sharing human hurts and pleasures. Glory to you for your wonderful love. Glory to you, eternal God; through Jesus Christ, Lord of lords, and King of kings, forever. Amen.

Confession

Understanding Father, we know your wish for us is that we keep the commandment to love our neighbor as ourselves. We humbly confess that too often we grow weary in well-doing, and so this morning we come with penitent hearts asking your forgiveness. Strengthen our resolve, O Lord, that we may lay aside the works of darkness, and put on the armor of light. We pray in Jesus' name. Amen.

Offertory Prayer

Receive these gifts, Almighty God, as evidences of our faith, as expressions of our love, as symbols of our thankfulness, and as proof of our commitment. Amen.

Hymns

"Wake, Awake For Night Is Flying"
"I Want To Walk As A Child Of The Light"

First Sunday Of Advent

Gospel Lesson: Matthew 24:36-44
Theme: Be Ready — The Son Of Man Is Coming

Call To Worship

Leader: Come, let us worship and bow down before the Christ who was, and is, and is to come,

People: for he is the Savior of the world, and the hope of the ages.

Invocation

Lord God, we come with our thirst to this oasis of living water. We come with our guilt to a forgiven and forgiving community. We come with hearts full of joy to this hour of celebration and love. Be with us in our worship, and enfold all that we are in the everlasting arms which reach out to us eternally; through Jesus Christ our Lord. Amen.

Confession

Lord, today we begin a season of preparation. We want to make ready our hearts for your coming. We must confess, however, that we are so intent on celebrating your advent so long ago, and speculating on when you will return, that we forget you are ready to come to us now. Forgive our blindness, awaken us to your presence, and come into our hearts now, Lord Jesus. Amen.

Offertory Prayer

Our Father, during this season in which we celebrate the love of God as expressed in the gift of your Son, it is fitting that we also express our love in a tangible way. Receive these gifts as our expression of that love. Amen.

Hymns

"O Come, O Come, Emmanuel"
"Lift Up Your Heads"

11

First Sunday Of Advent

Psalter: Psalm 25:1-10

Words Of Assurance

In this find strength: that God not only forgives the past, but gives a new vision for the future, and inspires a new commitment for the present.

Pastoral Prayer

O God of earth and altar, with whom the morning stars sang together to herald your first creation, this is the season of joy, but our ideals are crying still for our world to be made new. Your earliest voice declared, "Let there be light," but we have stood in its way and by our own willfulness have created shadows that enlarge the dark. Our days are clouded over by the threat of war, the decline of true religion, and the loss of clear meaning to life. So few give heed any longer to your call to us to be just and kind, and live in quiet fellowship with our God. In the words of the Psalmist then we pray: "Turn us again, O God of hosts, and cause your face to shine and we shall be saved."

We thank you, our Father, in this festive season, that in the midst of the ages you commanded light to shine into our darkness which brought to us knowledge of your divine being in the face of Jesus Christ. We bless you that that light increased in and through him, and down the countless years ever since he has brought release and pardon from sin through his unfailing grace; healing to all our hurts through the touch of his tender love; and the hope and promise of a new age of goodwill and fraternity for the whole inhabited earth.

Lord, we praise you for all these gracious benefits bestowed upon our common life, and we plead for help to prepare a wide room within us for the Child of Bethlehem, so that he may exercise his rule forever in our minds and hearts. Christmas is a time for deeper prayer and more costly devotion; challenge our wills to cast off the easy ornaments of sentimentality and make this time truly a celebration of the coming of eternal light to shatter the darkness and bring new life to all.

May he who came first as a little child, come now as more than a child — the Savior, victor over sin and death, the redeemer of the world, and the Prince of Peace. Come to each of us in some unexpected insight, some invasion of unlooked-for power, and work your transforming miracle in our hearts — faith for fear, courage for cowardice, strength for weakness, victory for defeat. Increase our confidence in you, burnish again our ideals that the fingers of the world have tarnished, give us brave hearts, and send us, who came here with plumes shorn and armor dented, into the world again rearmed with faith and strength for tomorrow's battles. We pray in the spirit of Christ. Amen.

Benediction
Go in peace, for the one who came to earth to rescue you will lead you through all of life, until at last he brings you to the home not made with hands, eternal in the heavens; and the blessing of God the Father, Son, and Holy Spirit be with you always. Amen.

Second Sunday Of Advent

First Lesson: Isaiah 11:1-10
Theme: The Peaceful Kingdom

Call To Worship

As we prepare for the coming of the Christ Child let us also prepare our hearts and minds for the coming of "The Peaceful Kingdom." The prophet Isaiah said: "The wolf shall live with the lamb ... the calf and the lion together, and a little child shall lead them." Come, let us praise God for the coming of *that* Child!

Invocation

Come, Christ Jesus, be our guest, and may our lives by you be blest! Come, God-with-us, and free us from false claims of the empires of this world. We are lonely for you and your peace. Come, Emmanuel, and dwell with us. Make us your people indeed, the people through whom you bring love and justice to the world. Amen.

Confession

O Lord, our God, we pray for the coming of your Peaceful Kingdom here on earth, but we bow before you this day with penitent hearts because we have been more a part of the problem than an instrument of your peace. We have not loved you as we ought, nor have we loved our neighbors as ourselves. Forgive us, we pray, and empower us to work for that Peaceful Kingdom, we pray in the name of the Prince of Peace, even Jesus Christ our Lord. Amen.

Offertory Prayer

O God, during this season in which we celebrate your love as expressed in the gift of your Son, it is with great joy and thanksgiving that we present our offerings to you that they may be used to bring word of your love to those who still live in darkness. By the power of your Holy Spirit may they be instrumental in bringing the Peaceful Kingdom a little closer. Amen.

Hymns

"O Come, O Come, Emmanuel"
"O Day Of Peace That Dimly Shines"

Second Sunday Of Advent

Second Lesson: Romans 15:4-13
Theme: The God Of Hope

Call To Worship

Leader: Let us prepare for the coming of the Lord.
People: We would be expectant, believing his promise.
Leader: Let us be diligent, faithful until the end.
People: We will be happy, celebrating his blessings.

Invocation

O God, who has set before us the great hope that your kingdom shall come on earth, and has taught us to pray for its coming, make us ever ready to thank you for the signs of its dawning, and to pray and work for that perfect day when your will shall be done on earth as it is in heaven; through Jesus Christ our Lord. Amen.

Confession

O God, we give you thanks for the gift of love which you have bestowed upon us with the coming of your Son, Jesus Christ, whose birth we are preparing to celebrate. We know that nothing can separate us from your love, for your love is stronger than all the forces of evil. Forgive us, therefore, when we doubt the power of your love, and trust instead in the power of might, the weapons of war and destruction. Strengthen our convictions and make us instruments of your peace. Amen.

Offertory Prayer

As those who watch and wait for the unfolding of God's promise of justice and integrity, we feel privilege and awe in offering our gifts and ourselves this day. Bless these gifts and those who share them; bless their use near and far, in the name of Jesus the Christ. Amen.

Hymns

"Hail To The Lord's Anointed One"
"Hope Of The World"

Second Sunday Of Advent

Gospel Lesson: Matthew 3:1-12
Theme: Prepare The Way Of The Lord

Call To Worship

Leader: A voice cries out: "Prepare in the wilderness a road for the Lord."

People: As we worship we will do so with reverent quietness.

Leader: Let us leave behind the rush of the season, and the strident voices of our commercial world.

People: Then we will hear the voice of the prophet and prepare the way of the Lord.

Invocation

O living Christ, in this season of lights, may we look to the Light of the World. In this season of music, may we hear the message of the angels. In this season of gift-giving, may we acknowledge the greatest gift of all. In this season of merriment, may we experience the joy of Jesus Christ. Amen.

Confession

Dear Lord, we confess that like the Pharisees of old we have often refused to believe that Jesus came for the salvation of all people, and to proclaim your love for everyone — rich and poor alike. Forgive us, we pray, for those times when we have failed to love everyone we meet, and teach us to refuse to accept the barriers our ancestors placed between people, or even those our society insists on erecting from time to time. Amen.

Offertory Prayer

We lift before you, O God, not these gifts alone, but all that we have and are. Use our gifts to multiply the effects of your work in the world. Use us to spread joy and love and peace and hope. We pray in Jesus' name. Amen.

Hymns

"Christ For The World We Sing"
"Fairest Lord Jesus"

Second Sunday Of Advent

Psalter: Psalm 24

Words Of Assurance
The Lord looks upon you with love, remembering your iniquities
no more, and filling your life with all good things.

Pastoral Prayer
"Angels announce with shouts of mirth,
Him who brings new life to earth.
Set every peak and valley humming
with the word, the Lord is coming."

It is our prayer, O Lord, that your divine presence may not be
obscured during the busyness and beauty of this season. Among the
lights of Christmas, may we see the Light of the World. Among the
jingles of Christmas, may we hear the songs of angels. Among the
gifts of Christmas, may we receive the greatest gift. Among the confusion of Christmas, may we feel the peace of God. Among the tinsel
of Christmas, may we see the beauty of holiness. Among the crowds
of Christmas, may we see the face of Jesus.

During this Advent season let us behold the full glory and wonder
of your love shining forth from the face of a babe nestled in the bosom
of his mother, Mary, and guarded by the faithful Joseph. They were
even more important to your plan than the shepherds and the Wise
Men. Thank you for the beautiful picture of family love and devotion
that this holy family still inspires. As we focus our family activities on
the celebration of Jesus' birth, help us to find serenity in the midst of
rushing, new surrender to the Christ even as we engage in Christmas
traditions. Free us to sing with our friends hopeful songs of peace and
good will, to dance with joyful delight, and to savor the freshness and
warmth of new intimacy and life because Jesus Christ, the Lord of
Life, is born again in us. Let us love you so much that we shall no
longer have room for irrational fears and impulses that lead us astray
and set us against one another. Let us not wallow in self-pity or wist-
ful sadness when memories of former days and departed loved ones
rush in upon us. Release us to reach out in love to those who need our

17

friendship, and to bring cheer to someone whose heart will be empty without the warmth of our thoughtful words and gifts. May nothing ever separate us from your Son, whose birth we shall soon celebrate. We pray all this in the name of your holy child, Jesus of Nazareth. Amen.

Benediction

As the followers of Christ, go forth now to become the instruments of his peace, the embodiment of his concern, the voices of his comfort, and the hands of his caring; and God the Father, Son, and Holy Spirit go with you. Amen.

Third Sunday Of Advent

First Lesson: Isaiah 35:1-10
Theme: The Pageant Of The Lord's Coming

Call To Worship

Leader: Behold! The pageant of our Lord's coming is unfolding beyond our expectations.

People: Desert places spring with water, the blind are gifted with sight.

Leader: Behold! The Lord comes and makes all things new.

People: The weak become strong, the silent now begin to speak.

Leader: Give praise to the Lord, people.

People: We give praise to the holy child of Bethlehem!

Invocation

Heavenly Father, on this third Sunday of the beautiful Advent season, we come anticipating a fresh experience of the presence of Jesus Christ among us. Open our eyes to behold his beauty; open our ears to hear his words; open our hearts to receive his presence; and open our hands to share his compassion. Amen.

Confession

Almighty God, you have called us to walk the King's Highway — the Holy Way, but we confess that far too often we have preferred to go our own way. Instead of joy and gladness we have found sorrow and sighing. By the power of your Holy Spirit, Lord, forgive our foolish ways, our false choices, and set our feet on the Way which will lead us into your eternal presence. Amen.

Offertory Prayer

O Lord, enable us, by these gifts, to spread the spirit of the loving Christ around the world, bringing sight to the blind, liberty to the oppressed, food to the starving, and hope to the poor. Amen.

Hymns

"O Come, O Come, Emmanuel"
"Lo, How A Rose E'er Blooming"
"O Day Of God, Draw Nigh"

Third Sunday Of Advent

Second Lesson: James 5:7-10
Theme: Patience In Suffering

Call To Worship

Leader: I waited patiently for the Lord; he inclined to me and heard my cry.

People: He put a new song in my mouth, a song of praise to our God.

Leader: Happy are those who make the Lord their trust.

People: I will commit my way to the Lord; and wait patiently for him.

Invocation

O Lord our God, most merciful and mighty: Fill our hearts with joy and our tongues with praise as we prepare to celebrate the festival of our Savior's birth. Let the Holy Spirit come upon us as we approach the mystery of his appearing in the flesh as a little child. Stir up in our hearts the precious gift of faith, that he may be born anew in us, and that his presence may shed abroad in our hearts the light of heavenly joy and peace. We pray in Jesus' name. Amen.

Confession

O Lord, as we come into your special presence, we bring with us the burdens of the past week. Many of us have deep concerns about our families, our health, and our material welfare. All of us come with the blight of sins which have been committed and with goals which have not been met.

Forgive our faults, we pray; give us strength to cope with our troubles and help us to dispel our needless worries, thus freeing us to worship and prepare ourselves for the challenges of the week ahead. Amen.

Offertory Prayer

O Lord, in the spirit of joy we offer to you our gifts. May they be used to bring to all the world the good news of your gracious love, manifested by the birth at Bethlehem. We also dedicate our lives so

20

that we might be for you a light unto the world, in the name of Christ our Lord, Amen.

Hymns
"It Came Upon The Midnight Clear"
"Come, Thou Long Expected Jesus"
"Give To The Winds Thy Fears"

Third Sunday Of Advent

Gospel Lesson: Matthew 11:2-11
Theme: Prepare The Way

Call To Worship

Leader: To those wandering in darkness,
People: Christ came as the Light of the World.
Leader: To those who are at odds with others and themselves,
People: Christ is the Prince of Peace.
Leader: To those who seek the presence of the divine,
People: Christ is Emmanuel, God with us.
All: Come, let us anticipate the advent of our Lord.

Invocation

Most Merciful God, who so loved the world as to give your only Son, so that everyone who believes in him may not perish but may have eternal life; grant unto us, we humbly pray, the precious gift of faith, whereby we may have power to overcome the world, and gain a blessed immortality; through Jesus Christ our Lord. Amen.

Confession

Almighty God, we who are aware of your power made known to us in the Babe of Bethlehem, realize that we ought to prepare the way for your coming into the lives of others. You have given us the task of witnessing to the hope for renewal that you hold out to all, but we confess that we have not always taken up our responsibility. Forgive us for our shortcomings, Lord, and encourage us as we try to proclaim the good news that Christ came into the world that everyone might have life, and have it abundantly. In Jesus' name we pray. Amen.

Offertory Prayer

Lord, through our offerings we commit ourselves anew to your ministry of healing and hope, both here in this place, and throughout the world. Accept these gifts with our prayers and with our concern. Amen.

Hymns

"What Child Is This?"
"Lift Up Your Heads"

Third Sunday Of Advent

Psalter: Psalm 40:1-11

Words Of Assurance

It will be said on that day, "Lo, this is our God, we have waited for him that he might save us. This is the Lord; we have waited for him; let us be glad and rejoice in his salvation."

Pastoral Prayer

Almighty God, our Heavenly Father, truly we want to walk as children of light — we want to follow Jesus. But sometimes our valleys seem so deep and dark that we despair of crawling out of them. We sometimes see the mountains as insurmountable obstacles rather than as vantage points of exhilarating beauty.

The rough places that we complain about are often of our own making. The deserts are hot and dry because we have failed to refresh ourselves at the springs of your Spirit.

Forgive, Lord, our wanderings and complainings as we welcome the liberating advent of Jesus into our lives.

God of surprise and goodness: in the commonplace, in a human child born in an animal shelter, your communication with us took on flesh and bone, lived itself out in our human history, so that we might have forever knowledge of your own self, and of your will and destiny for our human life. For the mystery and miracle of Christ's Advent, we rejoice and we thank you.

As the Christ was born of a human and was cradled in the rudeness of an animal shelter, grant again, we pray, the unexpected. May the Lord, who is the Spirit, be cradled within our hearts to be the wellspring of our inner beings. Be born, be born within us today so that we may be reborn.

O dayspring from on high, be the gift of a holy presence to strengthen the hearts of those for whom this season will not know its wished-for joy: the unemployed, and those who have no one with whom to share joy — the sick and those who must walk the valley of the shadow; those who experience fracture in their families. Come, Holy Child, and let your presence suffuse their lives with heavenly radiance.

We pray, too, that the Spirit of Jesus Christ will have a transforming impact on our society and our world — not only during the few weeks of the Christmas season, but throughout the year.

We lift these prayers in the name and in the Spirit of our Lord and Savior Jesus Christ. Amen.

Benediction

May the spirit of the season be that of the Holy Spirit; and may the peace of this season be that of the Prince of Peace. In the name of the Father and of the Son and of the Holy Spirit. Amen.

Fourth Sunday Of Advent

First Lesson: Isaiah 7:10-16
Theme: Immanuel

Call To Worship

It is an awesome thing to stand in the presence of God, to stand with feet on holy ground, to lift our hearts and voices in worship, to open our bodies and minds to divine healing, and to receive in our souls the truth of the ages. Come, let us worship together!

Invocation

O God, our Father, who has brought us again to the glad season when we commemorate the birth of your Son, Jesus Christ our Lord; grant that his Spirit may be born anew in our hearts this day and that we may joyfully welcome him to reign over us. Thus may we claim your promise of Immanuel — God with us. Amen.

Confession

Eternal God, we confess that in spite of all appearances to the contrary, we are unprepared for your coming. We have been carefully choosing gifts and wrapping them, planning our holiday trips, and preparing for the arrival of guests. Yet we have left the preparations for your arrival to chance. Help us now, even at this late hour, to open our minds and hearts to your Word that we may receive it afresh. So help us to be ready at your coming to welcome you with open hearts and expectant lives. We pray in Jesus' name. Amen.

Offertory Prayer

O God, you have given us the greatest gift of all in your Son, Jesus Christ. We can say, "Thank you, Lord," with our mouths, and it is right for us to do so. Yet we realize that those words can be said so easily that they may be meaningless. Therefore, we now give that phrase new emphasis by saying, "Thank you, Lord," with our gifts. Amen.

Hymns

"Come, Thou Long Expected Jesus"
"O Come, O Come, Emmanuel"
"Angels We Have Heard On High"

Fourth Sunday Of Advent

Second Lesson: Romans 1:1-7
Theme: Called To Belong To Jesus Christ — Son Of God

Call To Worship

Leader: Glory to God in the highest; and on earth peace, good will toward men.

People: For God so loved the world that he gave his only Son, that whoever believes in him should not perish but have eternal life.

Invocation

O God of love beyond telling, you gave your only begotten Son for the salvation of the world. As the Son was born for us, so may we be reborn for others. As the Son's life was poured out for the life of the world, so may we be spent in his service. As the Son was born the Prince of Peace, so may we be ambassadors for peace. May the Christ Child be imaged in our actions as we give ourselves in service to others.

All this we pray in the name of the one whose coming filled the heavens with glory to you in the highest. Amen.

Confession

Grant pardon, O God, if in our buying of gifts, we have forgotten The Gift; if in our enjoyment of brightly colored lights, we have closed our eyes to The Light; if in our singing of carols, we do not have a song in our hearts; if in our gatherings with friends, we neglect The Friend of All. Help us, O Lord, to know the true meaning of this season, and enable us to experience its joy fully. Amen.

Offertory Prayer

Our Father, since you have revealed the mystery of your saving love through Jesus Christ, make it possible, through our gifts, to reveal his marvelous mystery to those who have not heard or have not understood. Amen.

Hymns

"Angels From The Realms Of Glory"
"Hark! The Herald Angels Sing"
"The First Noel"

Fourth Sunday Of Advent

Gospel Lesson: Matthew 1:18-25
Theme: The Birth Of Jesus

Call To Worship

Leader: I have good news for you. Your Savior has been born —
Christ the Lord!

People: Glory to God in the highest, and peace to his people on earth.

Invocation

O God, our Father, while the world aches to hear your love-song, too often our songs of praise have been silent. Surprise us again, as you surprised the world at Bethlehem, with your way of turning things around. May we experience your grace and be ready for the coming of your Son, Jesus Christ our Lord. Amen.

Confession

Lord, with shame and sorrow we confess that we have not always made room for you in our lives. We have been so busy with family, friends, school, work, and play that we have not heard you knock. Help us this day to open wide the door that you may be born anew in each one of us. Let not the errors and offenses of the past cling to us, but pardon and set us free, that with purer purpose and a better hope we may renew our vows in your presence. We pray in Jesus' name. Amen.

Offertory Prayer

Almighty God, because you loved us so much that you gave your beloved Son, we respond in faith and trust. Because this love extends to all people who are in the world, we respond in generosity and hope. Bless these gifts we pray in Jesus' name. Amen.

Hymns

"O Come, All Ye Faithful"
"There's A Song In The Air"
"Infant Holy, Infant Lowly"

Fourth Sunday Of Advent

Psalter: Psalm 80:1-7, 17-19

Words Of Assurance

We celebrate the promise of the Christmas carol: "How silently, how silently, the wondrous gift is given! So God imparts to human hearts the blessings of his heaven. No ear may hear his coming, but in this world of sin, where meek souls will receive him still, the dear Christ enters in."

Pastoral Prayer

Dear God, "lowly in the manger laid," we are haunted that there was "no room in the inn" for Joseph, Mary, and Jesus the night Jesus was born. What an inhospitable world he entered! Might we have made it different had we been there?

We remind ourselves that we are all innkeepers of our hearts. We really want them to be inns where ultimate happiness is found. Instead, we are poor innkeepers who have allowed all sorts of guests to stay. We have given our best accommodations to the creators of sensate pleasure and feeling, those who abuse power and position, those who hide evil hearts under garments of elegance, those who cover their emptiness with sophisticated manners. Something is missing, for our hearts are not inns of ultimate happiness.

We need a baby in our midst, a baby fresh from the womb of your creation, a baby unblemished by selfishness, a baby freed to trust and love, a baby who excites hope in our weary hearts, and stirs recollections of childhood dreams and a lost innocence. Yet, where might we house such a baby?

Make room we must! Some old guests will have to go: the boastful who flaunt their power and position, the vendors of sensate pleasure who promise much and deliver little, those who lead us to compromise our ethical standards, who practice evil, and smell of death. We need your power to help us expel them all, for we truly want those guests who will bring us ultimate happiness. We know that not until we have cleansed the debris of bad thoughts and ill tempers from our hearts will we find a suitable place for the Christ Child.

And so we sing, "Cast out our sin and enter in: be born in us today." Then rejoicing will resound through the courts of heaven, for the Son of God will have found a suitable dwelling place. He will preside in our inn of ultimate happiness. Then we can say, "Christ is our life. Christ is our hope of glory."

All this we pray in the name of the Babe of Bethlehem, the Man of Galilee, the Prince of Peace, and the Savior of the World — even Jesus Christ our Lord. Amen.

Benediction
May the awe of Mary, the joy of the shepherds, and the wonder of the Wise Men be yours now and forevermore. The blessing of God the Father, the Son, and the Holy Spirit be upon you. Amen.

Christmas Eve/Day

First Lesson: Isaiah 9:2-7
Theme: The Coming King — Prince Of Peace

Call To Worship

Leader: Unto us a child is born, and unto us a son is given;
People: and the government shall be upon his shoulder;
Leader: his name shall be called Wonderful Counselor, Mighty God, Everlasting Father, Prince of Peace.
People: His authority shall grow continually, and there shall be endless peace.

Invocation

O Father, who declared your love to all humanity by the birth of this holy child at Bethlehem; help us to welcome him with gladness and to make room for him in our common days, so that we may live at peace with one another and in good will with all your family; through Jesus Christ our Lord. Amen.

Confession

O God, at Christmas we celebrate your presence, the promise that you are never far from us, and that you offer us peace. We must confess though that we have preferred platitudes to your peace, and in place of loving our neighbor we have practiced deceit and contempt. Forgive us, we pray, and teach us to live in such a way that Christmas will be a part of our lives every day of the year. Amen.

Offertory Prayer

O God, whose generosity has known no limits, and who has shared with us the gift of your Son, stir us by that act of love to in turn be generous and to share our gifts with others. Through Jesus Christ our Lord. Amen.

Hymns

"Hark! The Herald Angels Sing"
"Joy To The World"
"What Child Is This?"

Christmas Eve/Day

Second Lesson: Titus 2:11-14
Theme: Christ Our Hope And Redeemer

Call To Worship

Leader: Christ is born;
People: we give him glory!
Leader: Christ has come down from heaven;
People: we will receive him,
Leader: Christ is now on earth;
People: we will exalt him!

Invocation

Almighty God, by the birth of your holy child Jesus you gave us a great light to dawn on our darkness. Grant that in his light we may see light. Bestow upon us that most excellent Christmas gift of love to all people, so that the likeness of your Son may be formed in us, and that we may have the ever brightening hope of everlasting life; through Jesus Christ our Savior. Amen.

Confession

O God, you come to us while we are busy seeking other gods such as power, possessions, prestige, and you call us to return to you. Speak to us once more through the Babe of Bethlehem that we may see once again the errors of our ways. Overpower us with your love that we may be able to reflect that Light that came into the world at Christmas so long ago. Amen.

Offertory Prayer

Almighty God, Father of our Lord Jesus Christ, you have given everything to us in the incarnation of your Son. Receive these gifts as the signs of our gratitude for your love, and with them fulfill the purposes of your will. Amen.

Hymns

"Angels From The Realms Of Glory"
"Joy To The World"
"Go, Tell It On The Mountain"

Christmas Eve/Day

Gospel Lesson: Luke 2:1-14 (15-20)
Theme: The Birth Of Jesus

Call To Worship

Let our hearts be filled with joy and our voices with praise as we keep the festival of our Savior's birth. As we approach the mystery of the Holy Spirit born in history, may our hearts be stirred with the gift of faith. May Christ be born anew in us in joy, power, and peace.

Invocation

Almighty God, you have loved us as a father loves his children, and gathered us into your arms as a mother cradles her infant. We praise you for your coming among your people as a baby to live and grow in our care, and to care for us in your great love.

We give you thanks for Christmas and for the newness of life it contains. Especially we thank you for the gift of your Son whose birth we celebrate: for his life, for his death and resurrection, and in whom is our hope and our love. Amen.

Confession

Lord, on this day when we celebrate your coming into the world, the past seems so far away and the present so filled with problems. We know in our hearts that you are with us in our time of need, but we feel so alone that we don't listen to our hearts. Help us, Lord, to trust your promise, so that once again we may be aware of your holy presence within us, offering us the guidance we need in these troublesome times. Amen.

Offertory Prayer

O God, bless these gifts which we now offer that they may announce the good news of your love, heal those who are broken in body and spirit, and hasten the day of your justice and peace. In the name of the priceless gift of your Holy Child, we pray. Amen.

Hymns

"O Little Town Of Bethlehem"
"It Came Upon The Midnight Clear"
"Silent Night, Holy Night"

Christmas Eve/Day

Psalter: Psalm 96

Words Of Assurance

Fear not! For behold I bring you good tidings of great joy which shall be to all the people. For unto you is born this day, in the city of David, a Savior who is Christ the Lord.

Pastoral Prayer

Joy to the world! The Lord is come: let earth receive her king. We praise you and give thanks to you, O God, for the hope born into the world through Jesus Christ. Open our hearts to receive him, our ears to his promises, our arms to embrace the world for whom he was born, and our hands to do his work.

Joy to the world! The Savior reigns, let us our songs employ. O God, let our lives express the hope that Christ brings. Let our lips speak the love of Christ! Let our actions be devoted to peace on earth.

Joy to the world! Christ comes to make the blessings flow, as far as the curse is found. We pray, O God, for those who bear this day the sufferings of the world: for those who are wounded in spirit or broken in body; for those who grieve, and for those in lands torn apart by war; for those who are hungry, and for all who have lost all hope. Give to them, and to us, a renewed vision of your loving presence. Empower us with a willingness to serve others as Christ served.

Joy to the world! The Lord is come! Let these our prayers be joined with the praises of all heaven and earth, giving thanks this day for the wonders of your love ... the wonders of your love. In the name of Christ. Amen.

Benediction

May the awe of Mary, the joy of the shepherds, and the wonder of the Wise Men be with you now and forevermore, world without end. Amen.

First Sunday After Christmas/Holy Family

First Lesson: Isaiah 63:7-9
Theme: God's Saving Acts In History

Call To Worship

Leader: Make a joyful noise to the Lord, all you people.
People: We will worship the Lord with gladness.
Leader: Know that the Lord is God, it is he that made us, and we are his.
People: We are his people, and we belong to him.
Leader: The Lord is good; his steadfast love endures forever,
People: his faithfulness to all generations.

Invocation

It is fitting, O God of the ages, that as the year fades into history, we should come into your special presence. You have brought us through joys and sorrows, laughter and tears, prosperity and poverty, health and sickness. Through it all you are still our God and we are still your people. Consecrate this hour as one of special thanks for the past and one of heartfelt commitment for the future. Amen.

Confession

We confess, Lord, that we come this day with mixed feelings. The busyness and stress of the season are over, and in a way we are relieved. Yet some of us feel let down, even empty and depressed. Lord, as we come together in your house, bathe us in the glow of your abiding love, and encourage us by your continuing presence. We pray in Jesus' name. Amen.

Offertory Prayer

Receive our gifts, Lord, not only for what they are in themselves, but also as examples to our families concerning our priorities and values. Amen.

Hymns

"Love Came Down At Christmas"
"There's A Song In The Air"
"O God, Our Help In Ages Past"

First Sunday After Christmas/Holy Family

Second Lesson: Hebrews 2:10-18
Theme: Christ — One With Us

Call To Worship

This is the first Sunday after Christmas, and the last Sunday of the year. It is a time for thanksgiving, good cheer, and generosity. And why not? Christ has come to share our lives as one of us, to assure us that God is with us! Therefore, let our worship this day be one of joy and praise!

Invocation

Father, we are grateful for your Christmas gift of our Blessed Savior, for ... it is through his church that your Fatherly love is proclaimed; it is through his family that your lesson of love is taught; it is through his brothers and sisters that your gift of love is made present.

Father, may we be forever grateful for your Christmas gift of our Blessed Savior. Amen.

Confession

O God, our Father, we confess that in this holy season we have spent so much time adoring the Baby Jesus, that we sometimes act as though he always remained an infant, cradled in a manger. Remind us again, Lord, that Jesus came to walk among us, to share our human lives, to be our brother. Have mercy upon us and turn us from our foolish ways that we may truly be your disciples. Amen.

Offertory Prayer

O God, through our gifts may the foundation of Christ's Church be strengthened; through our gifts may the hope of Christ's people be brightened; through our gifts may the love of Christ's family be deepened. Amen.

Hymns

"There's A Song In The Air"
"Majesty, Worship His Majesty"
"Love Divine, All Loves Excelling"

First Sunday After Christmas/Holy Family

Gospel Lesson: Matthew 2:13-23
Theme: Holy Family

Call To Worship

To Mary and Joseph was entrusted the awesome responsibility of caring for the infant Jesus whose very life was threatened by a jealous king.

To each one of us is committed the incredible responsibility of sharing the love of God made known to us through Jesus Christ our Lord.

Let us worship the God who sent his Son for the world's redemption.

Invocation

Lord, we thank you for the Holy Family that cared for the infant Jesus in those turbulent days surrounding his birth, and who nurtured him into manhood so that he might fulfill your destiny for him. May this time of worship be a time for us to strengthen our commitment to family life, that we might do our part to show forth your love and concern for every member of our families. Amen.

Confession

Lord, forgive us when we expect life to be all smooth sailing, without rough seas to battle or storms to threaten. Remind us again of the difficulties Mary and Joseph confronted as they cared for the infant Jesus. Strengthen us for the living of these days with the assurance that Christ walks with us no matter what the future holds. Amen.

Offertory Prayer

O God, receive these gifts — these offerings which not only advance the cause of Christ, but leave a pattern for our families, a pattern of devotion and sacrifice. Amen.

Hymns

"Joyful, Joyful, We Adore Thee"
"For The Beauty Of The Earth"
"If Thou But Suffer God To Guide Thee"

First Sunday After Christmas/Holy Family

Psalter: Psalm 8

Words Of Assurance

We can ask God for the healing of our families because we are part of his family. "When we cry, 'Abba! Father!' it is the Spirit bearing witness with our spirit that we are children of God, and if children, then heirs of God and fellow heirs with Christ."

Pastoral Prayer

O Lord, our God, you have made plain your love to us by sending your Son into the world that we might live through him. Give to us, we pray, the precious gift of faith, that we might rejoice in his coming. May the song of the heavenly host be our song too: "Glory to God in the highest, and on earth peace, good will to all people."

O God of patience, slow us down. Pray us out of the rush of presents to be returned, out of the whirlwind of noisy gatherings. The world waited so long for your coming. Slow us down, Lord, so we may discover you.

O God of gentle presence, quiet us. Pray us out of electric carols on department store intercoms, out of ho-ho-ho's and bell-ringing Santas. How silently your gift was given. Quiet us, Lord, so we may hear the hush of a new mother's sleep.

O God of vigilance, awaken us. Pray us out of the routines that fatten our lives, out of the assumptions that dull our minds. Your new creation is so vulnerable. Awaken us, Lord, so we may hear the whispers in our dreams and spy the dangerous Herods in our midst.

Help us, Father, to become the kind of people who create homes which are loving, peaceful, and godly. May we be generous with our time — being willing to set aside our own hobbies and even our work to spend quality time with our loved ones. May we do so freely and ungrudgingly, setting a priority on those human relationships which really count.

May we be generous with our empathy — giving full attention to a son or daughter who is talking about a problem, or to a spouse who needs a listening ear. May we not simply nod absentmindedly, but may we really try to understand.

May we be generous with our love — expressing fully what we feel in our hearts. May we find delight in our relationships with each other, and may we repeat over and over again our expressions of endearment. May there be no doubt in the minds of all of our family members that they are cherished, appreciated, and loved.

O God, may we be generous with our prayers — bringing our deepest concerns and our happiest thanksgivings to your throne. May our family circle always include Jesus Christ, and may our family code always include the divine word.

O God, draw us closer to you as we lift these prayers in the name of your Son, Jesus Christ. Amen.

Benediction

Hear the Good News! This Jesus we worship is born anew in our hearts. His life makes this life worth living. Go in peace, and may Jesus go with you. Amen.

Second Sunday After Christmas

First Lesson: Jeremiah 31:7-14
Theme: Rejoice In Your Redemption

Call To Worship

Leader: Praise the Lord, all you people.
**People: We will glorify him; and make his ways known through-
out the earth.**
Leader: Declare that the Lord our God is a great God.
**People: He is worthy of our worship, and of the praises we sing
to his name.**

Invocation

O God of the Ages, source of all creation, and sustainer of all life,
we set aside this hour as a time of wonder, in which we reflect on the
mystery of life.

We set aside this hour as a time of thanksgiving, as we consider
the good things of the past year.

We set aside this hour as a time of worship, as we honor you as the
God of love and majesty.

We set aside this hour as a time of dedication, as we renew our
commitment to the healing of your world. Amen.

Confession

Almighty God, we know that we should be joyful, for you have
promised to redeem your people, and with the coming of Christ you
have kept your word. Yet it is still hard for us to keep from hating our
enemies, and even our sorrows give us a strange sort of satisfaction.
Forgive us, Lord, and set our hearts free so that we may not only experience the joy of our salvation, but may also help others to discover
that joy. Amen.

Offertory Prayer

We thank you, God of the Ages, for this opportunity of investing
in eternity; for your people will live forever and your kingdom will
never come to an end. Amen.

Hymns

"O God, Our Help In Ages Past"
"He Leadeth Me: O Blessed Thought"
"Good Christian Friends, Rejoice"

Second Sunday After Christmas

Second Lesson: Ephesians 1:3-14
Theme: Spiritual Blessings In Christ

Call To Worship
Hear, one and all, joyful and happy, lonely and afraid, friendless and trembling: Come, arise, shine, for your light has come! The Lord's Glory has risen upon us, and his Glory is seen in us.

Invocation
We are thankful, O God, that down through the ages you have spoken to people in a variety of ways; and that in Jesus Christ you came to reveal yourself more personally to us. We gather this day to hear you, experience you, and worship you. We are hungry, eager and waiting for your direction in our lives. Come be with us this day. Amen.

Confession
Heavenly Father, we have heard your word of salvation, and we have claimed the promise of redemption through your Son, Jesus Christ. We must confess, though, that we are weak, and while we want to follow your way, we are too often unwilling to inconvenience ourselves. Forgive us, Lord, and through this time of worship strengthen our resolve, and give us the courage and determination to follow our Lord and Savior, Jesus Christ. Amen.

Offertory Prayer
O Lord, we offer these gifts so that others, like us, may be privileged to hear the word of truth, thus experiencing the favor of God which both forgives and renews. Amen.

Hymns
"Spirit Of God, Descend Upon My Heart"
"O Master, Let Me Walk With Thee"
"We Would See Jesus"

Second Sunday After Christmas

Gospel Lesson: John 1:(1-9) 10-18
Theme: The Word Became Flesh

Call To Worship

Leader: The people that walked in darkness have seen a great light.
People: Those who live in a land of deep darkness, on them has light shined.
Leader: Arise, shine, for your light has come;
People: and the glory of God has risen upon us.

Invocation

As the Magi of old followed the light of a star to find the Light of the World, so we come this morning, our Father, seeking light. We need the light which overcomes the darkness of ignorance. We need the light that exposes evil. We need the light that gives comfort and dispels fear. We need the light that reveals the way to eternal life. Open our eyes, we pray, to the light you have given us, and may we not be content until we kneel before the Christ, who is the Light of the World. Amen.

Confession

Lord, don't despair of us. We can hardly believe it ourselves. Yet we know it is true. We have seen the Light that came into the world with the birth of Christ, but we still choose to live in darkness. We choose hate instead of love, greed in place of generosity, selfishness when we should be self-giving. Forgive us, Lord, and shine your Light upon us that we may be worthy of fellowship with you. Amen.

Offertory Prayer

O Lord, we who have received the Light of the World realize that many have not yet known that glorious privilege; so we give these offerings in order that others may see, may know, and may believe. Amen.

Hymns

"Christ Is The World's Light"
"Word Of God, Come Down On Earth"
"I Want To Walk As A Child Of The Light"

Second Sunday After Christmas

Psalter: Psalm 27

Words Of Assurance

May Almighty God, who caused light to shine out of darkness, shine in our hearts, cleansing us from all our sins, and restoring us to the light of the knowledge of his glory in the face of Jesus Christ our Lord. Amen.

Pastoral Prayer

Eternal God, our Father, as once you came to us in the majestic humility of Bethlehem, come now in the mystery of your Spirit to inspire our gratitude and trust. We bless you for all those influences of grace which have nurtured and sustained us through the seasons of our life. For precious memories, vital hope, the joy which you have set before us, and the challenges which beckon us to new insight and wisdom in our time, we give you thanks and praise. Draw us in our celebration to higher understanding and deeper faith in your way of costly love, that at each step of our journey we may know and feel your care and gracious leading.

As we remember with thanksgiving your coming among us as one of us, so also we seek your guidance to become ever more like you in word and thought and action. Keep alive in us a sense of novelty in your ways with us, so that we shall uncover something of the beauty and mystery of Christmas each day, finding you nearer than we expected and equal to every need. So may our new year mark a fresh beginning for us and a new venture for your work in us and through the fellowship of our faith.

Gracious Lord, you know the secret prayers and yearnings of our spirits. Help us to baptize these emotions in an ever-broadening concern for your world and all who share the way of our pilgrimage in it. We pray the healing of your spiritual grace on those ill in body, mind, or attitude. For those who are prisoners of their conscience and those who are imprisoned for conscience's sake in many lands, we pray the courage of a strong sense of your companionship and inner guidance. We lift up to you especially those whose needs for friendship and care have been unmet in this holiday season. Enlighten our perception and fire our will to serve them and each other with compassion and a graceful love.

Bind us together through the coming days, O Lord, in the fellowship of faith and love, teaching us to serve you with a glad and honest heart, through Christ our Lord. Amen.

Benediction

The Lord who in mercy forgives the past, and in hope sends us into the future, now grants us the assurance of his abiding presence. Go in peace, and the blessing of God the Father, the Son, and the Holy Spirit go with you. Amen.

Epiphany Of Our Lord

First Lesson: Isaiah 60:1-6
Theme: Jesus, The Light Of The World

Call To Worship

Leader: Nations shall come to Christ's light,
People: and kings to the brightness of his dawn.
Leader: They shall bring gold and frankincense,
People: and shall proclaim the praise of the Lord.
Leader: In our worship let us open our hearts to the Light of the World.
People: We too will praise the Lord, and expose our lives to the brightness of his dawn.

Invocation

Everlasting God, who brought the nations to your light, fill the world with your brightness, and make yourself known to every nation; through Jesus Christ, the true light, your Son and our Lord. Amen.

Confession

Lord, we know that you are continually trying to manifest yourself to us, but because we fail to see any bright lights in the sky guiding us or hear any angels speaking to us, we often think we walk alone with no one to give us direction. Forgive our shortsightedness and lack of faith. Speak to us once again in this time of worship that we may let our lights shine and give you the glory. Amen.

Offertory Prayer

O God, we thank you for the manifestation of your Christ among us, and for the life which he gives. We thank you for the sense of journey and adventure that comes when, like the Magi, we ride into the dark night following a star. Like those Wise Men of old we lay our gifts at your feet in adoration and praise. Amen.

Hymns

"O Day Of God, Draw Nigh"
"Arise, Shine Out, Your Light Has Come"
"Rise, Shine, You People"

Epiphany Of Our Lord

Second Lesson: Ephesians 3:1-12
Theme: Christ For The World

Call To Worship

Leader: Jesus said: "Other sheep I have, which are not of this fold: them also I must bring."

People: We have come to worship Christ, and receive our marching orders.

Leader: Jesus said: "Go and make disciples of all nations."

People: We will be true to our Lord for he has promised to be with us always.

Invocation

O God, your blessed Son came not to do his own will, but yours. Open our hearts and minds that we may know your will for us, and over all our fears let your plans prevail, that your will may be done on earth as it is in heaven. Amen.

Confession

Lord, we thank you for the gift of faith, and yet we confess that our fears often triumph over our desire to do your will. Fear of our enemies, and even our friends, frequently keeps us from bearing witness to your love and mercy. Sustain us by your Holy Spirit, we pray, Lord, or we will never have the courage to be your instruments in making disciples of all peoples. Amen.

Offertory Prayer

O Lord, use these offerings to shed your light on those sitting in darkness and to proclaim the good news of God's favor to all those who are living in despair. Amen.

Hymns

"How Shall They Hear The Word Of God"
"O Zion, Haste"
"We've A Story To Tell To The Nations"

Epiphany Of Our Lord

Gospel Lesson: Matthew 2:1-12
Theme: The Visit Of The Wise Men

Call To Worship

Leader: Where is the child who has been born king?
People: The Lord is in his holy temple. Let us pay him homage.
Leader: Yes, God is here! Let us celebrate his presence.
People: With God's help we will make our whole life a celebration.

Invocation

O God, by the leading of a star, you revealed your love to the people of the earth. Lead us, who know you now by faith, to your presence, where we may see your glory face to face. Amen.

Confession

Lord, when we think of those Wise Men of old, who journeyed so far under difficult circumstances to come and kneel before you, we are ashamed of how often we fail to make any effort or put ourselves to any inconvenience in order to come into your presence. Forgive us, we pray, and strengthen our resolve to make our whole lives a celebration of your goodness toward us. Amen.

Offertory Prayer

As the Wise Men of old brought their gifts of gold, frankincense, and myrrh to the Christ Child, so we offer ourselves and our substance, O Lord, for the advancement of your kingdom. Amen.

Hymns

"The First Noel"
"We Three Kings"
"There's A Song In The Air"

Epiphany Of Our Lord

Psalter: Psalm 72:1-17

Words Of Assurance
God is not willing that any should feel left out or unwanted, for he calls all to stand within the circle of his love.

Pastoral Prayer
Eternal Spirit, we would worship you this day with hospitable hearts, welcoming you to our minds and lives. Come, knock on the door and give us grace to open. Come to us in stimulating thoughts, clear insights, and illumined faith; in moving gratitude that makes us humble, in penitence that cleanses us, in a sense of vocation that challenges us. Come to us in a fresh vision of Christ, his grace and mercy, his call to our consciences, and his appeal to our strength.

At the beginning of a new year, full of dangers, yet full of possibilities, we pray that you will make us great enough for these great days. Against all our sins that defeat your holy purposes, we pray, but especially against the sins of littleness, meanness, prejudice, provincialism. Cast down our pride — national, racial, personal. Make us humble, understanding, cooperative members of our one humanity. Lift us above the petty to grasp the import of these momentous times.

For ourselves, one by one, we pray that we may be among the world's assets and not its liabilities. For strength to stand up in trouble, for courage to overcome temptation, for inward grace from divine resources to master life and not be mastered by it, we pray. Through joy and sorrow, success and failure, the world's favor and the world's enmity, through happy fellowship with those we love, and through bereavement when the bell tolls for them and us, God keep us steadfast, undefeated, undishonored, and unashamed.

Let your Light shine on all of us today, making plain some answers to our questions, some assurance for our doubts, some strength for our weakness, some vision of our duty. May we be more valiant and triumphant spirits because we have worshiped you here; we pray in the Spirit of Jesus Christ our Lord. Amen.

Benediction

We have followed a star to find him. He tells us that the light is no longer only in heaven. Indeed, we are the light of the world. Let your light so shine before all that they may see your good works, and give glory to your Father God who is in heaven; and the blessing of the Father, Son, and Holy Spirit be with you. Amen.

Baptism Of Our Lord (Epiphany 1)

First Lesson: Isaiah 42:1-9
Theme: A Light To The Nations

Call To Worship
In a world where there is much despair, we have a message of hope. In a world filled with tension, we have a message of peace. In a world of conflicting voices, we have a message from God. Come, let us worship together.

Invocation
O Source of Life, whose will it is that your people should be one in love and in truth, renew in your Church the gift of your Spirit of holiness. May we be filled with the diversity of your gifts, and be guided along the ways you choose toward the fullness of unity. We ask in the name of Jesus Christ. Amen.

Confession
Our Father, you have set before us the example and teachings of Jesus Christ, our divine Savior and our human brother, but we confess that we have been slow to learn, we have been hesitant to follow, we have been less than eager to imitate, we have been reluctant to sacrifice. Help us, by your grace, to hear his voice and to follow with enthusiasm. We pray in Jesus' name. Amen.

Offertory Prayer
O Lord, we offer these gifts so that others, like us, may be privileged to hear the word of truth, thus experiencing the favor of God which both forgives and renews. Amen.

Hymns
"God Of Grace And God Of Glory"
"O Jesus, I Have Promised"
"Dear Lord, Lead Me Day By Day"

Baptism Of Our Lord (Epiphany 1)

Second Lesson: Acts 10:34-43
Theme: The Good News For Everyone

Call To Worship

As the sun dispels the darkness, bringing light to an awakening world, so God's Son has come into the darkness of our condition to bring the light of truth and the warmth of life.

Invocation

Creating and Redeeming God, we come together to celebrate the Baptism of our Lord at which time you made known that your Son had come into the world for all people everywhere. We give you thanks for the gift of your Son, and that through him we too have an opportunity to be caring and supporting members of Christ's Body here on earth — the Church. Grant us all the will to work for our fellow-beings, serving them joyfully through the guidance of your Spirit, and guided by the example of our Master, Jesus Christ. In Jesus' name we pray. Amen.

Confession

Lord, remove from us anything that would make us deaf to your call. Cleanse us from anything that would close our minds to your truth. Purify us of anything that would harden our hearts to your beauty. Remove from us anything that would distract our attention from your still, small voice. Take away from us anything that would close our eyes to your smile. We pray in Jesus' name. Amen.

Offertory Prayer

O God, we consider it a privilege to be partners in the task of helping people to know and to love you. Bless both ourselves and our gifts in this great worldwide endeavor. Amen.

Hymns

"From All That Dwell Below The Skies"
"Take My Life, And Let It Be"
"Pass It On"

Baptism Of Our Lord (Epiphany 1)

Gospel Lesson: Matthew 3:13-17
Theme: The Baptism Of Jesus

Call To Worship

We worship Christ as the Lamb of God, for he takes away the sin of the world. We worship Christ as the eternal Word, for he embodies the nature and will of the Father. We worship Christ as the Light of the World, for he reveals the way to Life Eternal. Come, let us worship him.

Invocation

Almighty God, Father of our Lord Jesus Christ and our Father too, we remember that John the Baptist pointed out that Jesus Christ is the Lamb of God for not just a few, but for the whole world. So as we come to celebrate Jesus' baptism we would renew the vows we made or were made for us at our own baptism. We renew our covenant faithfully to participate in the ministries of the Church by our prayers, our presence, our gifts, and our service. By the power of your Holy Spirit strengthen us in this resolve. We pray in Jesus' name. Amen.

Confession

O Lord, our Heavenly Father, as we think upon your Son's baptism we recall the vows made on our behalf or that we ourselves made at the time of our baptism. We confess that contrary to those promises we have not always resisted evil, injustice, and oppression; nor have we put our whole trust in your grace. Forgive us, we pray, and strengthen our resolve to serve you as our Lord, all our days. Amen.

Offertory Prayer

O Lord, as we personally need the Holy Spirit to be effective in our Christian life and witness, so we also need your Holy Spirit's power to give vitality to these gifts. By your divine energy may these offerings of money become translated into a dynamic experience of your concern and love. Amen.

Hymns

"This Is The Spirit's Entry Now"
"Jesus! The Name High Over All"
"When Jesus Came To Jordan"

53

Baptism Of Our Lord (Epiphany 1)

Psalter: Psalm 29

Words Of Assurance

Remember that the God who set aside his Son for his holy work equipped him fully for the task, and he who calls us in Christ for our holy work will also enable us to fulfill it. Believe this promise and go forth to serve.

Pastoral Prayer

Gracious God, whose Spirit gives new life to us all: we give thanks for the countless ways you make yourself known to us. We remember how you saved Noah's family, how you led your people to freedom through the sea, how your Son was baptized, and how you wash away our sin. With joy and thanksgiving we tell of your mercy for all people, and join with all your sons and daughters in glorifying your name throughout the earth.

Remove the barriers and suspicions which divide us, and so move us by your Spirit that we may live in justice and peace. Teach us that there is but one body, and one Spirit, one hope of our calling, one Lord, one faith, one Baptism, and one God of us all.

Guard those who live with injustice, terror, disease, and death as their constant companions. Help us to eliminate the cruelty our neighbors bear. And strengthen those who spend their lives establishing equal rights and opportunities for all people.

O God, banish the fears of those whom we know who face difficult times. Whether they are hospitalized, weakened in advance age, frightened by their solitude, or tormented by the demands of everyday life, make such persons whole again so they may live to rejoice in your love.

Deliver from indifference and carelessness the newly baptized. Cause your sign of water to be, for those we welcome this day into the family of God, a perpetual testimony to your saving work and faithfulness. Help all of us, together with them, to serve you in trust and joy.

Grant this through your Son, Jesus Christ our Lord. Amen.

Benediction

Go forth to love and serve your neighbors in all that you do, and the grace of the Lord Jesus Christ, and the love of God, and the communion of the Holy Spirit be with you all. Amen.

Second Sunday After Epiphany

First Lesson: Isaiah 49:1-7
Theme: A Light To The Nations

Call To Worship

Leader: Sing to the Lord, all the earth.
People: Tell of his salvation from day to day.
Leader: Declare his glory among the nations.
People: His marvelous works among all peoples.
All: For great is the Lord, and greatly to be praised.

Invocation

Inspire us, O Lord God of all the earth, not only to sing to you, but also to tell of your salvation from day to day. Prepare us in this hour to declare your glory to our neighbor next door and to our neighbors across the ocean, affirming that indeed you do marvelous saving works, and that you are greatly to be praised and sincerely to be revered. Amen.

Confession

Almighty God, Lord of the universe, you have called us to proclaim the good news of your salvation to all the world, but we have found plenty of excuses to be content in our own little circle of friends. We have found it more comfortable to expect you to intervene and straighten out the world than to become involved ourselves. Forgive us, Lord, as we wait upon you to renew our strength, with hands and hearts ready to serve you now. Amen.

Offertory Prayer

Receive these gifts, Lord, with our prayer that they will be effective in proclaiming your Word and expressing your love to people who live close by and to people who live far away. Amen.

Hymns

"O Zion, Haste"
"Lift High The Cross"
"Heralds Of Christ"

Second Sunday After Epiphany

Second Lesson: 1 Corinthians 1:1-9
Theme: God Is Faithful

Call To Worship

Leader: The Lord our God calls us to discipleship.
People: Our God is faithful; we will follow him wherever he leads us.
Leader: We need never fear, for God will always be with us to guide and comfort us.
People: We trust the God of our salvation. We come to worship him and renew our commitment to him.

Invocation

Creating and Redeeming God, you have called us together in this place to be your people. We give you thanks for the opportunity once again to be caring and supporting members of your body. Grant us the will to work for our fellow beings, serving them joyfully through the guidance of your Spirit, and guided by the example of your service. In Jesus' name we pray. Amen.

Confession

We acknowledge, Lord, that we are often nonchalant in our worship. Our minds wander, our hymns are listless, our prayers are just words, we are corrupted by jealousies, and distracted by trivia. Forgive us, Lord, for our coldness and inattention, then direct our minds to your Word and warm our hearts by your Spirit. Amen.

Offertory Prayer

O Lord, receive these gifts with our gratitude and with our prayers. We give them with gratitude because we have received so much; we give them with our prayers because we know that only if your power accompanies them will they achieve their desired result. Amen.

Hymns

"Great is Thy Faithfulness"
"There's A Wilderness In God's Mercy"
"Amazing Grace"

Second Sunday After Epiphany

Gospel Lesson: John 1:29-42
Theme: The Lamb Of God

Call To Worship

John the Baptist exclaimed as he saw Jesus: "Look, here is the Lamb of God!" Two disciples heard him and they followed Jesus. We have come this morning to worship Jesus, the Lamb of God; let us also be prepared to follow him as faithful disciples. Come, let us worship.

Invocation

O Lord, our God, whose light no darkness has overcome, shine now into all the shadowed places of our lives, that in your shining we may see who we are to be, what we are to do, and where we are to go if we find ourselves in you. We pray through Jesus Christ, the Lamb of God, and the Light of the World. Amen.

Confession

Heavenly Father, we know that you sent your Son into the world as "the Lamb of God," that through him the world might be saved from sin and reconciled to you. However, we are too easily satisfied with the knowledge that you love us and that we are your children. We fail to live the kind of lives you expect of your children. Forgive us, Lord, and help us to find that abundant life reserved for those who know how to be your children fully and completely. Amen.

Offertory Prayer

Lord, we offer these gifts that through them we, like John the Baptist, might be witness to the coming of the Lamb of God that takes away the sins of the world. Use them, we pray, to go where we cannot go, communicating where we cannot speak, and touching lives we will never know. Amen.

Hymns

"Ye Servants Of God"
"Jesus! The Name High Over All"
"Just As I Am, Without One Plea"

Second Sunday After Epiphany

Psalter: Psalm 40:1-11

Words Of Assurance

Jesus said: "I have come that they may have life, and that they may have it abundantly." From him receive life and light, hope and peace, in this life and the life to come. Amen.

Pastoral Prayer

We are here today, O Lord, to celebrate your gift of a good creation. We ascribe to you all glory and power. May you bless your people with your peace.

O Most Holy Redeemer, we need you to hear us even though our complacency has made us deaf to you. We need you to receive us now even though our self-sufficient attitude has made us forget you. We need you to care for us because we have failed to care for each other.

Ever-living God, you have breathed into us the very breath of life. You beheld us even before we saw the light of day. It is to you, Creator of all, that we give our truest adoration, our highest praise, our purest love. You have not withheld your salvation. You have given your Son to rescue us. Though we can make no sacrifice, offer no gift in return for what you have done, we utter this prayer of heartfelt thanksgiving. Thank you for the life and light of Jesus. That light has pierced through the clouds of doubt and confusion. Thank you for family and friends whose love reminds us of your love. Thank you for your encouraging and empowering Spirit. Sometimes we are so filled with the Spirit we truly feel our youth being renewed and we soar like eagles. Our faith is full and sure and we are ready to go wherever you would send us. For these faith-filled times, we are most grateful. But we are not always so sure of ourselves or of you. Sometimes it is hard even to believe you are near. Sometimes it is impossible to take your promises seriously. When we are unable to pray and don't know what to ask, let your Spirit intercede for us. May the hearts, minds, and bodies of all women and men who serve you, whether close at hand or in distant places, be refreshed and supported by your loving Spirit.

Fill us now with your Holy Spirit that we might bring your love to our world. We pray in Jesus' name. Amen.

59

Benediction

May God give you a desire to serve him with daring courage, with a willing mind, and with a persevering heart; and the blessing of God the Father, Son, and Holy Spirit be with you. Amen.

Third Sunday After Epiphany

First Lesson: Isaiah 9:1-4
Theme: The Light Has Come

Call To Worship

Leader: God is forever calling us —
People: calling us from darkness to light;
Leader: calling us from where we are to where we should be;
People: calling us from despair to hope;
Leader: calling us from aimlessness to purpose;
People: calling us from silence to witness.
All: Come, let us worship together and hear that call!

Invocation

You know, Lord, that in our world there is much darkness: so much crime, so much anger, so many wars, so much anxiety. Help us through the inspiration of this time of worship, to experience the deep peace that can come only from you.

Yet we come not to escape the realities of the world, but to receive the strength and the power that we might show forth your Light, and be instruments in your hands to drive the darkness away. Enable us not only to be peace receivers, but also to become peace makers. Amen.

Confession

Our Father in heaven, the map is clearly marked, but we have lost our way. The way is brilliantly lighted, but we have closed our eyes. The truth is carefully explained, but we have become confused. Forgive us, Lord, for our lack of attention, for our slowness of mind, for our hardness of heart. Then put a new spirit within us igniting again our fervent desire to walk with you in holiness. We pray in Jesus' name. Amen.

Offertory Prayer

Receive these gifts, O God, with our prayer that they will be effective in reaching people who walk in darkness that they may see a great light, even Jesus Christ our Lord. Amen.

Hymns

"Come, Thou Almighty King"
"Christ, Whose Glory Fills The Skies"
"This Is My Father's World"

Third Sunday After Epiphany

Second Lesson: 1 Corinthians 1:10-18
Theme: Christian Unity

Call To Worship

Leader: Blest be the tie that binds our hearts in Christian love.
People: We have come to praise our redeeming Lord, who joins us by his grace.
Leader: Where charity and love prevail, there God is ever found.
People: All praise to our redeeming Lord, who joins us by his grace.

Invocation

O God, our Father, we are all your children; and we gather this day to praise your name and seek your blessing. Unite our spirits, we pray, in worship and fellowship. While we cannot all be of the same mind, may we be made one in love, and in devotion to your holy will. We pray in Jesus' name. Amen.

Confession

Almighty and Most Merciful God, we confess that we have been guilty of misdirected loyalties; we have broken the unity of your holy Church; and we have turned away from your will to our own selfish ways. Pardon our sins, heal all strife and discord, and make us all yours by redemption and grace; through Jesus Christ our Lord. Amen.

Offertory Prayer

Lord, as we give we join hands with brothers and sisters in this place and around the world, we accomplish things together that we could never do alone. We express our unity in you, O Christ. Amen.

Hymns

"All Praise To Our Redeeming Lord"
"Help Us Accept Each Other"
"Blest Be The Tie That Binds"

Third Sunday After Epiphany

Gospel Lesson: Matthew 4:12-23
Theme: Jesus Begins His Ministry

Call To Worship

The Lord our God calls us to turn from the past and to be his special people; to find in him joy and meaning, a new life here and now, and eternal bliss in the world to come. Come! Let us praise the Lord.

Invocation

O Lord, help us, as we come together to worship you, to hear the still, small voice, to feel the rustling of your Spirit, to experience the warming of our hearts, to understand the mysteries of our faith, and to recognize your presence among us, through Jesus Christ our Lord. Amen.

Confession

Lord, when we read how those first disciples responded to your call and followed you without hesitation we must confess that our own response has been less than a full commitment. We sometimes pretend to more knowledge of you and your will than we really have. Forgive us for our narrow vision and our limited love. Help us to expand our vision and our love until we are worthy to be called your disciples. Amen.

Offertory Prayer

Lord, in responding to your command to follow you, we have become aware that you have called us to serve a purpose in life greater than ourselves. Help us to achieve that purpose as we give of our time and talents daily and as we dedicate these gifts to the work of your Church around the world. Amen.

Hymns

"When Morning Gilds The Skies"
"Jesus Calls Us"
"O Young And Fearless Prophet"

Third Sunday After Epiphany

Psalter: Psalm 27

Words Of Assurance

The Lord our God is a forgiving God, taking away the sins of all who are repentant.

Pastoral Prayer

Our Father, who in Christ has come into the world as a saving Servant, and who calls us to be disciples in his name, we praise you for the glorious company of apostles, martyrs, and witnesses who carried the gospel beyond their own national borders into all nations. O God, we are breathless with wonder as we behold your life in Christ. Still you are going before us in everlasting truth and leading us with the power of your eternal Spirit. Yet you do patiently wait for us when we linger behind — confused, blinded, and leaderless. When we stumble in our sins, you raise us to the stature of righteousness. When in overconfidence we venture beyond our wisdom and strength, you look upon us as an understanding Friend. O Christ, of God, we thank you for your forgiveness and guidance. Help us to learn from you. Keep us close to the influence of your love and within hearing of your voice.

O Master of the good life, teach us to minister instead of waiting to be ministered unto, until we find our life in your joy and likeness. Send us forth day by day as those who know that you did become flesh to live redemptively on this earth. Keep us confident in discipleship wherein we die unto self and live unto you. Preserve us from jealousy of the gifts and attainments of others. Unite our differing talents in the doing of your will. Reveal the times in which we are to stand in faith or when we are to venture boldly in your name. Send us to the fields of humanity where we shall enter into the struggle between heartache and joy, shame and honor, despair and hope.

Sustain the spirit of those who know that they are close to heaven's door. Quicken the spirit of those who must make the decisions for many people. Break the hardness of heart of those who have turned from you.

And now we pray, O Lord, that you will cleanse the hearts of every person that the kingdoms of this world might indeed become the kingdom of your Son, our Lord and Savior, Jesus Christ. Amen.

Benediction
Having come to receive, go forth to give. Having come to be blessed, go forth to bless. Having come to learn, go forth to teach. Having come to pray, go forth to work; and the blessing of the Father, Son, and Holy Spirit go with you. Amen.

Fourth Sunday After Epiphany

First Lesson: Micah 6:1-8
Theme: Genuine Piety

Call To Worship

We who are so prone to define life in terms of money, of success, of pleasure: it is a good thing for us to excuse ourselves for a time from the confused arenas of this world, and to sit quietly at the feet of Jesus. Come, let us worship!

Invocation

O Holy God, creator of heaven and earth, enable us this hour to set aside all idols: all distractions and misconceptions of your being, all false gods and substitute saviors. May we worship you as instructed, in spirit and in truth; through Jesus Christ our Lord. Amen.

Confession

Almighty God, too long have we put our trust in creeds and ritual when we know what you really require of us. Yes, we have not always sought justice, nor have we been the kindest persons, and certainly we have not always walked humbly with you. Forgive us our shortcomings, we pray, and enable us to present ourselves, by our deeds, before you as children of light rather than darkness. Amen.

Offertory Prayer

O Lord, we offer unto you these gifts of gratitude for all you have done for us. With them we pledge ourselves to serve one another in love and kindness, not only by words but also by deeds, in Jesus' name. Amen.

Hymns

"O Worship The King"
"What Does The Lord Require"
"Lord, I Want To Be A Christian"

Fourth Sunday After Epiphany

Second Lesson: 1 Corinthians 1:18-31
Theme: Christ — The Power And Wisdom Of God

Call To Worship
Our God has power, but grants freedom. Our God passes judgment, but prefers mercy. Our God is self-sufficient, but delights in us whom he has created in his own image, and with whom he shares all things good and beautiful.

Invocation
Our Father, we pause again amid the hectic schedule of our busy lives, to seek strength and guidance. The more feverishly we work, the more we need rest. The more frantic our schedules, the more we need this time of worship and contemplation. The more conflicting voices there are in our lives, the more we need the quieting influence of your Spirit. So we cherish this hour knowing that it will revitalize our lives and renew our spirits. Amen.

Confession
Almighty God, we have been warned of the peril that comes from worshiping other gods, but we still bow before the idol of knowledge. We think that we can learn enough to build our own kingdom here on earth, and we forget that only with the wisdom that comes from you will we receive the power to overcome the forces of darkness. Forgive our foolishness, we pray, and grant us a new understanding of the power of the cross of Jesus Christ, our Lord. Amen.

Offertory Prayer
Heavenly Father, through the message of the Cross of Christ we have found the power of God. Now with these gifts we wish to share our blessings and the good news of Jesus Christ. Receive our offerings, and enable them to make a positive impact on our world. Amen.

Hymns
"Immortal, Invisible, God Only Wise"
"In The Cross Of Christ I Glory"
"Wellspring Of Wisdom"

Fourth Sunday After Epiphany

Gospel Lesson: Matthew 5:1-12
Theme: Life Under The Reign Of God

Call To Worship

"Grace to you and peace from God our Father and the Lord Jesus Christ." Open your eyes and see the surprising love of God. Open your ears and hear the startling news of Jesus Christ. Open your hearts and sing the praises of the Lord.

Invocation

As citizens of Galilee gathered on a grassy hillside to hear the teachings of Jesus, so we have gathered to hear the words of life. Our setting may be much more formal, our clothing a different style, and we have hymnals, Bibles, and musical instruments; but our human needs are the same. Speak to our hearts, Lord, and bring us into your presence so that we, too, may learn the secrets of genuine living. Amen.

Confession

We know, Father, that those who feel no guilt cannot be forgiven, that those who feel no need cannot be filled. Therefore, we come into your presence today with humble hearts and open hands, asking that you will first pardon us by your grace, and then bless us with your presence. Through Christ our Lord we pray. Amen.

Offertory Prayer

O Heavenly Father, as the gift of your Son has inspired our gifts, may our giving in turn motivate others to give of themselves, thus inspiring an ever-widening circle of love and concern. Amen.

Hymns

"Take Time To Be Holy"
"Come, Thou Fount Of Every Blessing"
"A Charge To Keep I Have"

Fourth Sunday After Epiphany

Psalter: Psalm 15

Words Of Assurance

Our God is both wise and caring: afflicting the comfortable and comforting the afflicted.

Pastoral Prayer

God, we bow before you this morning, knowing that you hear every prayer. We know that in all of Creation, you are the source of life. You are the one who set the light swirling between the galaxies. The breath of your Spirit pulses through all life. You have even become flesh among us. We praise you, Lord, that in all your wonder, you have not forgotten us.

We need your presence in this place. Week after week, we are weary. Being faithful seems so complicated, and in the long run, doesn't seem to make so much difference. We are consumed by our own lives, our own betrayals, our own frustrations. Every sorrow weighs us down. Too often, life seems to be a role we play, and truthfully, Lord, we're tired of pretending.

Move among us now. In this place, let us hear your Spirit whisper. Let us feel the presence of your life. Let the radiance of your light shine on our faces. Help us turn aside false voices. Help us ignore the doom and gloom of the world, and hear the promise of your Word. Remind us that we are not alone. We are united by the Spirit in Jesus Christ, who moves among us now. Let your truth and mercy surround us like a circle of friends, guiding us, holding us up, pointing us to new ways.

As we are strengthened, Lord, help us witness. Help us grasp other hands, helping those who are weary. We forget how much good work there is to do. There are homeless folks to shelter, hungry folks to feed, orphan children to care for. There are battles to be stopped, and violence to be halted. Unite us, strengthen us, empower us with your Spirit of Life, so that we can overcome the forces of death. Help us stand together to do the work you have set before us. Help us encourage and inspire one another, so that your Word will continue to bring life.

We ask all this, knowing that you are faithful, and that even now, your Spirit is among us. Amen.

Benediction

Go forth in faith, ready to enter the doorways God is opening; prepared to accept the challenges he is offering; willing to make the sacrifices he is asking; and the blessing of God the Father, Son, and Holy Spirit go with you. Amen.

Fifth Sunday After Epiphany

First Lesson: Isaiah 58:1-9a (9b-12)
Theme: True Worship

Call To Worship

Leader: Give thanks to the Lord, for he is good.
People: His steadfast love endures forever.
Leader: Come into his presence with praise and thanksgiving.
People: Shall we come before him with offerings?
Leader: He has told us what is good.
People: And what does the Lord require of us?
All: To do justice, to love kindness, and to walk humbly with our God.

Invocation

O Lord, we gather here in eager anticipation that through the experience of worship our comprehension of you will be expanded and our lives will be enriched. Having thus been personally restored, send us away, equipped and eager to make a positive impact on our world that we may truly glorify you by working for justice and freedom, by feeding the hungry, and housing the homeless. Amen.

Confession

Most Merciful God, we know that we have fallen short of your expectations of us. Too often have we worshiped you with our lips only, while in our daily lives we have gone about business as usual. We have not loved our neighbors as we should. We have avoided the hungry and the homeless. We have turned the other way to avoid becoming involved when we have seen injustice. Forgive us, Lord, and renew a right spirit within us. Amen.

Offertory Prayer

Accept, Lord God, these our sacrificial offerings. May they be symbolic of the totality of our lives, which we commit to you and to the welfare of others. Amen.

Hymns

"Where Cross The Crowded Ways Of Life"
"What Does The Lord Require"
"Breathe On Me, Breath of God"

Fifth Sunday After Epiphany

Second Lesson: 1 Corinthians 2:1-12 (13-16)
Theme: True Wisdom Of God

Call To Worship
To worship is to think God's thoughts after him; to open the windows of the soul to the cool winds of the Spirit; to recognize a dimension of existence which transcends the world we touch and see; to sensitize our wills to the fruitful plan God has for our lives. Come, let us worship!

Invocation
Our Father, as we come to worship, we ask for both holy boldness and genuine humility.

Make us confident to approach your presence, knowing that you love your children and have invited us to share all good things.

At the same time, may we come with a humble spirit, knowing that as your children we can request but we cannot demand; we can ask but cannot order; we can pray but dare not require. Through Jesus Christ our Lord, we pray. Amen.

Confession
O Lord our God, we are aware of your wisdom, majesty, and power, and yet when the going gets rough we are tempted to go it alone, relying on our own strength and power. Forgive us, God, and give us the courage to trust in you, to follow your way. Free us from our fears by the power of your love. Amen.

Offertory Prayer
Lord, it is our prayer that these gifts will make a difference: that because of our generosity lives will be changed, souls will be saved, bodies will be fed, living conditions will be improved, and minds will be enlightened. Amen.

Hymns
"Wellspring Of Wisdom"
"Ask Ye What Great Thing I Know"
"O Spirit Of The Living God"

Fifth Sunday After Epiphany

Gospel Lesson: Matthew 5:13-20
Theme: Discipleship

Call To Worship

God calls us to play an important role in the life of planet earth. Through Christ, he has called us to be lights in the present darkness and salt in the current state of decay. Let us, in this hour of worship, dedicate ourselves anew to our high calling and prepare ourselves for the task ahead.

Invocation

We are grateful, Spirit of the living God, for this moment when we can slow down the pace of our lives and can come to be refreshed and restored. Clear our minds, ease our tensions, open our hearts, and touch us with your healing peace. Amen.

Confession

God of all goodness and light, we confess that we have not always been like light to the world or salt to the earth. We have not always acted in ways that show our faith. There have been times when our own wills were stronger than yours. We have failed to love our neighbors. Forgive us, Lord God, so that by your grace our light might shine before all people. Amen.

Offertory Prayer

O Lord, someone has said that it is better to light one candle than to curse the darkness. Through these gifts we light but a very small candle, but we ask that you will use it to bring enlightenment in our dark world, the enlightenment which frees people from illiteracy, from oppression, from hunger, from hopelessness and from godlessness. Amen.

Hymns

"This Little Light Of Mine"
"The Voice Of God Is Calling"
"I Am Thine, O Lord"

Fifth Sunday After Epiphany

Psalter: Psalm 112

Words Of Assurance

In this be confident: that the grace of God is active enough to forgive, and the love of God is powerful enough to transform.

Pastoral Prayer

Almighty God, you spoke your Word in the beginning and gave us life, you spoke your Word in Jesus Christ and brought us wholeness. We rejoice that by your grace your Word continues on the lips of women and men. We give thanks for words which stirred our hearts to respond to you: for loving and gentle words which assured us of our worth; for thanksgivings that bond us together more closely in gratitude; for a friend's rebuke that inflicted a moment's pain before showing us a better way; for a stranger's needful request that summoned us to follow that way of discipleship more faithfully; for that right word at the right time that disclosed something of the holy mystery; for the lines of hymns and prayers that mustered our unspoken praise; and for the words of scripture that tell and retell your goodness. By your Holy Spirit make our words sufficient to give thanks, through Jesus Christ our Lord.

Ever-present God, you are the source of our lives and the destiny of our pilgrimage. Teach us by your Holy Spirit the gracious language of your kingdom while we are yet at a distance. Grant us your love that we may speak with caring; your mercy that we may declare forgiveness; your gentleness that we may speak with patience. Give us courage to tell of the hope that leads us on the way toward the kingdom preached and taught by Jesus Christ our Lord.

Ever-eloquent God, in each generation you raise up women and men to speak your Word and make known your desire to bless. Send forth your Holy Spirit that they may speak in power. We pray this morning for teachers: encourage them and give them wisdom to behold the vast importance of their nurturing work. We pray, too, for students and teachers in our colleges: let your wisdom appear among the many lessons and lectures that they may rejoice in the challenges before them. We pray for the prophets of our day: though their words disturb us, strengthen their voices that your people might rightly hear the call to a more costly righteousness. We pray for poets and writers: enliven their imaginations to discover the subtle movements of your grace. You watch over your Word, O God. Let it come among us in power, through Jesus Christ our Lord, in whose name we pray. Amen.

Benediction
Go now to complete your worship through service. Go in the power of the Spirit of God to be the Church in the world; and the blessing of God the Father, Son, and Holy Spirit be upon you. Amen.

Sixth Sunday After Epiphany

First Lesson: Deuteronomy 30:15-20
Theme: Choose Life

Call To Worship

Leader: Seek the Lord while he may be found. Call upon him while he is near.

People: Too long have we followed the devices of our own hearts.

Leader: God has set before us life and death, blessings and curses.

People: We would choose life, loving the Lord our God, obeying him and holding fast to him.

Leader: Come then and let us worship together.

Invocation

We have heard your invitation, Lord, to seek first your kingdom and your righteousness. Enable us now, as we come into your house, to leave behind our contentions and our jealousies, our greediness and our blind ambitions, our anxieties and our tensions. May your kingdom become a reality within us as we seek to make your righteousness our own. Amen.

Confession

O God of resurrection and power, we are aware that sometimes our love grows cold and our commitment becomes lukewarm. We have wandered from your path, and the enthusiasm we once knew fades into lethargy.

Help us, Ever-creating God, to rekindle the flame that yet smoulders within us, to recapture the love we once knew, to experience again the breathless wonder of a vibrant faith. In Jesus' name. Amen.

Offertory Prayer

Giver of all that we have and are, take our gifts and our lives, and use them to make Jesus Christ known, loved, and followed both here and throughout the world. In our Savior's name. Amen.

Hymns

"Sing Praises To God Who Reigns Above"
"Breathe On Me, Breath Of God"
"I Am Thine, O Lord"

Sixth Sunday After Epiphany

Second Lesson: 1 Corinthians 3:1-9
Theme: Working Together For God

Call To Worship

Leader: It is a good thing to come before the Lord,
People: to submit ourselves before the most high God.
Leader: For God alone can save us, God alone can change us.
People: God alone can teach us how to truly live and how to truly love.

Invocation

We come to you, O God, as a company of diverse people. We are young and old, men and women, single and married, achievers and strugglers, believers and doubters. But we come with common purposes: to worship and adore you, to hear your Word, to affirm our faith, to offer our gifts, and to commit ourselves anew to work together for you and your kingdom. Amen.

Confession

O Lord, you have called us to be your disciples, dedicated to your service, presenting ourselves as living sacrifices. We have been unwilling followers who have failed to live up to your expectations. Forgive us, we pray, and enable us to serve you faithfully all our days. Amen.

Offertory Prayer

Forbid, Lord, that as we bring our gifts we should withhold ourselves, for who we are is more basic than what we have. Amen.

Hymns

"O Church Of God, United"
"Blest Be The Tie That Binds"
"Blest Be The Dear Uniting Love"

Sixth Sunday After Epiphany

Gospel Lesson: Matthew 5:21-37
Theme: Importance Of Personal Relationships

Call To Worship
Come, let us seek the beauty of soul that never fades; the treasure that rust cannot destroy; the satisfaction that will never sour with age. Come, let us seek the blessings of the Lord.

Invocation
Dear Lord, you have given us eyes to see light, minds to know truth, and hearts to choose goodness. Enable us to use these gifts to honor you. Help us to be open to your presence, willing to be transformed to Christ-likeness, faithful to respond to your direction. We pray in Jesus' name. Amen.

Confession
O Lord, we really do want to be kind, loving, and compassionate in all our dealings with other people, but time and again we find ourselves being angry, judgmental, and self-righteous. Forgiving Father, create in us clean hearts, and open our eyes that we may see that everyone we meet is our brother or sister. Help us to become a loving people so that we may truly share in your eternal kingdom. Amen.

Offertory Prayer
Heavenly Father, we rejoice in the many blessings you have given us, and we are grateful for this opportunity to bless others through sharing our love, our talents, and our material possessions. Amen.

Hymns
"In Christ There Is No East Or West"
"All Praise To Our Redeeming Lord"
"Help Us Accept Each Other"

Sixth Sunday After Epiphany

Psalter: Psalm 119:1-8; 33-48; 129-144

Words Of Assurance

Christ, the Light of the World, is a saving light, for he reveals the means of forgiveness.

Pastoral Prayer

O God, whose Spirit searches all things, and whose love bears all things, encourage us to draw near to you in sincerity and in truth. Save us from a worship of the lips while our hearts are far away. Save us from the useless labor of attempting to conceal ourselves from you, for you search and know our hearts.

Enable us to lay aside all those cloaks and disguises which we wear in the light of day, and here to bare ourselves, with all our weakness and failures and sin, before your sight.

We thank you, O God, for making yourself and your love so real to us. There are many concrete ways that we see you and know you. But the most real way is when we know you in other people. Thank you for the people we know who are authentic and whose love is the real thing. Most of all we think of Christ. How could you become more real to us? You became a man. You loved as we love, felt the burdens of poverty and sorrow, and even faced a real death like we face. How far you have gone to make yourself real to us! How thankful we are!

Thank you, too, for our friends, who are sometimes painfully honest, for their advice has often been good and their evaluations have often been just.

Thank you even for problems which seem to have no solution, for these have caused us to draw on spiritual reserves which might otherwise have gone untapped. For all these things we thank you and praise you.

Upon the altars of our intercession we lay our anxious concern for this storm-tossed world. We are burdened by the tumult and bloodthirstiness of the nations. Ours is the sin, O God, the sin of all of us, that violence stalks the earth. Before it is too late, we beseech you, bring the people to penitence and the rulers of the people to wisdom,

81

that in the day of our opportunity we may choose light not darkness, law not slaughter, brotherhood not enmity, peace and not war.

We offer our prayers in the name and Spirit of Christ our Lord and Savior. Amen.

Benediction

Leave this place with a profound sense of the presence of God. May this awareness give you boldness in your service, peace in your relationships, humility in your successes, and hope in your failures. May the blessing of God the Father, Son, and Holy Spirit accompany you always. Amen.

Seventh Sunday After Epiphany

First Lesson: Leviticus 19:1-2, 9-18
Theme: Moral Holiness

Call To Worship

God has summarized hundreds of moral directives in one word: love! Without love, our worship will consist of meaningless motions and empty words. Therefore, let us cast our anger and hatred, suspicion and jealousy aside, and let us worship in the spirit of love.

Invocation

We know, Lord, that while others look upon outward appearances, you look upon the heart, so we ask that as we prepare for worship our motives will be purified, our minds will be receptive, and our hearts open to the direction of your Holy Spirit. Amen.

Confession

O Lord, how often we have read and heard of your great love for all humankind, and especially for the poor and people with special needs. Yet we have gone on our merry way concerned mainly about our self and our own needs. We have stood in awe of the rich and looked with contempt upon the poor and outcast. Forgive us, we pray, and help us to respond with love to everyone we meet, following more closely in the footsteps of our Master, even Jesus Christ our Lord. Amen.

Offertory Prayer

We bring these gifts to you, O Lord, and pray that you will take our love and make it represent the Christ in whose name we serve and share. Amen.

Hymns

"Dear Lord, Lead Me Day By Day"
"Take Time To Be Holy"
"The Gift Of Love"

Seventh Sunday After Epiphany

Second Lesson: 1 Corinthians 3:10-11, 16-23
Theme: Christ The Sure Foundation

Call To Worship

In the course of a week we hear so much news: news of war and rebellion; news of injustice and repression; news of murder and embezzlement. Come now and let us hear the Good News, the gospel of our Lord and Savior, Jesus Christ.

Invocation

O God, it may seem that we are seeking you, but in reality we know that you are seeking us. Jesus said: "Behold I stand at the door and knock; if anyone hears my voice and opens the door, I will come in to him and eat with him, and he with me." Help us, O Lord, to hear your voice that we may open our hearts so you can come in and dwell with us. Through Jesus Christ our Lord. Amen.

Confession

Dear Lord, when the storms of life beat all around us, and all the things we have counted as important slip away from us as sand between our fingers, then it is that we realize how foolish we have been not to build our lives on the one sure foundation — even Jesus Christ our Lord. Forgive our foolishness, we pray, and enable us to plant our feet upon Christ the solid Rock, in whose name we pray. Amen.

Offertory Prayer

Once again, Lord, we offer our selves, our time, our talents, and our resources. Make us useful for your kingdom, through Jesus Christ our Lord. Amen.

Hymns

"My Hope Is Built"
"How Firm A Foundation"
"Guide Me, O Thou Great Jehovah"

Seventh Sunday After Epiphany

Gospel Lesson: Matthew 5:38-48
Theme: Christian Perfection

Call To Worship
Come! Let us worship God. Let us turn from fear to confidence. Let us turn from despair to hope. Let us turn from uncertainty to faith. Come, let us worship the Almighty!

Invocation
O Lord, amid the clatter of our noisy world, with the sirens, screams, and shoutings, may we hear your still, small voice. Amid the turbulence of our inner emotions, with their contending desires and troublesome impulses, may we feel the gentle urgings of your Spirit; through Jesus Christ our Lord. Amen.

Confession
Heavenly Father, through your Son you have shown us what we are called to do as your children. But we must confess that try as we must we still find it difficult to love our enemies and not to retaliate in kind when someone takes advantage of us. Forgive our waywardness, O God, and teach us to love as Jesus loved. Amen.

Offertory Prayer
We bring these gifts to you, O Lord, and pray that you will take our love and make it represent the Christ in whose name we pray. Amen.

Hymns
"I Want A Principle Within"
"We Are Climbing Jacob's Ladder"
"Help Us Accept Each Other"

Seventh Sunday After Epiphany

Psalter: Psalm 98

Words Of Assurance

If anyone is in Christ, he is a new creation; the old has passed away, behold the new has come.

Pastoral Prayer

O God, whose glory shone in the face of Jesus Christ as the Light of the World, shine into our lives as the light of grace and truth. We have heard your call to be his disciples and to some degree we have responded. Jesus has captured our imaginations about our possibilities for personal growth and development. We like the kind of power he displayed in healing the sick of body, mind, and soul. We covet his mental brilliance in answering critics and distorters of his words, deeds, and motives. We are amazed at his costly steadfastness, his unswerving purpose in serving you. He set new levels of dedication and obedience for us all.

Yet as much as we love him, admire him, and want to be his disciples, we are not sure that we are willing always to be thus identified, to pay whatever cost of rejection, accusation, and misunderstanding that might result. Truthfully, we find pockets of resistance within ourselves to walking fully in his light. We dislike the discomfort of going against popular opinions and beliefs, of being considered different, even weird and queer.

We had thought that following Jesus would make life easier, more peaceful, even tranquil. We understood not how the claims of the gospel set people against one another — father against son, mother against daughter, neighbor against neighbor — unless they all acknowledge his Lordship. We did not see how his gospel of peace and justice, freedom, cooperation, sharing, and acknowledging the basic worth of all would kindle so much hatred and antagonism. We failed to see the threat of the gospel to the powerful who lord it over the poor and weak, how it sets the "haves" against the "have-nots," the rich against the poor, the high against the low. Now we're beginning to understand what Jesus meant when he said, "I came not to bring peace but a sword."

86

Help us, O God, to strive to be among those who make a saving difference in the world, even at the cost of misrepresentation or ridicule or even laying down our lives for your truth. Let us be the light of the world, even when others try to put it out. When others examine our lives, may they find enough good works to give glory to our Father in heaven. Let us never forget that Jesus said, "If any one would be my disciple, let him deny himself, and take up his cross and follow me." To his cross and our cross let us ever be true, until we hear from him those blessed words, "Today, you shall be with me in paradise."

All this we pray in the name of Jesus Christ our Savior. Amen.

Benediction
Go back to the world in peace. Love and serve the Lord. Rejoice in the power of God in your life; and may the grace of our Lord Jesus Christ, the love of God, and the fellowship of the Holy Spirit be and abide with you and those you love, both now and forevermore. Amen.

Eighth Sunday After Epiphany

First Lesson: Isaiah 49:8-16a
Theme: God Of Comfort And Compassion

Call To Worship

Leader: Greetings! Let us open our hearts to the transforming power
of God.

**People: Our hearts are open to receive his special word for us
this day.**

Leader: Let us open our spirits to the revelation God has for us.

**People: We seek to be transformed so that Christ's ministry be-
comes our own.**

All: Let us sing praise to God!

Invocation

Receive us, Lord, as we submit to you our hearts for cleansing,
our souls for renewing, our inner selves for regenerating, the core of
our being for transforming, by the power of your Holy Spirit. Amen.

Confession

Almighty Comforter, you have promised to be with us to uphold
and strengthen us no matter what happens in our journey through life.
So often, though, we try to go it alone, and then we blame you for
deserting us. Forgive us our foolishness, Lord. Open our eyes so that
we may see the error of our ways, and our faith may be strengthened
by your presence in our lives. Amen.

Offertory Prayer

Lord, we give ourselves in these gifts with the hope that you will
use us and them in wonderful ways to build up your Church, and to
draw others to Christ with us. Amen.

Hymns

"How Firm A Foundation"
"Be Still, My Soul"
"Trust And Obey"

Eighth Sunday After Epiphany

Second Lesson: 1 Corinthians 4:1-5
Theme: Stewards Of God

Call To Worship

Leader: We have come to praise God, who has done wonderful things among us.

People: In Jesus, the Christ, God has shown us love, giving light for our darkness, and strength for all our days.

Leader: Sing praises to God's name.

People: We will bow down before God in prayer, and open our hearts to God's saving word.

Invocation

God of grace and creative power, you have given us minds to seek you and hearts to love you. Enhance our poor powers, we pray, so our spirits may reach to your Spirit; so our hearts may beat with the compassion of your heart; and we may worship you in purity and peace. Amen.

Confession

O Lord, Jesus Christ, you have called us to be your disciples, to be stewards and servants, but we must confess that we have not always acted in ways that are trustworthy. With shame and sorrow for our shortcomings, we ask your forgiveness, and pray that you will grant us a new vision of what we can and should do for the building of your kingdom. Amen.

Offertory Prayer

O Lord, we pray that with your power working through these gifts, miracles will take place: miracles of families being reunited; miracles of young people finding a cause; miracles of addictions being conquered; miracles of lives being changed; through Jesus Christ our Savior. Amen.

Hymns

"Take My Life, And Let It Be"
"Forth In Thy Name, O Lord"
"Heralds Of Christ"

Eighth Sunday After Epiphany

Gospel Lesson: Matthew 6:24-34
Theme: Worry

Call To Worship
Jesus said: "Come to me all you who are weary and heavy laden, and I will give you rest." Come now to Jesus. Come and honor him. Come to be blessed by him. Come to be transformed by him.

Invocation
O Lord, equip us to worship you as our gracious God, serve you as our worthy Lord, and trust you as our faithful companion. Lead us to new insights and discoveries; to old, proven truths and certainties; to renewed vision and purpose. We pray in Jesus' name. Amen.

Confession
Dear God, our lives are filled with concern about all the things you have told us not to worry about. We are so occupied with what we shall eat and drink, what we shall wear, where we will live that there is little time for anything else. Give to us that faith which will free us from these worries and enable us to straighten out our priorities, so that we may be worthy workers for your kingdom. Amen.

Offertory Prayer
Gracious God, may these gifts reach and touch those who are hurting, those who are filled with longing for a sign of hope, with the message of your love. Amen.

Hymns
"God Will Take Care Of You"
"Leaning On The Everlasting Arms"
"I Sing The Almighty Power Of God"

Eighth Sunday After Epiphany

Psalter: Psalm 37:1-11

Words Of Assurance

Do not try to punish yourselves or live in nagging regret. Instead, accept for yourselves the complete healing offered by Jesus when he said: "Your sins are forgiven; rise, take up your pallet and walk."

Pastoral Prayer

O God, you are our refuge. When we are exhausted by life's efforts, when we are bewildered by life's problems, when we are wounded by life's sorrows, we come for refuge to you.

O God, you are our strength. When our tasks are beyond our powers, when our temptations are too strong for us, when duty calls for more than we have to give to it, we come for strength to you.

O God, it is from you that all goodness comes. It is from you that there comes to us the spur of high desire and the restraint of conscience. It is from you that there has come the strength to resist temptation and to do any good thing.

And now as we pray to you, help us to believe in your love, so that we may be certain you will hear our prayer. Help us to believe in your power, so that we may be certain you are able to do for us above all that we ask or think. Help us to believe in your wisdom, so that we may be certain you will answer, not as our ignorance asks, but as your perfect wisdom knows best.

God of peace, we beseech your blessing upon this torn and broken world. We live in a time of hate, mistrust, fear, and violence. Bless us with your Holy Spirit that we may follow in your ways and create a world where all may live in peace.

We pray in Jesus' name. Amen.

Benediction

Let this be your assurance, that God will walk with you. Let this be your resolve, that you will walk with God. And the blessing of God the Father, the Son, and the Holy Spirit go with you. Amen.

Transfiguration Of Our Lord

First Lesson: Exodus 24:12-18
Theme: On The Mountain With God

Call To Worship

Leader: Seek the Lord, while he may be found.
People: We have come into the house of the Lord that we might find him.
Leader: Come into his presence with thanksgiving.
People: We will make a joyful noise to him with songs of praise.

Invocation

God whose power and wonder are far beyond our imaginations, enfold us in the awe, the majesty, the mystery of this time of worship.

Open us to hear your Word, and to see your love working its healing powers in this community and our world. May others experience your light and your truth through all that we say and do, we pray in Jesus' name. Amen.

Confession

Almighty God, as your people of ancient times pledged to do your will and be obedient to your laws, so have we committed ourselves to be faithful followers of your Son. So too, Lord, as your children of old failed to keep their word, so have we neglected your commandments and chosen to follow the desires of our own hearts. Forgive us, we pray, and as we come to this mountaintop experience of worship enable us to renew our commitment and strengthen our faith in you that we may go forth into the world to do your will. In Jesus' name we pray. Amen.

Offertory Prayer

Lord, may these gifts glow with your love, bringing a ray of warmth and illumination into a world which is continually threatened by darkness. Amen.

Hymns

"Open My Eyes, That I May See"
"How Can We Name A Love"
"Seek The Lord"

92

Transfiguration Of Our Lord

Second Lesson: 2 Peter 1:16-21
Theme: Christ's Glory

Call To Worship

Leader: The Lord is king; he is exalted over all people.
People: We will praise his great and awesome name.
Leader: Mighty King, the Lord, is a lover of justice.
**People: We will extol the Lord our God and worship at his holy
mountain, for the Lord our God is holy.**

Invocation

Our Father, enable us, as we gather in your presence, to shut out
anything that would distract our worship; to reject anything that would
shut our ears to your Word; to overcome anything that would dull our
sensitivity to your holy presence; to decline anything that would diminish our love for you and for each other. Amen.

Confession

Almighty and Everlasting God, time and again we have felt your
presence close to us. We have heard you speak to us through your
Holy Word, through your messengers, and in time of worship and
prayer. We confess though that often we have failed to witness to others the meaning of your presence. We have been too timid or too selfish to share the glory of your epiphany. Forgive our weakness, O Lord,
and strengthen us that we might bear witness to your glory, and be as
a lamp shining in a dark place to bring your love to others. Amen.

Offertory Prayer

Lord, we offer our gifts as tokens of our love and as expressions of
our faith. Use them and us, we pray, to bring light to those who dwell
in darkness. Amen.

Hymns

"Christ, Whose Glory Fills The Skies"
"When Morning Gilds The Skies"
"To God Be The Glory"

Transfiguration Of Our Lord

Gospel Lesson: Matthew 17:1-9
Theme: We Behold His Glory

Call To Worship

Leader: Behold the King of Glory waits.
People: We will enter his gates with thanksgiving and his courts with praise.
Leader: It is good for us to be here.
People: Yes, for we would see Jesus, and behold his glory, the glory of the Father's only Son.

Invocation

We are grateful, Almighty God, that you have called us to come apart from the rush, the busyness, the clamor of our everyday world, and to be with you in this holy place. As we worship may we capture a greater vision, and commit ourselves enthusiastically to the tasks which you have chosen for us to do. We pray in Jesus' name. Amen.

Confession

God, you speak to us in so many ways, but we are not listening because we hear only what we want to hear and listen only to those voices with which we agree. You show yourself to us in so many people, but we do not see because in our eyes these persons do not appear to be worthy. Cure our deafness and heal our blindness, we pray, that we may behold the glory of your love and hear the voice that will direct us in the path that leads to your kingdom. Amen.

Offertory Prayer

Our Heavenly Father, as we behold your glory, made known to us through your Son, Jesus Christ, we humbly present these offerings that they might be a blessing to others even as you have blessed us. Amen.

Hymns

"Christ, Upon The Mountain Peak"
"O Wondrous Sight! O Vision Fair"
"Love Divine, All Loves Excelling"

Transfiguration Of Our Lord

Psalter: Psalm 99

Words Of Assurance

The grace of God not only cleanses us but also changes us. His love renews as well as restores. When we ask for forgiveness we are also submitting ourselves for reformation.

Pastoral Prayer

O God of unsurpassed radiance and splendor, you are light itself, and in the power of your light "we live and move and have our being." You are, indeed, the light of the whole world and the darkness can never put it out. Today, we are troubled by clouds of darkness rolling in, an impenetrable fog that conceals familiar boundaries and landmarks. We feel exposed to all sorts of danger and confusion, and need your light to shine upon us in many ways.

Let the warmth of your light lift the fog of our confusion and brighten our days. Clarify and illumine our perception of how we can grow as persons, reaching our potential as your children. We are powerless to see you until you activate the photocells of our souls with the light of your truth. May our spiritual circuits be connected by faith with your inexhaustible energy and love so that we are never defeated or discouraged.

We confess our need for moral cleansing and purification, both personally and as a nation. As the sun's light mysteriously energizes the trees of the forest to absorb the poison of carbon-dioxide from the air and give back life-sustaining oxygen, so we need you to cleanse the impurities of our thoughts, feelings, and behavior, that we may show forth your goodness through the way we live. Let us be exposed to your light in Jesus Christ that his likeness is formed on the undeveloped films of our lives. Then, with Saint Paul, we can declare, "It is no longer I who live, but Christ lives in me." Thus may the warmth of your love take away the chill from our hearts even as the heat of the solar energy takes the bite out of winter days.

Lord, we are troubled when the daily news reminds us that the fierce struggle between the powers of light and darkness continues, often at high levels of government, the citadels of education, and the bastions of economic interests. We see the conflict between light and darkness in the struggle of nations and races to free themselves from tyranny. May ours be a liberating strife, based on your truth that sets us inwardly free, regardless of outward tumult, the truth that affirms all children to be children of your creation, endowed not only with rights, but also, great potential to be co-creators with you of a far better world.

All this we pray in the name and for the sake of Jesus Christ our Lord. Amen.

Benediction

May your life be a light to the people around you. May they be enriched by the good things you do, and give grateful praise to your Father in Heaven.

And now may the love of God the Father, Son, and Holy Spirit abound in your life and be with you always. Amen.

Ash Wednesday

First Lesson: Joel 2:1-2, 12-17
Theme: A Call To Prayer, Fasting, And Repentance

Call To Worship

Leader: The day of the Lord is coming.
People: We come to prepare ourselves for his coming.
Leader: Return to the Lord, your God, for he is gracious and merciful.
People: We know he is slow to anger, and abounding in steadfast love.
All: **We will repent of our sins and seek the Lord's forgiveness.**

Invocation

O Lord, God of our salvation, assist us mercifully with your help that we may enter with joy upon the meditation of those mighty acts through which you have given unto us life and immortality, through Jesus Christ our Lord. Amen.

Confession

O God, maker of everything, and judge of all that you have made, from the dust of the earth you have formed us and from the dust of death you would raise us up. By the redemptive power of the cross, create in us clean hearts and put within us a new spirit, that we may repent of our sins, and lead lives worthy of your calling; through Jesus Christ our Lord. Amen.

Offertory Prayer

O God, you see and know not only the gifts that we bring, but also the love with which they are given. Accept our offerings and our devotion to your service, and increase in us the works of faith and love; through Jesus Christ. Amen.

Hymns

"Out Of The Depths I Cry To You"
"I Surrender All"
"When I Survey The Wondrous Cross"

Ash Wednesday

Second Lesson: 2 Corinthians 5:20b—6:10
Theme: Reconciliation With God

Call To Worship

Leader: Now is the acceptable time; now is the day of salvation.
People: **We come to repent of our sins and to accept the grace of God.**
Leader: Bless the Lord who forgives all sins.
People: **God's mercy endures forever.**

Invocation

Grant us, O Lord, in all our ways of life your help, in all our perplexities of thought your counsel, in all our dangers of temptations your protection, and in all our sorrows of heart your peace, through Jesus Christ our Lord. Amen.

Confession

O Lord, we come before you humbly confessing that we have fallen short of what you would have us be. We have put obstacles in the way of those seeking you, rather than love. We have lacked patience, kindness, truthful speech, and genuine love. Forgive us, we pray, and lead us in paths of righteousness for your name's sake. Amen.

Offertory Prayer

O Gracious God, you have accepted us such as we are and the way we are. We ask you now to receive these offerings such as they are and dedicate them to the purposes for which they have been given. Through Jesus Christ our Lord. Amen.

Hymns

"Lord, Who Throughout These Forty Days"
"I Surrender All"
"Pass Me Not, O Gentle Savior"

Ash Wednesday

Gospel Lesson: Matthew 6:1-6, 16-21
Theme: The Life Of Righteousness

Call To Worship

Leader: Beware of practicing your piety before others in order to be seen by them.

People: We come before the Lord our God with humble and contrite hearts.

Leader: When you pray, do not pray so that you may be seen and heard by others.

People: We lift up our hearts and voices to our Father in heaven.

All: Bless the Lord, O my soul, and forget not all God's benefits.

Invocation

We come into your presence, Father, offering nothing but ourselves: with hands ready to receive, minds waiting to be nourished, and lives eager to do your will. Amen.

Confession

A Litany Of Penitence

All: Most Holy and Merciful Father, we confess to you and to one another, and to the whole communion of saints in heaven and on earth, that we have sinned by our own fault in thought, word, and deed; by what we have done, and by what we have left undone.

Leader: We have not loved you with our whole heart, and mind, and strength. We have not loved our neighbors as ourselves. We have not forgiven others, as we have been forgiven.

People: Have mercy on us, Lord.

Leader: We have been deaf to your call to serve, as Christ served us. We have not been true to the mind of Christ. We have grieved your Holy Spirit.

People: Have mercy on us, Lord.

Leader: We confess to you, Lord, all our past unfaithfulness: the pride, the hypocrisy, and impatience of our lives.

People: We confess to you, Lord.

Leader: Our self-indulgent appetites and ways, and our exploitation of other people. Our anger at our own frustration, and our envy of those more fortunate than ourselves.

People: We confess to you, Lord.

Leader: Our excessive love of worldly goods and comforts, and our dishonesty in daily life and work.

People: We confess to you, Lord.

Leader: Our negligence in prayer and worship, and our failure to commend the faith that is in us.

People: We confess to you, Lord.

Leader: Accept our repentance, Lord, for the wrongs we have done: for our blindness to human need and suffering, and our indifference to injustice and cruelty.

People: Accept our repentance, Lord.

Leader: For our waste and pollution of your creation, and our lack of concern for those who come after us.

People: Accept our repentance, Lord.

Leader: Restore us, good Lord, and let your anger depart from us.

People: Favorably hear us, for your mercy is great.

Leader: Accomplish in us the work of your salvation,

People: that we may show forth your glory in the world.

Leader: By the cross and passion of your Son our Lord,

People: bring us with all your saints to the joy of the Resurrection. Amen.

Words Of Absolution

Leader: In the name of Jesus Christ, you are forgiven!

People: In the name of Jesus Christ, you are forgiven!

Offertory Prayer

O Lord, with this offering we dedicate ourselves to live as faithful and obedient citizens of your holy kingdom. Amen.

Hymns

"Dear Lord And Father Of Mankind"
"Depth Of Mercy"
"Take Up Thy Cross"

Ash Wednesday

Psalter: Psalm 51:1-17

Words Of Assurance

Give thanks to God who reconciles us to himself in Christ, who closes the gap we could never bridge, and who gives to us the ministry of reconciliation.

Pastoral Prayer

O God, our Father, who sent your only Son to bring your saving life to a sin-filled world, open the eyes of our souls to behold your immeasurable love. We have no merit to plead our need. In his sacrifice you are forever offering redemption to your children. Guide our minds to learn of your Christ, and incline our hearts to believe in him.

We confess that among the bountiful material blessings we have often wasted and lost the gifts of the Spirit. When your hands opened to provide food for the soul, we turned to forbidden fruit that left us hungry and ill in spirit. We have been busy about many things and have neglected the one thing needful for the salvation of our souls. We come empty, weak, and disillusioned to you, our God, to hear the eternal story of the cross, forever new with its power to transform and bless.

O Christ, forbid that we should pass unheeding before the cross, standing amidst each life and event of our day. With contrite hearts we come to you in the assurance that if our sins be as scarlet, you can make them white as snow. Teach us then to examine our hearts, and lead us to surrender all things deceitful and unbrotherly or unsisterly. Take from us all contempt, envy, and covetousness. May we not grieve but love your Holy Spirit.

We ask it all in the name of Jesus Christ our Lord, and our Savior. Amen.

Benediction

The salvation of God has been offered to you this day. By the grace of our Lord Jesus Christ, receive now the wholeness that comes only from God, and walk in the light of his fellowship. In the name of the Father, and of the Son, and of the Holy Spirit. Amen.

First Sunday In Lent

First Lesson: Genesis 2:15-17; 3:1-7
Theme: Temptation

Call To Worship

Leader: Draw near to God and he will draw near to you.

People: The Lord is near to all who call upon him, to all who call upon him in truth.

Leader: Let not loyalty and faithfulness forsake you; write them on the tablet of your heart.

People: God is Light, and in him is no darkness at all. If we walk in the Light, we have fellowship with one another.

Invocation

Father, as we come into your presence on this first Sunday of Lent, break down any temptations that hinder us from worship: temptations to ill-feeling between ourselves and others, temptations to feelings of guilt or indifference between ourselves and you, temptations of discouragement and anxiety that could preoccupy our minds and dull our receptivity to your Spirit. We pray in Jesus' name. Amen.

Confession

In your presence, O God, as nowhere else, we acknowledge the gravity of our sin. We have talked better sense than we have lived; we have judged others more harshly than we have judged ourselves; we have piously implored you for more light when more than enough has been granted; we have sought to inflate ourselves by deflating the deeds and accomplishments of others whose example threatens us. Give us moral courage to face our sins and then let your pardoning and restoring love ignite in us the spirit of new life in Jesus Christ our Lord. Amen.

Offertory Prayer

Realizing that every privilege carries a duty, and every blessing implies a responsibility, we return some of our gifts as a service to others; through Jesus Christ our Lord. Amen.

Hymns

"All My Hope Is Firmly Grounded"
"Dear Jesus, In Whose Life I See"
"In The Cross Of Christ I Glory"

First Sunday In Lent

Second Lesson: Romans 5:12-19
Theme: New Beginnings

Call To Worship
You who are seeking God, do you know that he is this moment seeking you? God is the Good Shepherd who seeks, the Visitor who knocks, the Father who welcomes. Come, let us respond to his urgent invitation and rejoice in his gracious welcome.

Invocation
Lord, we come into your presence as a people who are often alienated: sometimes alienated from people of other races, nationalities, and creeds; sometimes alienated from our neighbors next door and down the street; sometimes alienated from the members of our own family; and sometimes alienated from you, our God. Now as we worship we ask for the healing salve of your love, and the reconciling power of your Holy Spirit, so that in the quietness of this hour we may find true peace with each other. Amen.

Confession
Holy and Merciful God, we confess with shame those times when we have failed to be your faithful people, when we have made an empty show of our religion, when we have judged others and been blind to our own sins, when our words have been substitutes for justice and kindness, when times of testing have come and we were weak. Forgive us, we pray, and by the power of your Spirit make us strong for all that is to come; through Jesus Christ our Lord. Amen.

Offertory Prayer
O Loving Father, help us ever to honor you with our substance, and show forth our thanks, not only in words, but by our gifts and our deeds; through him who came not to be served, but to serve, and to give his life a ransom for many, even Jesus Christ our Lord. Amen.

Hymns
"Ye Servants Of God"
"Spirit Of God, Descend Upon My Heart"
"Take Up Thy Cross"

First Sunday In Lent

Gospel Lesson: Matthew 4:1-11
Theme: Temptation

Call To Worship

Leader: It is written: "One does not live by bread alone, but by every word that comes from the mouth of God."

People: We come seeking the Bread of Life.

Leader: It is written: "Do not put the Lord your God to the test."

People: We come to strengthen our faith and renew our spirits.

Leader: It is written: "Worship the Lord your God and serve only him."

People: We would see Jesus and him only would we serve.

Invocation

O Lord, our God, in this season of Lent as we turn our eyes toward the cross, we ask that we may see clearly the sacrifice you have made for us, and then may see just as clearly the sacrifice we must make for others; through Jesus Christ our Lord. Amen.

Confession

Gracious God, we seek your pardon and forgiveness for all our faltering steps. We have hesitated in seeking your glory. We have tarried where we are, rather than accept the challenge of discipleship. We have left compassionate words unsaid, held back on forgiving words, and loosened our lips with trivial and hurting words. Renew us as we seek to listen again to the words of Jesus. Forgive us our timid discipleship. In the name of Jesus Christ. Amen.

Offertory Prayer

Come to our aid, Lord, as we try to sort out our priorities in life. Help us always to put first things first, and help us to place our trust in those things that are eternal. Amen.

Hymns

"We Are Climbing Jacob's Ladder"
"What A Friend We Have In Jesus"
"Make Me A Captive, Lord"

First Sunday In Lent

Psalter: Psalm 32

Words Of Assurance

Rejoice in the Lord, for he can both forgive and transform. His grace is adequate to deal with past failures and present weakness. Amen.

Pastoral Prayer

O God, our Father, whom the night cannot hide nor evil drive away, we come in this time of worship that in your presence we may find the cleansing and sanctifying light of the cross. We thank you for the old and ever-new gospel of our Lord Jesus Christ. It comes to us with fresh truths and new judgments for our living. The stories of your shame and suffering and death, O Lord, strip from us our false goodness and lead us out of our poverty of spirit to the Fountain of Life.

May the contemplation of the sins which led to your crucifixion cause us to examine ourselves humbly and in repentance, O Christ. Deliver us from the vain things which have power over us. Forgive us our sins and help us by your Spirit to walk with confidence as trusted followers for whom you care eternally.

We remember, dear Lord, how in the midst of the pain of body and soul you did care for others, even your enemies. Give us grace to let our own discomfort or hardships bring appreciation of the needs and distress of others. Have mercy upon the sick that they may obtain the faith to endure and receive strength from medicine and sleep. Let your healing powers embrace those who are wounded in spirit or ill in mind. May the fearful have hope and courage. Teach the careless and calloused the sensitivity which remembers you.

Arouse, O God, within your people a zeal to bring the message of your love in Jesus Christ to their fellow beings. Let not your Church become content with present blessings or accomplishments.

Lord, we are yours — may we, therefore, remain restless until everyone is found whom you desire in your flock. Call us and lead us, Good Shepherd, through the gate that leads to eternal life. In your holy name we ask it. Amen.

Benediction

Let love be genuine, hate what is evil, hold fast to what is good; and the blessing of God the Father, Son, and Holy Spirit be yours. Amen.

Second Sunday In Lent

First Lesson: Genesis 12:1-4a
Theme: God's Call

Call To Worship

Leader: Draw near to God and he will draw near to you.
People: We come before the Lord with praise and thanksgiving.
Leader: God is calling you over the tumult of life's wild restless sea.
People: We will open our ears and our hearts that we may hear God's summons.
All: Praise be to God!

Invocation

Almighty God, our hearts are stirred with gratitude and our mouths are opened in praise. You dispel our fears and replace them with confidence. You take away the night of despair and awaken us to a morning of bright hope. You call us from a life of self-indulgence to a life of helpful and healing service. Hear our praise and accept our worship, in the name of your Son, even Jesus Christ our Lord. Amen.

Confession

Gracious God, our Creator, we come before you a rebellious people. We have denied your intentions for us; we have preferred our ways to Christ's way; we have disobeyed your commandments; and we have worshiped ourselves and the things we have made. Forgive us, restore in us the knowledge of who we are, and make us alive to serve you in faith, obedience, and joy; through Jesus Christ our Lord. Amen.

Offertory Prayer

Almighty and Everlasting God, we offer our gifts as a sign of our determination to be open to your mysterious presence, and to place our lives in the service of your purposes of reconciliation and healing in our broken and hurting world. In our lives and in our world, may your kingdom come, now and forever. Amen.

Hymns

"I Am Thine, O Lord"
"Take Up Thy Cross"
"Make Me A Captive, Lord"

Second Sunday In Lent

Second Lesson: Romans 4:1-5, 13-17
Theme: Victory Through Faith

Call To Worship

Leader: Come, let us give praise to the Lord.

People: We come, for God has given us life, and in him we live and move and have our being.

Leader: Come, let us raise our songs to the Lord God Almighty.

People: We come, for he has redeemed us from despair and has given us a high calling through Jesus his Son.

Invocation

We thank you, O God, for the light which wakes us morning by morning; for the light of learning which brings knowledge; but most of all we thank you for the divine light which is reflected in the face of Jesus Christ and which enlightens our lives by the Holy Spirit. Strengthen our faith, we pray, that we may claim the promises made to your people, through Jesus Christ our Lord. Amen.

Confession

O Merciful Father, who in compassion for your sinful children sent your Son Jesus Christ to be the Savior of the world, grant us grace to feel and lament our share of the evil which made it needful for him to suffer and die for our salvation. Help us by self-denial, prayer, and meditation to prepare our hearts for deeper penitence and a better life. Give us a true longing to be free from sin through the deliverance wrought by Jesus Christ our only Redeemer. Amen.

Offertory Prayer

Enable us, Lord, to express our true gratitude by the way we live as well as by the way we give; through Jesus Christ our Lord. Amen.

Hymns

"To God Be The Glory"
"Victory In Jesus"
"Faith Of Our Fathers"

Second Sunday In Lent

Gospel Lesson: John 3:1-17
Theme: God's Love And Our Response

Call To Worship
Jesus is the Word made flesh, who came to live among us. Jesus is the Way, the Truth, and the Life. Jesus is the Lamb of God who takes away the sin of the world. Come, let us worship him. Come, let us praise him!

Invocation
Forbid, O God, that we should forget, amid our earthly comforts, the pains and mortal anguish that our Lord Jesus endured for our salvation. Grant us a true vision of all that he suffered: his betrayal, his lonely agony, his false trial, his mocking and scourging, the torture of the cross; that remembering his suffering and death, we may give ourselves wholly to you; through Jesus Christ our only Lord and Savior. Amen.

Confession
Most Merciful God, who knows the thoughts of our hearts: we confess that we have sinned against you, and done evil in your sight. We have neglected your Word, and transgressed your holy laws. Forgive us, O Lord, and give us grace and power to put away all hurtful things, that, being delivered from the burden of our sins, we may bring forth fruits worthy of repentance, and henceforth may always walk in your holy ways; through Jesus Christ our Lord. Amen.

Offertory Prayer
Gracious God, we are awed by your goodness to us. Hear us now, as we offer ourselves and our gifts that your will might be done on earth. Amen.

Hymns
"Savior, Like A Shepherd Lead Us"
"Ask Ye What Great Thing I Know"
"He Touched Me"

Second Sunday In Lent

Psalter: Psalm 121

Words Of Assurance

The Lord is near to the brokenhearted, and saves the crushed in spirit. The Lord redeems the life of his servants; none of those who take refuge in him will be condemned.

Pastoral Prayer

Eternal Spirit, whom we could not seek unless you had first sought us, give us responsive hearts today. Unless you come down the little stairways of our lives into the humble place where we abide, we shall miss you. We pray not for a change in you, but in ourselves. Make us receptive to your presence. Make us sensitive to all that is noblest in our own lives through which you come to us. Make us attentive to the still, small voice by which you speak to us. Give us for the reward of our worship this morning another hour of communion with you, from which we shall go forth knowing that we have been in your presence.

Speak to us through conscience. Let some authoritative word of righteousness come to some heart here that needs it. Startle us out of our complacency. Summon us to ideals that we have forgotten. Refresh us with the memory of knightly hours when we dedicated ourselves to things worth living and dying for. O Spirit of the living God, challenge our consciences.

Speak to us through our ambitions. Shame us from low motives of greed and selfish acquisition. Help us to set our hearts once more on things above where Christ dwells. Lift us up to dream nobler things for our world, and send some young lives from this place, we beseech you, to consecrate their strength and their minds to the building of the kingdom of God.

Our Father, we pray for our church. Let us not become content with present blessings or accomplishments. Lord, we are yours — may we, therefore, remain restless until everyone is found whom you desire in your flock.

All this we pray in the Spirit of Christ. Amen.

Benediction

If you have heard God's claim upon your life, respond in faith, receiving with joy his promise, and yielding your whole being to his transforming power; and go in peace in the name of the Father, and of the Son, and of the Holy Spirit. Amen.

Third Sunday In Lent

First Lesson: Exodus 17:1-7
Theme: Is God With Us?

Call To Worship

Leader: Come, God's people. Come with your difficulties.
People: **We come with our troubles because this is a place of healing.**
Leader: Come, too, with your successes.
People: **We come with our joys for this is a place of celebration.**
Leader: Come with your sins as well.
People: **We come as we are for this is a place of forgiveness and hope.**
All: **Come, let us worship together!**

Invocation

Lord, we have asked for, and received, our daily bread; feed us now with the Bread of heaven. We have asked for, and received, the water from the well; give us now the water that bubbles up from within, the water which flows to eternal life. Amen.

Confession

Almighty God, you have freed us from slavery to sin; you have led us through the wilderness of despair; you have faithfully provided for our daily needs. Yet we humbly confess that when things don't go exactly our way we feel you have deserted us. Forgive our faithlessness, O God, and help us to realize that it is we who so often have deserted you. We pray in Jesus' name. Amen.

Offertory Prayer

Almighty God, because we know that you are always with us, and that it is through us you plan to carry on the work of your kingdom here on earth that we present these offerings. Bless them, we pray, and bless the ministries of your Church as we strive to do your will. Amen.

Hymns

"Great Is Thy Faithfulness"
"Leaning On The Everlasting Arms"
"He Lives"

Third Sunday In Lent

Second Lesson: Romans 5:1-11
Theme: Our Hope — Reconciliation With God

Call To Worship

Leader: Come, let us sing for joy to the Lord.
People: Let us shout aloud to the rock of our salvation.
Leader: Let us come before him with thanksgiving,
People: and extol him with music and song.

Invocation

Help us, O God, to experience your presence today; to be overwhelmed by your transcendent majesty; to be comforted by your overshadowing wings; to be uplifted by your incomprehensible love. Give us, through worship, a new vision and a new hope, through Jesus Christ our Lord. Amen.

Confession

O God, have mercy on us. Blot out our transgressions, wash us thoroughly from our iniquities, and cleanse us from our sin. We know our transgressions, and our sin is ever before us. We know that we have done that which is evil in your sight. Forgive us, we pray. Create in us clean hearts, O God, and put a new and right spirit within us. In Jesus' name we pray. Amen.

Offertory Prayer

Realizing that many in our community and around the world are seeking an answer to their deepest needs, we present these offerings to bring the good news to everyone who will hear. Amen.

Hymns

"To God Be The Glory"
"My Jesus I Love Thee"
"Blessed Assurance"

Third Sunday In Lent

Gospel Lesson: John 4:5-42
Theme: Jesus, Savior Of The World

Call To Worship

Leader: The hour is coming, and is now here, when the true worshipers will worship the Father in spirit and truth.
People: For the Father seeks such as these to worship him.
Leader: God is Spirit, and those who worship him must worship in
spirit and truth.
**People: Great is the Lord, and greatly to be praised; he is to be
revered above all gods.**

Invocation

As we come to worship and grapple with your Word, our Father,
we realize that we are likely not only to be blessed, but also to be
disturbed; not only to be comforted, but also to be confronted; not
only to be soothed, but also to be sent. Open our eyes, O Lord. Help us
to apply your Word, and expand our understanding. We ask in Jesus'
name. Amen.

Confession

Lord Jesus, we confess that often we have been more interested in
quenching our physical thirst than in seeking the living water from
you. We have been concerned about food for our bodies, and ignored
the Bread of Life which would strengthen us to do your will. Forgive
us, we pray, and grant us the wisdom and the courage to be more
worthy disciples. Amen.

Offertory Prayer

Lord, because we care, because we have hope, because we have
faith, because we love, we bring these offerings. Amen.

Hymns

"Jesus, Keep Me Near The Cross"
"Fill My Cup, Lord"
"O Zion, Haste"

Third Sunday In Lent

Psalter: Psalm 95

Words Of Assurance

If we confess our sins, God is faithful and just, and will forgive our sins and cleanse us from all unrighteousness.

Pastoral Prayer

O God, who in fatherly wisdom has given us freedom to lock or unlock our hearts' doors, teach us the secret of an open heart. Let our waiting for your knock become a reverent desire to please you as loving children. When words fail us and our thoughts are barren, teach us to be still and know that you are all in all. If our soul's image of you is uncertain, put your arms around us. May we feel the strength of your majesty and the reassurance of redeeming love.

O Spirit of the Eternal, at times we find it easy to commune with you. When beauty and joy flood our life, and you provide our creature comforts in abundance, we are thankful. When life is healthy and strong and our efforts meet with success, let us not fail to see the deeper meaning in your blessings for us. Save us then from pride and make our life a song of praise.

Lord of mystery and holiness, often we find it hard to commune with you. In mercy and patience bend close to the mists of uncertainty until we recognize that it is the Lord. When we are overwhelmed by our weakness and failure, come to us as a friend of sinners. If we feel no need of prayer, reveal your fingerprints upon every gift and the marks of Christ's sufferings upon the world's sorrows and broken hopes. When we seek your face and remember grievances which keep one of your children from your altar and fellowship, show us the way of reconciliation. When anxieties press in to suffocate the breath of the Spirit, give us faith to breathe deeply the winds of heaven's promises. When burdens oppress us, be like a shadow of a mighty rock in the heat of a desert. If any of us are beset by doubt, then let us reach out in mind and spirit until we feel your timeless heartbeat near our hearts. Let us not be afraid to follow the reasoning of faith when it outreaches the reasoning of our minds. May radiance upon our faces be the sign that we have been with you.

Now send us out to make goodness attractive and righteousness lovable. Forgive us that we should ever so misrepresent Christ, that the world should not see him in us. We ask it in the Spirit of the Master, Jesus Christ our Lord. Amen.

Benediction

May your weariness give way to strength, and may your failures be transformed into victory, through the hope of the gospel and the courage of God's living Spirit; and the blessing of God the Father, Son, and Holy Spirit go with you. Amen.

Fourth Sunday In Lent

First Lesson: 1 Samuel 16:1-13
Theme: The Lord Looks On The Heart

Call To Worship

Come, let us prepare our hearts and minds to worship the Lord our God. The Lord does not look at our outward appearance, but on the heart. So come, let us open our hearts and minds to the power and influence of God's love and care.

Invocation

Our Father, as we gather for an experience of worship, we ask that you will help us prepare. Remove, we pray, our masks of pretense; take away our resentments; overcome our indifference; remove our preoccupations; and dispel our fears; through Jesus Christ our Lord. Amen.

Confession

O Lord, the Cross shouts to us that you have not given up on us, that you have forgiven us, that you have died for us. We come before you now with penitent hearts to claim that forgiveness. Our lives have been so cluttered with the love of things, that we have not heard your Word of Love. We have been so emotional over personal conflicts, that we have not received forgiveness. We have been so caught up in impressing people, that we have not been impressed by your sacrifice.

Lord, we must confess that we have found it easy to judge people by their outward appearance, and have failed to look within the heart to see them as brothers and sisters, loved by you even as we are. Forgive us, Merciful God, and create in us clean hearts; through Jesus Christ our Lord. Amen.

Offertory Prayer

O Lord, help us always to translate our vision into reality; to transform our good intentions into good deeds; and to express with our gifts what we feel in our hearts. Amen.

Hymns

"Breathe On Me, Breath Of God"
"Help Us Accept Each Other"
"O Love That Wilt Not Let Me Go"

Fourth Sunday In Lent

Second Lesson: Ephesians 5:8-14
Theme: Living As Children Of Light

Call To Worship
God, who said, "Let light shine out of darkness," has not only given us the brightness of a new day, but has given us the light of the glory of his knowledge in the face of Jesus Christ. Come, let us come to the light!

Invocation
God of light, in whom there is no darkness, and who made the sun to shine, wake us not only from the night of rest, but wake us also from our night of doubt and fear.

Bathe our lives in the light of the truth taught by your Spirit and revealed in Jesus Christ, our Lord, whom we praise forever. Amen.

Confession
Gracious God, we confess that though we have seen the Light of the World, often we have preferred to walk in darkness. Forgive our foolish ways, and help us always to keep our eyes upon you that we may not stumble on our journey to walk in the footsteps of our Lord and Savior, Jesus Christ. Amen.

Offertory Prayer
Because Christ is the light of our lives, we present these gifts. Because Christ has called us to reflect this light and to share his love with a stumbling world, we give these offerings. Amen.

Hymns
"Trust And Obey"
"When I Survey The Wondrous Cross"
"I Want To Walk As A Child Of The Light"

Fourth Sunday In Lent

Gospel Lesson: John 9:1-41
Theme: Open Our Eyes That We May See

Call To Worship

We come together to worship the God of Love. We come to hear his message of Love. We come to thank him for his great gift of Love. We come to reflect on the awesome power of his Love. Come, let us worship!

Invocation

We know, O God, that without your help our search is in vain, our efforts are useless, and our worship is cold. Warm our hearts, strengthen our wills, and sharpen our minds, so that your name will be honored and our faith will be firmly established. Amen.

Confession

O Lord, our God, we have pledged ourselves to follow in the Master's footsteps, but time and again we have stumbled; blinded by the cares and concerns of this world we have failed to see the Light of the World. Extend your strong hand and lift us up, Lord. We have wandered far from your will. Incline us by the pressure of your will to return to our spiritual home. We pray in Jesus' name. Amen.

Offertory Prayer

Come to our aid, Lord, as we try to sort out our priorities in life. Help us always to put first things first, and help us to place our trust in those things that are eternal. Amen.

Hymns

"Precious Lord, Take My Hand"
"Be Thou My Vision"
"Open My Eyes, That I May See"

Fourth Sunday In Lent

Psalter: Psalm 23

Words Of Assurance

This is the message we have heard from him and proclaim to you, that God is light and in him is no darkness at all. If we walk in the light, as he is in the light, we have fellowship with one another, and the blood of Jesus his Son cleanses us from all sin.

Pastoral Prayer

Eternal Spirit, hope of the souls that seek you, strength of the souls that find you, we worship you, praying for that inner refreshment and renewal which only your presence can bring. Through another week the world has towered above us with its turbulence, and we have grown anxious, fearful, perplexed, inadequate. We need some shepherd to lead us in green pastures and beside the still waters, restoring our souls. Surprise us today with some unexpected gift of your grace, some needed insight and guidance, some vision of new possibilities, some fresh resource of strength and courage. Let this visit to your sanctuary be to some of us the beginning of a new era, as though once more at the burning bush your voice said to us, "The place whereon you stand is holy ground."

We pray for inner, spiritual victory over our lives. Grant us this triumph when we face hardship. We dare not ask to be spared life's difficulties and tragedies. Whatever strength of character we have achieved, whatever fortitude and patience we possess, has come from handling hardships. But we pray that we may rise above it, be superior to it, have power to transcend it, that we may build it into the fabric of our characters and weave it into the texture of our souls.

Grant us victory, we pray, over our temptations. Have mercy upon us, for we are exceedingly beset by enticements to evil. May the good life, revealed in Christ, shine in our eyes today with an attractiveness that evil cannot have. Above all, we pray that we may so handle ourselves that we may not hurt and harm others. You have woven into our lives those whom we deeply love, so that whatever we do, we do also to them. Help us to be our best for their sakes, and may we never by our weakness injure and despoil them.

As thus we pray for ourselves, we pray for the world, and especially for all those who labor for the good of humankind. We pray, too, for your Church, O God. Make the Christian Church more Christian. May the Spirit of Jesus descend upon her and invade all who represent her, that the day of the Lord's victory may come at last.

All this we pray in the Spirit of Christ. Amen.

Benediction

Let love be genuine, hate what is evil, hold fast to what is good; and the blessing of God the Father, Son, and Holy Spirit be yours. Amen.

Fifth Sunday In Lent

First Lesson: Ezekiel 37:1-14
Theme: We Live When God's Spirit Is Within Us

Call To Worship

The Lord calls us to worship, not for his sake, but for ours; for in worship our lives take on a new dimension. We become more aware of divine realities; we readjust our priorities and goals; we raise our ethical standards; and we see ourselves as people with eternal significance. Come! Let us worship!

Invocation

Creator God, rekindle within us the presence of your Holy Spirit. Create in us a clearer understanding of the depths of your grace. May your Spirit breathe within us the love and joy that warms our often cold and lifeless hearts. Renew a right spirit within us, and empower our lives until we become the new creation you have promised to those who believe in you; through Jesus Christ our Lord. Amen.

Confession

O Lord, we spend so much of our time worrying about material things that we have no time for spiritual concerns. We wonder about so many needs, and we forget that you already know we have need of these things. Little wonder that our souls are withering like a bag of dry bones. Forgive us, Lord, and renew a right spirit within us that we might truly live for you. Amen.

Offertory Prayer

O Lord, through our offerings we express the new creation in us. Darkness has given way to light; self-centeredness has been replaced by concern and love; greed has given way to generosity; the old has been overwhelmed by the new. Amen.

Hymns

"In The Cross Of Christ I Glory"
"My Faith Looks Up To Thee"
"Breathe On Me, Breath Of God"

Fifth Sunday In Lent

Second Lesson: Romans 8:6-11
Theme: The Spirit Is Life

Call To Worship

Come, let us celebrate life — body life and soul life, private life and corporate life, this life and the life to come; and let us honor God, the source of all life.

Invocation

O God, source of all life, we thank you for your abiding love. As we come to you this day renew within us an awareness of who we are as your people. May this be a time of new insight and new resolution to live in the way of the One who came not to be served but to serve, even Jesus Christ. Free us now from wandering of mind and restlessness of heart that we might worship you in spirit and in truth. Amen.

Confession

Almighty God, how often we have stood by the grave of loved ones and mourned their death as though it was the end of life. Grant us a renewed faith in the promise that your Son came into the world that whosoever believes in him might have eternal life. We pray in Jesus' name. Amen.

Offertory Prayer

Father, grant that in our giving, as in all our other ways, we may be led by the Spirit of Christ dwelling in us. Amen.

Hymns

"Holy Spirit, Truth Divine"
"He Lives"
"Surely The Presence Of The Lord"

Fifth Sunday In Lent

Gospel Lesson: John 11:1-45
Theme: Jesus, The Resurrection And The Life

Call To Worship
Jesus said: "I am the Resurrection and the Life. Those who believe in me, even though they die, will live, and everyone who lives and believes in me will never die."

Come, let us worship the Lord of Life, and lift up our hearts and voices in praise and thanksgiving to the Almighty.

Invocation
Eternal God, we pray to you with a sense of wonder. You are far beyond our ability to comprehend or define, yet you come to us as Parent and Friend. We pray now that you will direct our minds to your Son, Jesus Christ. Help us to capture his vision of goodness, truth, and love. Enable us to take that Spirit of his into our daily round of affairs. Through him may we live life in a new dimension, and through lives transformed by him, may this broken world find its way to truth and peace. Amen.

Confession
Lord, because we have failed to turn to you in our deepest time of need, we have suffered needlessly. We come now with penitent hearts asking to be forgiven for our foolishness. We bring to you our discouraged hearts, asking hope. We bring to you our wavering commitment, asking renewal. We bring to you our puzzled wills, asking direction. We bring to your our loneliness, asking love. Through Jesus Christ our Savior, we pray. Amen.

Offertory Prayer
O God, you see and know not only the gifts we bring, but also the love with which they are given. Accept our offerings and our devotion to your service, and increase in us the works of faith and love, through Jesus Christ our Lord. Amen.

Hymns

"Victory In Jesus"
"When I Survey The Wondrous Cross"
"Jesu, Jesu"

Fifth Sunday In Lent

Psalter: Psalm 130

Words Of Assurance

In this be confident: that the grace of God is active enough to forgive, and the love of God is powerful enough to transform.

Pastoral Prayer

Gracious God, through whose faithfulness and providential care we are sustained from day to day, help us to come before you with complete honesty and sincerity. Your divine holiness and majesty strike us with awesome wonder. In the light of your presence show us a love that will vanish all our fears and doubts, and make us to be at home with you. Let us know your comforting compassion, your unconditional acceptance, however undeserving we may be. Seldom are we loved enough or valued enough, safe enough or powerful enough. Our needs are not only insatiable, they often conflict with one another. We often compete and fight with those whose love we most need and want. We sometimes use our powers to coerce and command, and we are left with empty hands and bleeding hearts. In our rage we discover how fragile is the gift of reason, how brittle the thread of sanity. We need serenity to discipline our passions. We need the quiet patience that nurtures friendship, the relinquishment of desires that quiets striving and brings peace and contentment.

As we continue this Lenten journey with Jesus Christ, give us the power to bring all of life, all of self under his guidance and control. Let us follow Jesus through his Gethsemane of anguish and temptation, feel the humiliation and rejection of his cross-bearing, the terror of his torture, the loneliness of his death. You know how we would rather sleep than watch, and we pray that we do not enter temptation. Always our flesh is weak. Help us never to betray our Lord with some kiss of death or deliver him over to his enemies for a purse of silver and gold. And if by chance or willful neglect we miss the mark of our high resolution and intent, then smile on us, O Christ, as you did to Peter when he followed afar off and swore to your enemies that he never knew you. See some solid rock of possibility within us as you did in him, and on that rock build your temple of the Spirit, a temple of love and forgiveness, light and hope.

Let this be a time truly of repentance and personal preparation to celebrate the resurrection of Jesus Christ our Lord. Make us mindful of the multiplied missions of people who have never heard the good news of salvation through him. As we share in the benefits of his suffering passion, give us grace to share your saving love with others. Only then will your kingdom come and your will be done on earth as it is in heaven. We pray in the name and for the sake of Jesus Christ our Lord and Savior. Amen.

Benediction

The salvation of God has been offered to you this day. By the grace of our Lord Jesus Christ receive now the wholeness that comes only from God, and walk in the light of his fellowship. Amen.

Sunday Of The Passion (Sixth Sunday In Lent/Palm Sunday)

First Lesson: Isaiah 50:4-9a
Theme: Turning The Other Cheek

Call To Worship

Leader: He was oppressed, and he was afflicted,
People: yet he did not open his mouth;
Leader: like a lamb that is led to the slaughter, and like a sheep that before its shearers is silent,
People: so he did not open his mouth.
Leader: They made his grave with the wicked, and his tomb with the rich,
People: although he had done no violence, and there was no deceit in his mouth.
Leader: Come, let us worship the One who was wounded for our transgressions, crushed for our iniquities.

Invocation

O Lord, as your followers shouted hosannas and spread their clothing and palm branches to greet you on that first Palm Sunday, so we open our lips in praise and spread our lives before you in sacrifice.

May we not forget, Lord, that before the week was over you were beaten, tortured, mocked, and spat upon.

Help us to understand, Lord, that between the victories of Palm Sunday and Easter you underwent this humiliation for us.

With humble and contrite hearts we bow before you in this hour to offer our prayers of thanksgiving for your life, death, and resurrection. Amen.

Confession

Lord, we confess that often we leave this time of worship with loud hosannas still ringing in our hearts, and shouts of acclamation coming from our lips to praise the King of kings, only to find by the end of the week we have been swayed by the crowd and our hosannas, as well as our actions, cry out, "Crucify him!" Forgive us, Lord, and strengthen our faith that we may remain true disciples. In Jesus' name we pray. Amen.

Offertory Prayer

Lord, as you made your triumphal entry into Jerusalem, we pray that you will make a triumphal entry into our hearts and lives. By your Holy Spirit enable us to be faithful disciples praising you not only with our lips, but by our deeds and by our giving for the sake of others. Amen.

Hymns

"All Glory, Laud And Honor"
"What Wondrous Love Is This"
"Hail, Thou Once Despised Jesus"

Sunday Of The Passion (Sixth Sunday In Lent/Palm Sunday)

Second Lesson: Philippians 2:5-11
Theme: The Humility Of Jesus

Call To Worship
Praise to him who comes in the name of the Lord. Shout with joy, for your King is coming! He proclaims peace to the nations and healing to the end of the earth. Hosanna in the highest. Honor and praise to Christ our King!

Invocation
Almighty God, today when we remember the day on which Jesus rode in triumph into the city of Jerusalem, we pray that now and always he may triumph in our hearts. We praise you that he came into the world not as a conquering ruler, but as the Messiah to save us from our sins and reveal to us the God of the universe as the God of love. Help us to do our part that the day will come when every knee shall bow, and every tongue confess that Jesus Christ is Lord. Amen.

Confession
We confess, Lord, that our worship often lacks the enthusiasm of the early followers who shouted "Hosanna" in the streets of Jerusalem. So often we worship out of a sense of obligation rather than of enthusiastic desire. The smile is not on our faces, and the spring is not in our steps. Fill us, Lord, with a sense of awe and wonderment in your presence, and help us to celebrate with joy your mighty acts among us. Amen.

Offertory Prayer
As we give, we remember Jesus Christ our King. We remember that he devoted his life to doing good. We remember that he designated his death as a sacrifice. We remember that he appointed us to carry on his work. As we give, we remember Jesus Christ. Amen.

Hymns
"All Praise To Thee, For Thou, O King Divine"
"Take Up Thy Cross"
"At The Name Of Jesus"

Sunday Of The Passion (Sixth Sunday In Lent/Palm Sunday)

Gospel Lesson: Matthew 26:14—27:66 or Matthew 27:11-54
Theme: Dark Gethsemane

Call To Worship

Leader: Hosanna to the Son of David!
People: Hosanna in the highest!
Leader: Blessed is the One who comes in the name of the Lord.
People: Hosanna in the highest!

Invocation

Lord God, we gather to praise you this morning, as did the believers in the streets of Jerusalem so many years ago. May our hosannas be genuine, and may our devotion be sincere. Amen.

Confession

Gracious Lord, we humbly confess that your kingship has not always been evident in our lives. We have not always been obedient to your authority and we have failed to reflect your character in our thoughts and actions.

Forgive us, we pray, for our betrayal of your trust in us and strengthen us that we may be more worthy disciples of our Lord Jesus Christ. Amen.

Offertory Prayer

Almighty God, we know that our most generous gift stands pale alongside your sacrifice through Christ. Nevertheless we wish to respond in some meaningful way. So we give in faith, knowing that you will receive our offerings with your benediction and will use them to share your love. Amen.

Hymns

"Lift Up Your Heads, Ye Mighty Gates"
"Go To Dark Gethsemane"
"Precious Name"

Sunday Of The Passion (Sixth Sunday In Lent/Palm Sunday)

Psalter: Psalm 31:1-16

Words Of Assurance

For this be thankful, and in this be confident: that Jesus Christ through sacrifice and humility accomplished more than all the armies that ever marched and all the bombs ever dropped, and all the violence ever perpetrated in the name of truth.

Pastoral Prayer

Hosanna! Blessed is the One who comes in the name of the Lord! With multitudes of disciples we greet you and rejoice at your coming. So many moments sound forth your presence among us, and thus we rejoice when despair is overcome by hope; when the season of indifference gives way to warmth and tenderness; when the warm breezes of spring quicken our forgotten energies; when a friend says the right thing only a friend could say to us; when our prayers at last are answered. However you signal your life among us, whenever your goodness appears to us, we give you thanks and pray, come and abide with us forever, through Jesus Christ our Lord.

As you entered the city vast crowds rejoiced to see you, and before you cried out our ancient longings for peace. Even now we pray for peace. Deliver us, O God, from violence of terrorism and curse of war, from the human sin that builds enmity among the people of the earth. Make keen the minds and strong the hands of those in all nations who work for peace, that we may learn to live together in your love, through Jesus Christ our Lord.

We rejoice today with our hosannas and palms, but we know that Friday will bring a cross and cries for crucifixion. As we begin this holy week, we pray you will send your Spirit upon us that we may walk the way of the cross bravely and honestly. Keep our eyes upon the One who comes in the name of the Lord, and do not let us look away in fear or shame. Quiet the small concerns that distract us from this pilgrimage. Comfort those who tremble in the shadow of death. Give direction to those who are confused, that we may together walk from the shadow of betrayal, through a dark tomb and into the brilliance of resurrection hope, through Jesus Christ our Lord.

All this we pray in the name of Jesus Christ, our Triumphant Lord. Amen.

Benediction

As you walk the streets of your life, may you continue to sing hosannas and honor Christ as the sovereign and ruler of your life; and the blessing of God the Father, Son, and Holy Spirit go with you. Amen.

Holy/Maundy Thursday

First Lesson: Exodus 12:1-4 (5-10), 11-14
Theme: The Passover

Call To Worship
The loud hosannas of Sunday have faded into oblivion. Jesus has gathered his disciples for the Passover Feast. Let us now join in that event of remembrance.

Invocation
Lord, we gather at your table as did your disciples so long ago. Open our eyes that we may see our role as servants. Open our mouths that we may praise you for your victory over sin and death. Open our hearts that we may welcome your presence in our lives. We pray in Jesus' name. Amen.

Confession
Merciful God, we confess that like Judas we have betrayed you for the sake of material gain. Like Peter we have denied you rather than sharing our faith in you. By your Spirit make us to be faithful disciples, through Jesus Christ our Lord. Amen.

Offertory Prayer
Lord, in response to your love which is so amazing, so divine, we offer you our souls, our lives, our all. Amen.

Hymns
"Here, O My Lord, I See Thee"
"For The Bread Which You Have Broken"
"Just As I Am, Without One Plea"

Holy/Maundy Thursday

Second Lesson: 1 Corinthians 11:23-26
Theme: The Institution Of The Lord's Supper

Call To Worship

Leader: The grace of the Lord Jesus Christ be with you.
People: And also with you.
Leader: Christ commands his disciples to partake of the bread and the cup in remembrance of him.
People: Christ has prepared a feast of love for us. We remember with thanksgiving.

Invocation

Lord, we gather together tonight around your table that we might commune with you. We know that your work on earth is not yet completed, and that you are relying on your disciples to extend your loving arms until they embrace the whole wide world. Tonight we would rededicate ourselves to you and to that task. Amen.

Confession

Gracious God, we humbly confess that we have not loved you with all our heart and mind and soul and strength; nor have we loved our neighbors as ourselves. Forgive us, we pray, and by your Spirit within us make us more worthy disciples of our Lord Jesus Christ. Amen.

Offertory Prayer

O God of our salvation, as you accepted the total and perfect sacrifice of your Son, we ask that you will receive these sacrifices, however partial and faulty they may be; through Jesus Christ our Lord. Amen.

Hymns

"Bread Of The World"
"For The Bread Which You Have Broken"
"Become To Us The Living Bread"

Holy/Maundy Thursday

Gospel Lesson: John 13:1-17, 31b-35
Theme: Servant Leadership

Call To Worship
Christ showed us his love by becoming a humble servant. Let us draw near to God as we remember his death and resurrection, and his command to love one another.

Invocation
O God, in mystery and silence you are present in our lives, bringing hope out of despair, courage out of weakness, peace out of turmoil. We thank you that you do not leave us alone, but walk with us as our companion and friend. Help us to pay attention to the gentle guidance of your Spirit that we may know the joy you give your people. Amen.

Confession
Most Merciful God, we confess that often our spirit has not been that of Christ. Where we have failed to love one another as he loves us, where we have pledged loyalty to him with our lips and then betrayed, deserted, or denied him, forgive us we pray. By your Spirit make us faithful in every time of trial; through Jesus Christ our Lord. Amen.

Offertory Prayer
O God of our salvation, having received the benefits of the greatest sacrifice ever made, by the greatest person who ever lived, we respond by giving our sacrificial gifts for the greatest cause ever known. Amen.

Hymns
"I Come With Joy"
"Jesu, Jesu"
"Now Let Us From This Table Rise"

Holy/Maundy Thursday

Psalter: Psalm 116

Words Of Assurance

Leader: Believe the Good News: In the name of Jesus Christ, you are forgiven!

People: In the name of Jesus Christ, you are forgiven!

All: Glory to God. Amen.

Pastoral Prayer

Almighty God, we gather this evening in remembrance of your Son, Jesus Christ, who gave his life for us. As we partake of the bread and the cup make us mindful of your presence and your indwelling Spirit in our lives. Grant that in all our ways and doings we may remember that you see us, and may we always have grace to know and perceive the things you would have us do, and the strength to fulfill them.

O Lord, Jesus Christ, who for our sake underwent want and shame, we confess most humbly that we have refused to share the burden of your cross, that we have denied you rather than face mockery, and have sought comfort and security. Forgive our sins, help us to amend, and give us courage to endure.

O God, our Heavenly Father, you are always kind to us; you give us life and health and every good thing which we enjoy. We thank you that you have made this earth so beautiful, and that there is so much in it for us to love, and so many things to make us happy. May we think of this world as your world, and remember that you are on earth as in heaven. Since you are always near to take care of us, may we never be afraid, except of grieving you and robbing ourselves or others of the gladness of life.

God of truth, free us from all hypocrisy and dishonesty. May all that we say and do issue from a trained and understanding love deep within us. May we respond wisely and unselfishly to the immediate needs of those around us and throughout the world. May we labor for goodness here and now in our daily contacts with others. As we profess brotherhood, may we be a brother or sister to all persons, especially to those who least attract us. As we cherish freedom may we restrain ourselves so that we do not interfere with the rights and privileges of our fellows. As we cry for justice, may we practice fairness in all our relations and activities. As we yearn for love to rule the world, may we be severe with our own faults, and gentle with the failings of others. O God, make our thinking a brave and active part of your saving truth.

We ask it in the name of Jesus Christ our Lord and Savior. Amen.

Benediction

Go in peace. May Jesus Christ, who for our sake became obedient unto death, even death on a cross, keep you and strengthen you this night and forever; and the blessing of God the Father, Son, and Holy Spirit be with you. Amen.

Good Friday

First Lesson: Isaiah 52:13—53:12
Theme: The Suffering Servant

Call To Worship

Leader: Come, let us kneel before the cross with awe.
People: We behold the Lamb of God who takes away the sins of the world.
Leader: All we like sheep have gone astray; we have all turned to our own way,
People: and the Lord has laid on him the iniquity of us all.
All: Praise be to God!

Invocation

Almighty God, we bow before you in humble recognition that Christ died on the cross for our salvation. We give you thanks for your love as expressed in the death of your Son, Jesus Christ, and pray that as his disciples we may joyfully take up our cross daily and follow him. Amen.

Confession

Lord Jesus Christ, come into the brokenness of our lives with your healing love. We bow before you in true repentance for our sins which have separated us from you. By the power of your Holy Spirit melt our hard hearts and consume the pride and prejudice which keeps us from expressing your love through us to others. We pray in Jesus' name. Amen.

Offertory Prayer

Lord, in humility we bring our gifts to you and ask that you will use them and us to proclaim the message of your death and resurrection to a needy world. Amen.

Hymns

"O Sacred Head Now Wounded"
"What Wondrous Love Is This"
"In The Cross Of Christ I Glory"

Good Friday

Second Lesson: Hebrews 10:16-25
Theme: Forgiveness

Call To Worship

Leader: Come, God has promised that he will remember our sins no more.

People: We come with true hearts in full assurance of faith, with our hearts sprinkled clean from an evil conscience.

Leader: Let us consider how to provoke one another to love and good deeds.

People: We come together to encourage one another. Praise be to our Redeemer.

Invocation

Almighty God, we come together as part of your family for whom Christ was willing to be betrayed into the hands of sinners, and to suffer death upon the cross; who now lives and reigns with you and the Holy Spirit, one God for ever and ever. Amen.

Confession

Lord, we confess that from time to time we have been guilty of neglecting to meet with our fellow Christians to worship and encourage one another. Forgive us, we pray. Yes, we have often failed to provoke one another to good deeds. As we stand before the cross on which our Savior died for us, it is with shame and sorrow that we recognize our shortcomings. Renew a right spirit within us, we pray, for the sake of Jesus Christ our Lord.

Offertory Prayer

Almighty God, accept these our tithes and offerings as an expression of our love, and with them our lives that we may be used by you to spread your love throughout the world. Amen.

Hymns

"O Love Divine, What Hast Thou Done"
"Beneath The Cross Of Jesus"
"Are Ye Able"

Good Friday

Gospel Lesson: John 18:1—19:42
Theme: The Crucifixion Of Jesus

Call To Worship

Behold the Savior of humankind nailed to the shameful tree; see where he bows his sacred head! He bows his head and dies! O Lamb of God, was ever pain, was ever love like this?

Invocation

Almighty God, we come together in recognition that your Son, Jesus Christ, gave himself up on the cross in order that the whole world might be reconciled to you. Even as we glory in his supreme sacrifice we hear his call for us to take up our cross and follow him. Amen.

Confession

Lord, be our strength, for we know that we have stumbled time and again as we have tried to carry our cross. Be our guide as so often we have lost the way as we struggle to follow the Master. Be our comforter as we have stood beneath the cross and bewailed the sins of the world which led to the crucifixion of our Lord. Amen.

Offertory Prayer

Almighty God, as Christ in obedience offered himself for the good of all, so we offer ourselves and our gifts so we can share with others the love he came to express. Amen.

Hymns

"Alas! And Did My Savior Bleed"
"He Never Said A Mumbalin' Word"
"O Crucified Redeemer"

Good Friday

Psalter: Psalm 22

Words Of Assurance

On the night that he was betrayed Jesus said to his disciples: "Do not let your hearts be troubled. Believe in God, believe also in me."

Pastoral Prayer

O God, who redeemed us through the mystery of the cross; we bow before you in reverent gratitude for the revelation of your love declared in Jesus Christ. We praise you that he shared our common life and humbled himself and became obedient unto death, even the death of the cross. We bless you that he bore our griefs, carried our sorrows, and triumphed over sin and death. We glorify you that through his perfect and sufficient sacrifice on the cross there is pardon for the penitent, power to overcome for the faithful, and transformed life for all who truly turn to him.

Give us grace to yield ourselves in glad surrender to the Lord Jesus. May we share his spirit of obedience to your will, his consecration to the welfare of humanity, and his passion that your kingdom may come and your will be done on earth as it is in heaven. So may Christ dwell in our hearts and reign there as our divine Redeemer. Amen.

Benediction

May our Lord Jesus Christ, who for our sake became obedient unto death, even death on a cross, keep you, now and forever. Amen.

Easter Day (Resurrection Of Our Lord)

First Lesson: Acts 10:34-43 or Jeremiah 31:1-6
Theme: Jesus Christ — Lord Of All or Everlasting Love

Call To Worship

Leader: Come, let us praise the Lord.
People: Let us worship our Risen Savior.
Leader: For death has given way to life,
People: despair has been replaced by hope,
Leader: grief has been replaced by joy,
People: and darkness has been dispelled by light.
All: Christ is Risen, Alleluia!

Invocation

God, our Father, by raising Christ your Son, you conquered the power of death and opened to all who believe in him eternal life. We pray that each person here may truly share the joy of Easter, experiencing in mind and in soul the stirrings of new birth and believing with unwavering confidence in the promise of the life to come. Amen.

Confession

We know, Father, that the good news of the resurrection is not to be kept a secret, hidden away as the private promise to a few. Rather it is to be a universal communication of hope and joy to all people. Where we have failed in our commitment to make known your eternal love to all the world we now ask your forgiveness, and pray that through your Holy Spirit we may rededicate ourselves to this task. Amen.

Offertory Prayer

In commitment to the worldwide proclamation of the good news of the resurrection of Jesus Christ, we dedicate these offerings of love. Amen.

Hymns

"Easter People, Raise Your Voices"
"Christ Is Risen"
"We've A Story To Tell To The Nations"

Easter Day (Resurrection Of Our Lord)

Second Lesson: Colossians 3:1-4
Theme: New Life In Christ

Call To Worship

Leader: Come, Holy Spirit, fill the hearts of your faithful.
People: Kindle in us the fire of your love.
Leader: Jesus said: "I am the resurrection and the life."
People: We come seeking that new life in Christ.

Invocation

Almighty God, as you opened the tomb on Easter morning, proving to the world that you can bring forth life from death and joy from mourning, we ask that you will also work a mighty miracle in our lives. May our hearts be filled with the joy of resurrection, and may Christ's life vibrate through all that we do, all that we say, and all that we think. Amen.

Confession

Almighty God, we have claimed the new life in Christ but time and again we have set our minds on things on earth rather than on things that are above. Forgive us, we pray, and through your Holy Spirit help us to rise above the material things that surround us that we may truly enter into your kingdom now and for all eternity. Amen.

Offertory Prayer

Father, we give these gifts as an act of celebration: celebrating the resurrection of our Savior, celebrating our own new life, and celebrating the worldwide proclamation of the good news to all people everywhere. Amen.

Hymns

"Christ Is Alive"
"The Strife Is O'er, The Battle Done"
"Thine Be The Glory"

Easter Day (Resurrection Of Our Lord)

Gospel Lesson: John 20:1-18 or Matthew 28:1-10
Theme: The Resurrection Of Jesus

Call To Worship

Leader: Christ is risen!
People: Christ is risen indeed!
All: Alleluia!

Invocation

Our Father in heaven, this is the best day of the year, for we celebrate the best day of all time. Jesus, who was dead, is alive, and we, who will one day die, will live again. Darkness has yielded to light, and evil has been defeated by the holy. May this hour reflect the joy of the event we celebrate, and may our lives be flooded with your hope. Amen.

Confession

Forgive us, Father, for sometimes living as if Easter had never taken place. We have allowed prophecies of doom to darken our thinking. We have wrung our hands helplessly because of the evil which surrounds us. We have allowed the pain of bereavement to blind us to the promise of reunion. Enable us, Lord, to cast aside the dark attitude of despair and gloom, and may we reflect in our lives the joyful reality of the resurrection. Amen.

Offertory Prayer

Almighty God, we offer these gifts as an affirmation of life and hope: the new life we have in Christ, the new confidence we have toward the future, and our desire for all people everywhere to share this joy. Amen.

Hymns

"Christ The Lord Is Risen Today"
"He Lives"
"O Sons And Daughters, Let Us Sing"

Easter Day (Resurrection Of Our Lord)

Psalter: Psalm 118:14-29

Words Of Assurance

For God so loved the world that he gave his only Son, that whoever believes in him should not perish but have eternal life.

Pastoral Prayer

Ever-living God, we hail you in the risen Christ who brings to our dark world the glory of an eternal morning. Your deathless life shines above the crosses of sin, bursts through the tombs of death, and is reflected by the beauty of springtime. We would touch you, O Unseen Presence, with the hands of doubt, and behold you with the eyes of faith. Stir our souls with joy as you move among us. Let us, like Mary, hear you calling us by name in the midst of waiting sorrow and longing loneliness. Where our heartstrings have ceased to sing, let the resurrection songs of victory awaken new melodies of hope. Be the living Master who goes before us, healing the wounds of sin and lifting up the truth of life that would claim our love.

Eternal God, we thank you for the cloud of witnesses from days gone by who surround our worship here; for every memory of strong faith, humane service, and Christ-like character. Deepen our gratitude for sacrifices made by those who have gone the King's Highway before us, persons who found in your church refreshment and comfort, peace and restoration, challenge to service and strength to render it. Give us grace to see the need of our children, and our children's children, and let not the heritage of the gospel fail them because of our slackness or infidelity.

Grant unto your Church, O God, a new sense of your power and a holy passion to glorify you among all persons, and to let your kingdom come and your will be done; through Jesus Christ our Lord. Amen.

Benediction

For this amazing day, may God's name be praised! And may the creative love of God, the power of Jesus' resurrection, and the sustaining grace of the Holy Spirit be with you and with the ones you love, wherever they may be, this day and always. Amen.

147

Second Sunday Of Easter

First Lesson: Acts 2:14a, 22-32
Theme: Testimony To The Risen Lord

Call To Worship

Leader: Praise the Lord! Praise the Lord, O my soul!
People: I will sing praises to my God all my life long.
Leader: The Lord is gracious and merciful,
People: slow to anger and abounding in steadfast love.
Leader: The Lord is good to all,
People: And his compassion is over all that he has made. Amen.

Invocation

Lord of life, Conqueror of death, you draw all people to you and by your resurrection you restored to humanity all that we had lost through sin.
All praise is yours, now and throughout eternity. Amen.

Confession

Almighty God, forgive, we pray, our unbelief, our laziness, our failure to follow the leading of your Son, Jesus Christ. When we are challenged, we turn away. When we are threatened, we cling to ourselves. Merciful Father, pardon our sin, and give us new Spirit to live life in faith, obeying your Word made known to us in Jesus Christ our Lord. Amen.

Offertory Prayer

Our Father, as you took Christ's sacrifice and filled it with your life and power, so use our gifts and transform our lives, that we may be the living presence of your return on earth, now and always. Amen.

Hymns

"Jesus Shall Reign"
"In The Garden"
"God Whose Love Is Reigning O'er Us"

Second Sunday Of Easter

Second Lesson: 1 Peter 1:3-9
Theme: A Living Hope

Call To Worship

Leader: Praise the Lord, all you nations!
People: Extol him, all you peoples!
Leader: For great is his steadfast love toward us,
People: and the faithfulness of the Lord endures forever.
All: Praise the Lord!

Invocation

O God our help in ages past, our hope for years to come, our shelter from the stormy blast, and our eternal home: we thank you that through the resurrection of Jesus you have made known your presence with us through all the trials and tribulations of this life. Be our guide while life shall last, and our eternal home. Amen.

Confession

God of mercy and power, love and holiness, we ask that you will reach down and meet our needs. We need spiritual healing — grant us pardon. We are confused — grant us guidance. We are depressed — grant us encouragement. This we ask in the name of him whom you sent to walk among us, doing miracles and signs of the kingdom; even Jesus Christ, our Savior. Amen.

Offertory Prayer

O living Christ, you are our hope for this life and the life to come. We present these gifts and pray that they may be used to bring hope to those living in the darkness of despair and confusion. Amen.

Hymns

"O God Our Help In Ages Past"
"Rejoice, The Lord Is King"
"The Strife Is O'er, The Battle Done"

Second Sunday Of Easter

Gospel Lesson: John 20:19-31
Theme: The Doubter

Call To Worship

Leader: Give thanks to the Lord, for he is good.
People: His steadfast love endures forever.
Leader: It is better to take refuge in the Lord,
People: than to put confidence in mortals.
Leader: Let those who are wise give heed,
People: and consider the steadfast love of the Lord.

Invocation

O Lord, our God, Easter has come, and the hallelujahs have been drowned out by the cries of the world. We believe in the risen Christ, but we cry out, "Help thou our unbelief." We come this morning for that reassurance that will enable us to shout with Thomas, "My Lord and my God!" Amen.

Confession

O God, forgive us we pray for our doubts and our wavering beliefs. Strengthen our faith and keep us constantly aware of your abiding presence that we might know your peace that passes understanding. Amen.

Offertory Prayer

O Lord, our God, send down your Holy Spirit upon us to cleanse our hearts, hallow our gifts, and perfect the offering of ourselves, through Jesus Christ our Lord. Amen.

Hymns

"He Is Lord"
"Crown Him With Many Crowns"
"All Hail The Power Of Jesus' Name"

Second Sunday Of Easter

Psalter: Psalm 16:5-11

Words Of Assurance

The disciples rejoiced when they saw the Lord. Jesus said to them, "Peace be with you."

Pastoral Prayer

Eternal God, who holds in your hands the destiny of every living thing, we worship you. Thanks be to you for the note of victory that fills our souls today! Thanks be to you for our living Lord over whom death had no dominion! For the rich heritage of faith that life is ever lord of death, and that love can never lose its own, we give you thanks. Strengthen our believing. Confirm our confidence in you and life eternal.

We thank you for all things excellent and beautiful that make faith in immortality more sure. For our friends who have loved us, our homes that have nourished us, for the heights and depths of the human spirit, full of promise and prophecy, for all victories of right over wrong, and above all for Christ, who has brought life and immortality to light, we give you thanks. Join to our company today those whom we have loved and who live with you in the house not made with hands. Gather us into the fellowship of your Church, both militant and triumphant, as we sing our praise to you

We pray for those defeated souls to whom the note of victory sounds distant and unreal. You see them here, known to you, not to us, spirits frustrated by circumstance, overwhelmed by temptations, facing griefs too heavy for their unaided strength. O Lord, who can make the barren place rejoice and the desert to bloom like the rose, redeem some stricken souls here from defeat to victory.

Replenish with new hope all who are discouraged about the world, who find faith in the ultimate victory of righteousness difficult. So often might triumphs over right, and the good is undone by evil that, like our Master on his cross we cry, "My God, my God, why have you forsaken me?" O God, to whom a thousand years are but as yesterday when it is past, and as a watch in the night, speak to us and refresh our souls with a new hope. Lift our vision above the immediate. Say to us

151

this Easter season that no Calvary can finally defeat Christ. May Easter not represent to us only an historic victory, but may it mean a present triumph in our souls — the living Christ our inspiration and our strength, so that we live, and yet not we, but Christ lives in us, the hope of glory. In that sustaining faith, may we, too, like our Master, overcome the world. We pray in the name of Christ. Amen.

Benediction
Go in peace, be alert to the presence of the living Christ, and the blessing of God the Father, Son, and Holy Spirit be upon you. Amen.

Third Sunday Of Easter

First Lesson: Acts 2:14a, 36-41
Theme: Call To Repentance

Call To Worship
You who are seeking God, and you who are avoiding him; you who need to be comforted in your affliction, and you who need to be afflicted in your comfort; whatever your needs, this church opens its doors and bids you welcome. Come, let us praise the Lord.

Invocation
O God, the source of all true joy: Grant a vision of our risen Lord, that we may know your peace which passes understanding, which the world can neither give nor take away, and that pure joy which shall make radiant all our duty and all our toil; through the same Jesus Christ our Lord. Amen.

Confession
Forgive us, Father, if we have become discouraged and disheartened. We have failed to express in our lives the reality of the living Christ; we have acted as if Easter never happened. Restore to us, we pray, the glory of Easter, the joy of the resurrection, and the victory of new life in Christ. Amen.

Offertory Prayer
O Lord, with joy and thanksgiving we offer to you these symbols of our lives, and pray that you will use them to your glory. Amen.

Hymns
"Standing On The Promises"
"Amazing Grace"
"Love Divine, All Loves Excelling"

Third Sunday Of Easter

Second Lesson: 1 Peter 1:17-23
Theme: A Call To Holy Living

Call To Worship

Every Sunday is set aside as a special time to celebrate the Resurrection of our Lord and Savior, Jesus Christ. Even as we celebrate, let us also be about the business of setting our minds on things that are above and not on things that are on earth. Come, let us worship together.

Invocation

We realize, Lord God, that your presence is always with us. But our everyday activities crowd in on us, and we don't often think about you. We have come here today so we can pray without interruption, so we can meditate without distraction, so we can listen to your Word without interference. Help us to direct our minds and souls, we pray in Jesus' name. Amen.

Confession

Lord, we know that we have been called to love one another deeply from the heart, but we confess that we do not always find this easy. Send your Holy Spirit upon us that we may be born anew through your living and enduring Word. Forgive us for our past weakness and strengthen us to press on toward the goal of our high calling in Christ Jesus. Amen.

Offertory Prayer

O Lord, accept these gifts as signs of our faith, as proof of our concern, as symbols of our devotion, and as expressions of our gratitude. Amen.

Hymns

"Rejoice, Ye Pure In Heart"
"Fairest Lord Jesus"
"Lord, I Want To Be A Christian"

Third Sunday Of Easter

Gospel Lesson: Luke 24:13-35
Theme: Christ Walks With You

Call To Worship
The dawning of each new day is a celebration of creation, and the dawning of every Lord's Day is a celebration of Resurrection. Come! Let us join the celebration praising God for life itself and thanking God for the new life we share with the Son.

Invocation
O God, who commanded light to shine out of darkness, and who through your Son has illumined the path to eternity, dispel the darkness of our ignorance and guilt. Bring us out of the woods of dark despair, and lead us on the road to joy; through Christ our Lord. Amen.

Confession
Lord, like the disciples on the Emmaus Road we often are blinded by self-pity and overwhelmed by grief so that we fail to recognize your presence. Open our eyes that we may see you in all that we do and wherever our journey through life may lead us. Amen.

Offertory Prayer
O Gracious God, you have given us new life in Christ, and now we offer unto you these gifts as a visible expression of our grateful hearts. Amen.

Hymns
"On The Day Of Resurrection"
"O Master, Let Me Walk With Thee"
"He Lives"

Third Sunday Of Easter

Psalter: Psalm 116

Words Of Assurance

All thanks and honor to Christ who, when we are lost, seeks us out; who, when we are in despair, gives us hope. Amen.

Pastoral Prayer

Almighty God, who has promised to those who love you such good things as pass our understanding, make us conscious today of your presence, your goodness, and your power.

Sovereign God, we confess to you who we are: we are not the people we like others to think we are; we are afraid to admit even to ourselves what lies in the depths of our souls. But we do not want to hide our true selves from you. We believe that you know us as we are, and yet you love us. Help us not to shrink from self-knowledge; teach us to respect ourselves for your sake; give us the courage to put our trust in your guidance and power.

We also confess to you, Lord, the unrest of the world to which we contribute and in which we share. Forgive us that so many of us are indifferent to the needs of others. Forgive our reliance on weapons of terror, our discrimination against people of different races, and our preoccupation with material standards. Forgive us for being so unsure of our Good News and so unready to tell it. Raise us out of the paralysis of guilt into the freedom and energy of forgiven people.

Thank you, God, for the invitation to come to the One who is the Way, when we have lost direction, to the One who is the Truth, when our pluralistic world sees everything as relative, to the One who is the Life when our lives seem threatened.

Please help us to share with you the brokenness of our lives. Be a refuge for us in the storms of uncertainty about decisions we must make, in the waves of conflict in our homes and families, in the swirls of too much to do and not enough time to accomplish our dreams.

Open our eyes to the needs of others. Help us to minister comfort to the sick and bereaved. Remind us to pray for our political leaders. Bring peace to the war-torn, justice to the oppressed, and help us to share with the naked and hungry.

We offer these prayers in the name and for the sake of Jesus Christ our Lord and Savior. Amen.

Benediction

Go in peace and in the knowledge that God's gift of new life in Jesus Christ is yours; and may the grace of our Lord Jesus Christ, the love of God, and the fellowship of the Holy Spirit be with you always. Amen.

Fourth Sunday Of Easter

First Lesson: Acts 2:42-47
Theme: Life Among The Believers

Call To Worship

God reveals himself not to the person who is self-sufficient or self-righteous, but to the one whose mind is open, whose will is receptive, and whose soul is humble. In that spirit, let us come in worship before the Lord.

Invocation

We come, Almighty God, seeking your light and your truth. We need your light because we are surrounded by darkness. We need your truth because we are bombarded by falsehoods. Open our minds and open our hearts, that we may be taught by your Word and may be enlightened by your Spirit. Amen.

Confession

Lord, when we read how those early Christians devoted themselves to your teachings, to fellowship, to the breaking of bread, and to prayer, we realize how much we have neglected our spiritual life. Forgive us, we pray, and through the power of your Holy Spirit draw us nearer to you and to one another by cultivating spiritual disciplines in our lives. Amen.

Offertory Prayer

Consecrate, Lord, not only the gifts we give, but the hands that have earned them, the love that has shared them, and the causes that have inspired them. Amen.

Hymns

"Come, We That Love The Lord"
"When Morning Gilds The Skies"
"The Church's One Foundation"

Fourth Sunday Of Easter

Second Lesson: 1 Peter 2:19-25
Theme: When We Suffer Unjustly

Call To Worship

In a world where good people often suffer, and evil ones seem to prosper, we come before Almighty God searching for understanding and seeking for power to live Christ-like lives. Come! Let us worship together.

Invocation

We ask for your help, Lord, as we come here to worship. Help us as we listen, that we may not close our ears to truth that makes us uncomfortable. Help us as we sing, that we may mean with our minds what we say with our lips. Help us as we pray, that our spirits may truly communicate with your Spirit. In Jesus' name we pray. Amen.

Confession

O Lord, how often we have cried out to you in anger and distress when we have suffered unjustly while doing what is right. We have failed to see that Christ set us an example when he unjustly suffered the agony of the cross that the world might be drawn closer to you. Forgive our shortsightedness, we pray, and grant us the courage and the strength to follow our Redeemer's example by putting our trust in you who judges justly. Amen.

Offertory Prayer

O God, of whose bounty we have all received, accept our offerings and so follow them with your blessing that they may promote peace and good will, and advance the kingdom of our Lord and Savior Jesus Christ. Amen.

Hymns

"All Praise To Our Redeeming Lord"
"Out Of The Depths I Cry To You"
"And Are We Yet Alive"

Fourth Sunday Of Easter

Gospel Lesson: John 10:1-10
Theme: The Good Shepherd

Call To Worship

Leader: The Lord is my shepherd, I shall not want.
People: He makes me lie down in green pastures;
Leader: he leads me beside still waters;
People: he restores my soul.
Leader: Come, let us worship the Good Shepherd!

Invocation

O Lord, hear our faltering words, and turn them into songs. Take our unspoken desires, and transform them into prayers. Listen to our incoherent thoughts, and accept them as praise. We ask in Jesus' name. Amen.

Confession

Lord, we thank you for revealing yourself to us as the Good Shepherd. All we like sheep have gone astray, seeking our own path rather than following you. With grateful hearts we praise you for the countless times you have sought us out and set our feet back on the path that leads to your eternal home. Amen.

Offertory Prayer

O God, as we present these offerings we express our love and support for the Church of Jesus Christ which is built on the foundation of Christ and is dedicated to extending his work in our world. Amen.

Hymns

"The King Of Love My Shepherd Is"
"Savior, Like A Shepherd Lead Us"
"Great Is Thy Faithfulness"

Fourth Sunday Of Easter

Psalter: Psalm 23

Words Of Assurance

The Lord is gracious and merciful, slow to anger and abounding in steadfast love.

Pastoral Prayer

O God, in this time of worship help us to realize our unity with all who put their trust in you. All our lives you have been leading us, even when we did not know it. The simple things we take for granted — food, shelter, home and friends, work and play, the beauty of the world we see, the interest of the thoughts we think — all are yours, your gifts to us for our welfare and happiness. But they cannot do for us all that you desire unless we realize that they come from you. Open our eyes, we beseech you, that we may see you as you are. You who has formed us for yourself, reveal yourself to us this day.

Father of Spirits, we come to you today, conscious of our weakness, asking that you make us strong. Free us from the tyranny of the little and the near, the haste that is too busy to enjoy, the restlessness that we can bring nothing to completion. May we realize that beneath all changes of time and space, all limits of knowledge, all instability of will, the foundation of God standeth sure!

The Lord knows those who are his. Help us to be still and know that you are God. Deliver us from the fear that separates us from you — the fear of the known, the greater fear of the unknown. Strengthen us with power in the inner person, that, renewing our life from your divine life, we may be free indeed. In this world so full of unanswered questions and of unforeseen dangers, may we find in you a safe refuge and a sure defense. You who have set eternity in our hearts, grant us this day and always your peace! Watch over us all, so that day in and day out we may delight in your presence, and ever do your will; through Jesus Christ our Lord. Amen.

Benediction

Go in peace. Let your faith make a difference. Encourage one another; and may the grace of the Lord Jesus Christ, the love of God, and the fellowship of the Holy Spirit be with you always. Amen.

Fifth Sunday Of Easter

First Lesson: Acts 7:55-60
Theme: In The Face Of Persecution

Call To Worship

Leader: "Are you able," said the Master, "to be crucified with me?"
People: Lord, we are able.
Leader: "Are you able," still the Master whispers, "to believe that Spirit triumphs?"
People: Lord, we are able. Our Spirits are thine.

Invocation

Lord, we do not pray for tranquility, nor that our trials and tribulations may cease. We pray for your Spirit and your love, and that you will grant us strength and grace to overcome adversity; through Jesus Christ our Lord. Amen.

Confession

Lord, like Peter on the night of your betrayal, we too have failed to identify ourselves as your disciples when challenged by those who scoff at your message of love and good will. Forgive us for past failures and loosen our tongues that we may always confess boldly that Jesus Christ is Lord. Amen.

Offertory Prayer

O God, along with our offerings, we also give ourselves for your service. Please use all that we give and all that we are to make the world better and spread the good news of your love to all people. Amen.

Hymns

"Are Ye Able?"
"Faith Of Our Fathers"
"I Need Thee Every Hour"

Fifth Sunday Of Easter

Second Lesson: 1 Peter 2:2-10
Theme: A Chosen People

Call To Worship

To those who are wandering without direction, Jesus is the Good Shepherd. To those who need a source of strength, Jesus is the true vine. To those who see no light at the end of the tunnel, Jesus is the door to a fuller life. To those who would be builders of God's kingdom, Jesus is the chief cornerstone. Come! Let us worship together!

Invocation

All week long, our Father, we have heard the cacophony of conflicting voices; we have been enmeshed in the busyness of our work; we have been torn by the urgency of many responsibilities; we have been anxious about many things. It is good for us to come here for a while, to set aside this time for meditation and worship, to sit beside the still waters, and to hear the gentle voice of the Good Shepherd. Amen.

Confession

O God, like the foolish one who built his house on sand, we have seen everything come tumbling down around us because we failed to lay a sure foundation with Christ as the cornerstone of our lives. Help us to build anew on Christ the solid rock. Then when the storms come and the winds blow we will be able to stand firm in our faith. Amen.

Offertory Prayer

O Lord, as we offer our gifts, we offer also our lives in renewed dedication to you. Help us to make them an offering fit for your use. Amen.

Hymns

"Christ Is Made The Sure Foundation"
"The Church's One Foundation"
"Standing On The Promises"

Fifth Sunday Of Easter

Gospel Lesson: John 14:1-14
Theme: Jesus, The Way

Call To Worship

Leader: Jesus said: "I go to prepare a place for you ... where I am, there you may be also."

People: Like the disciples of old, we cry out: "Show us the way, Lord."

Leader: Jesus said: "I am the Way, and the Truth, and the Life."

People: Praise be to God who has revealed himself in his Son, Jesus Christ.

Invocation

O God, who has taught us to keep all your heavenly commandments by loving you and our neighbors, grant us the spirit of peace and grace, that we may be both devoted to you with our whole heart and united to each other with a pure will; through Jesus Christ our Lord. Amen.

Confession

O Lord, our God, you have told us not to let our hearts be troubled, but to believe in you and in your Son, Jesus Christ. Still our hearts cry out for reassurance, and our steps falter as we strive to follow Jesus. Forgive our weakness, we pray, and by the strength of your Holy Spirit help us to be unwavering in our faith that we may be worthy witnesses, able to carry on the works of Jesus. Amen.

Offertory Prayer

Lord, you blessed the common things of life, such as bread and wine, and made them holy sacraments, revealing yourself through them. We ask that you will take these common coins and bills, making them sacraments, holy and set apart, for the revelation of your love. Amen.

Hymns

"Blessed Assurance"
"Come, My Way, My Truth, My Life"
"Dear Lord, Lead Me Day By Day"

Fifth Sunday Of Easter

Psalter: Psalm 31:1-16

Words Of Assurance

Jesus said: "Let not your hearts be troubled. Believe in God, believe also in me."

Pastoral Prayer

Almighty God, our Heavenly Father, you who have bent chaos to your will and have established order in the midst of the dark deep, we turn to you that we might better know you; that we might in this moment share the deep thoughts within us with you, and in that sharing find ourselves reordered; that we might bring the chaos within us to you and in your hovering Spirit find our battered lives recreated.

Eternal God and Lord, by your power even death has died, and we rejoice in the new life won by Jesus Christ. The arrogance of cruel people, the timidity of frightened disciples, the injustice of mindless crowds, all are now overcome, all wrongs are righted, and we can believe in the future. For this we praise you, and pledge you our very lives.

We thank you for the great multitude of your blessings, but we do not turn to you and beg for more. We turn to you in prayer and devotion for in your presence, in your company, our hearts are at rest, life has a direction, and our work has power.

Grant, O Lord, that we may serve you as we have been served: seeing each person as special, observing each person as unique from every other, listening to each person with our hearts as well as our ears; helping and being helped in ways that maintain the dignity of the helper and the helped.

All this we pray in the name of Jesus Christ our Lord. Amen.

Benediction

Jesus said: "The one who believes in me will also do the works that I do...." Go forth as co-workers with Christ; and the blessing of God the Father, Son, and Holy Spirit be yours. Amen.

Sixth Sunday Of Easter

First Lesson: Acts 17:22-31
Theme: The Unknown God Made Known

Call To Worship

Let us call upon the name of the Lord our God, for it is a good thing to praise the one who is our maker. He is the God of justice, of hope, and of love; the one from whom we have come, by whose power we live daily, and to whom we will one day return.

Invocation

Father, we ask that during this hour you will lead us in your Way; you will teach us your Truth; and you will share with us your very life; so that your name may be honored, our lives may be enriched, and your world, through us, may be blessed. Amen.

Confession

Heavenly Father, we confess that we have been blind to the divine presence in our midst. We have been searching for you, yes groping for you, and have failed to realize that you are not far from us. Open our eyes, Lord, that we may see you all about us in your creation, and sense your very presence in our lives. We pray in Jesus' name. Amen.

Offertory Prayer

We are concerned, Father, that our children and grandchildren will be instructed in the faith, that this church will have a dynamic witness in this community, and that the poor and needy around the world will know that Jesus lives. Because of these concerns, and of others, we present these gifts. Amen.

Hymns

"I Sing The Almighty Power Of God"
"Sing Praise To God Who Reigns Above"
"Rise, Shine, You People"

Sixth Sunday Of Easter

Second Lesson: 1 Peter 3:13-22
Theme: Witness To The Hope That Is In You

Call To Worship

Come, let us worship the One who is the Alpha and the Omega, the Beginning and the End; the One who has left us, and yet is still with us; the One who has come, and yet is to come; the One who has conquered, yet will conquer still.

Praise be to God!

Invocation

Perform great things in us, Father. Expose us in the light of your truth. Hold us in the arm of your strength, and send us away with a new resolve to witness to your presence in our lives; through Jesus Christ our Lord. Amen.

Confession

Heavenly Father, we are eager to be good, but when we suffer for doing what is right we are intimidated. When asked to defend or define the hope that is within us we become angry and sometimes irreverent. Forgive us, we pray, and through the power of the resurrected Christ grant us a clear conscience that when we are maligned we may love our enemies to shame. Amen.

Offertory Prayer

O Lord, for the light we have received, we give thanks. For the opportunity to share with those who struggle in darkness as we do, we share what we have. Amen.

Hymns

"Go Forth For God"
"Lord, Speak To Me"
"Pass It On"

Sixth Sunday Of Easter

Gospel Lesson: John 14:15-21
Theme: The Promise Of The Holy Spirit

Call To Worship

Leader: Christ promised that he would not leave his followers alone.
People: Praise God for his presence with us now and always.
Leader: Christ promised that because he lives, we will live also.
People: Praise God for Christ's presence in our lives.
Leader: Come, let us worship the Father, the Son, and the Holy Spirit.

Invocation

Almighty God, may we, like the early disciples, experience among us the presence of the Risen Christ. May we be filled with awe at the miracle of resurrection. May we be amazed at the grace that restores us after we have fallen. May we be inspired by the challenge that sends us out as messengers of hope in a hurting world. We pray in Jesus' name. Amen.

Confession

Father, forgive us when inner distractions interrupt our worship, and coldness of heart quenches your Spirit. Help us to focus our undivided attention on your divine Word, and warm our souls with a holy enthusiasm. We pray in Jesus' name. Amen.

Offertory Prayer

Lord, through the generosity of our gifts, may we prove that the Spirit of Christ's love and concern is flowing through us. May these gifts travel where our feet cannot go, and may they reach out where our hands cannot extend. Amen.

Hymns

"God Will Take Care Of You"
"Jesus, Lover Of My Soul"
"Because He Lives"

Sixth Sunday Of Easter

Psalter: Psalm 66:8-20

Words Of Assurance

Jesus said: "I am coming to you ... because I live you will live also."

Pastoral Prayer

Our Most Gracious Heavenly Father, whose Spirit meets us in the valley of shadows as well as on the mountaintop of triumph, we come before you in this time of worship, praying that you will sustain our spirits this day.

Sustain us as we seek to understand ourselves. We pledge ourselves to the cause for which your Son gave himself; but then, in unguarded moments, we reveal attitudes and actions unworthy of his love. Speak to our hearts of your forgiving grace; set our minds on the lofty heights of fulfillment; and send us on our way.

Sustain us, O Lord, in our relationships with our fellows. Plant within our hearts the seeds of trust that will allow us to reach out unafraid to those around us. Give us vision to see the refinement that is part of every heart, though it might not be perceived at first glance. Remove from us, O Lord, feelings of suspicion, bitterness, mistrust, and cynicism that rise against our souls like waves that pound the rocky shore.

Sustain us, O God, in life at home with our families. So often we close the door of our minds when we enter the sanctuary that is our dwelling place. Alert us, we pray, to the intimate needs that go unnoticed day after day because we are preoccupied with less important concerns. Let love flow unchallenged through the dry, parched land, that we might glimpse what it means to speak of the redemptive love of Christ.

Sustain our Spirits now. Hear our innermost thoughts and bring your healing Spirit forth to meet the uncountable needs that are ours today. This we pray in the Spirit of Christ. Amen.

Benediction

Go forth in joy, for the Father has created you; in peace, for the Son has redeemed you; in strength, for the Spirit has renewed you; and the blessing of God be with you always. Amen.

Ascension Of Our Lord

First Lesson: Acts 1:1-11
Theme: Christ Knows No Bounds

Call To Worship

Leader: Christ has risen!
People: Christ will come again!
All: Praise be to God!

Invocation

Almighty God, your blessed Son, our Savior Jesus Christ, ascended
far beyond this earth that his love, his hope, his peace might know no
bounds. Help us to perceive that he still abides with us and his Church
on earth even to the end of the world. Amen.

Confession

O God, our understanding is so limited, and what we do not fully
understand we often refuse to believe. Deepen our understanding, we
pray, and help us where we cannot fully comprehend to walk by faith,
trusting in our Lord, Jesus Christ. Amen.

Offertory Prayer

Eternal God, with these gifts we dedicate ourselves anew to you.
Consecrate them, we pray, for the work of our kingdom, and consecrate for us the resolutions we make in this hour that will lead us into
true understanding and fruitful service. Amen.

Hymns

"Crown Him With Many Crowns"
"Christ For The World We Sing"
"The Head That Once Was Crowned"

Ascension Of Our Lord

Second Lesson: Ephesians 1:15-23
Theme: Coming To Know Christ

Call To Worship

Leader: Ascribe to the Lord glory and strength.
People: To the one seated at the right hand of God be glory and blessing forever and ever. Amen.

Invocation

God, our Father, we come before you seeking a spirit of wisdom and understanding. Help us to grow in faith and in the knowledge of our Lord and Savior, Jesus Christ. Amen.

Confession

All-powerful God, how often we rely on our own strength alone, and then wonder why we fail. Forgive our foolish ways, and keep us ever near to you, the source of our strength and power, through Jesus Christ our Lord. Amen.

Offertory Prayer

O Lord, enable these gifts, by the power of your Spirit, to convey your love and ours: healing the sick, feeding the hungry, comforting the sorrowing, and proclaiming the good news that Jesus lives. Amen.

Hymns

"Jesus Shall Reign"
"What A Friend We Have In Jesus"
"Christ Whose Glory Fills The Skies"

Ascension Of Our Lord

Gospel Lesson: Luke 24:44-53
Theme: The Commission

Call To Worship

We come together at the beginning of another week to prepare ourselves to go forth and fulfill our commission to proclaim repentance and forgiveness of sins in the name of Jesus Christ. Let us come expectantly that we might receive the power from on high that God has promised.

Invocation

Gracious God, we know that your Son, Jesus Christ, once walked upon the earth, confined by time and space. Grant us faith to realize his presence among us now unfettered by space and time, in the name of Jesus Christ our ascended Lord. Amen.

Confession

Where we have failed, O Lord, to proclaim with glad hearts your Word of repentance and forgiveness we ask your forgiveness. Make us to know the joy of your salvation that we may comfort the sorrowing, strengthen the faint of heart, and restore the wayward to ways of life and peace. Amen.

Offertory Prayer

O Lord, we have taken seriously your commission to go throughout the world with your message of repentance and forgiveness. While many of us are limited in our ability personally to go beyond our own community, we present these gifts to support the work of those who do take your Word throughout the world. Amen.

Hymns

"All Hail The Power Of Jesus' Name"
"Ask Ye What Great Thing I Know"
"I Want To Walk As A Child Of The Light"

Ascension Of Our Lord

Psalter: Psalm 47

Words Of Assurance
The beautiful miracle of the living God's resurrection power is that it is present in us now, breaking through the daily deaths caused by our selfishness.

Pastoral Prayer
Almighty God, giver of all grace, the refuge of all who flee to you, the helper of those in need, and the one sure resource in times of trouble: hear us now, we pray, as we approach you through worship and adoration.

Ever-living God, we give you thanks this day that your eternal Christ, who once dwelt on earth, ascended into glory where, freed from the bonds of time and space, he is present with us everywhere and at all times. Forgive us wherein we have held on to half-truths, smugly congratulating ourselves that we are not as others. Forgive us for closing out insight with the attitude that we have already arrived at the truth. Forgive us wherein we have accepted the cliches that are bandied about as defenses for our consciences.

Open our minds to the call of love, that we may measure our attitudes and responses by this standard. Forbid that we should shunt aside concern for others as a pretense for minding our own business. Help us to avoid the arrogant spirit that causes us to feel self-made. Enable us through prayer and worship to reassess the reasons we like to give why we have succeeded and others have failed. May we have the empathy to feel what it means to be a minority, to be caught in the squeeze of our automated industrial age without developed skills, to be unable to pay the rent, to be unemployed without hope of a job. Almighty God, whose essence is love, draw back the curtains behind which we, in a false security, congratulate ourselves, that we may try again to see whether or not we have any right to feel acceptable in your sight.

As we attempt to follow our Master, Jesus Christ, as faithful disciples, keep us ever mindful of our commission which, just before his ascension, he gave to all who would follow him: that we should take his gospel of love into all the world, making disciples, and baptizing them in the name of the Father, the Son, and the Holy Spirit. Send your Holy Spirit upon us that we might have the courage and the strength to carry out his command. We pray in Jesus' name. Amen.

Benediction
Go forth with great joy knowing that God goes with you; and the blessing of God the Father, Son, and Holy Spirit be yours. Amen.

Seventh Sunday Of Easter

First Lesson: Acts 1:6-14
Theme: God's Messengers Come To Us In Our Time Of Indecision

Call To Worship

Leader: God is Spirit.

People: And we who worship him must worship him, in spirit and in truth.

Invocation

Most Merciful Father, who has willed that your children should dwell in families, we praise your name for all the joys of family love and comradeship. Enable us, of your great mercy, so to open unto you the doors of our abodes that you yourself may dwell therein, and your blessing may rest constantly upon them; through Jesus Christ our Lord. Amen.

Confession

Father, inner distractions often interrupt our worship, and we allow coldness of heart to quench your Spirit. Forgive us, we pray. Help us to focus our undivided attention on your Divine Word, and warm our souls with a holy enthusiasm. Amen.

Offertory Prayer

O God, we present these gifts that they might be used by you to bring hope where there is despair, insight where there is blindness, love where there is hate, justice where there is oppression, and faith where there is unbelief. Amen.

Hymns

"For The Beauty Of The Earth"
"Our Parent, By Whose Name"
"Help Us Accept Each Other"

Seventh Sunday Of Easter

Second Lesson: 1 Peter 4:12-14; 5:6-11
Theme: The Power Of God To Overcome

Call To Worship

From a world in which many feel that no one cares, we come to worship One who has given us a living community, the Church. At a time when it is hard to be sure that we haven't lost our way, we lift our voices to adore the Christ who is The Way.

Come! Let us worship.

Invocation

We have come, O God, to celebrate the power of love: the love we know in our families, the love we experience in our church, the love we enjoy among friends, and even among complete strangers. We praise you for this love, for we know that all of it has its source in your great heart, and that it reached its fullest expression in Jesus Christ our Lord. Amen.

Confession

Lord, we know that we can express our love in many ways: by a gentle touch, by an accepting smile, by a note of greeting. Yet so often we have failed to express this love to our neighbors. We ask your forgiveness, Father, and pray that by your grace we may do better from now on. Amen.

Offertory Prayer

Lord, some are called to go to the ends of the earth to share the good news and the good deeds of Jesus Christ. Others of us have been called to stay at home and support them with our prayers, our gifts, and our concern. Whatever our role, may we perform it with enthusiasm. Amen.

Hymns

"Jesus, The Very Thought Of Thee"
"Jesus Shall Reign"
"Pass It On"

Seventh Sunday Of Easter

Gospel Lesson: John 17:1-11
Theme: Eternal Life Is To Know God

Call To Worship
Let us come before the Lord with minds open to his Truth, with hearts receptive to his Love, and with wills subject to his Spirit.

Invocation
As we worship this morning, our Heavenly Father, we pray that your Spirit will be our strength, your Word will be our guide, your Love will be our comfort, and your promises will be our hope. Amen.

Confession
Is it possible, Lord, that we get along so well because we never really take a stand? Could it be that people never raise their eyebrows at us simply because we try so hard to conform? Is it conceivable that others never ask about the hope that is in us because the evidence of that hope is not obvious? Could it be that people do not challenge our faith because they are not aware of that faith?

If these things are true, Lord, we stand humbled before you, begging that you will forgive our timidity, and beseeching you to help strengthen the courage of our convictions. Amen.

Offertory Prayer
O God, how selfish we would be if, having found the way, we would not point it out to others; and if, having known the truth, we would keep it secret; or having seen the light, we would leave our brothers and sisters in darkness.

Receive, then, these gifts, that others may find, and know, and see the truth of the living God, through Jesus Christ our Lord. Amen.

Hymns
"Your Love, O God"
"Easter People, Raise Your Voices"
"O Crucified Redeemer"

Seventh Sunday Of Easter

Psalter: Psalm 68:1-10, 32-35

Words Of Assurance

As a father pities his children, so the Lord pities those who fear him.

The Lord is gracious and merciful, slow to anger and abounding in steadfast love.

Pastoral Prayer

O God, our Father, we would thank you for all the gifts with which you have filled our lives; for the daily miracle of light and shadow, work and rest, life and love; for high thoughts which uplift us and for pure hopes which bind and beckon us to you. We would thank you for disappointments and failures which have humbled us, for pain and distress which have taught us our need of you, but most of all for our faith in you and for the fullness of joy which your presence brings. You have opened your heart to us in great mercy; may we open our hearts to you in penitence and gratitude.

From our meditations here may we learn that these lives of ours, so frail and fallible, may be shaped after a noble pattern. So may we rise to your expectations of us. So may we endeavor this and every day to be what you desire, to do what you have commanded, listening to the inner voice of your Spirit, searching the depths of our hearts, leaving no spot uncleansed and sparing no sin from which it may cost us more to part.

We would put ourselves at the side of your Son, our Savior, that from him we may learn the secret of the well-balanced life, the life which yields to his restraint yet loses none of its fire and force.

We make intercession for all your people, near and far: for our brothers and sisters and companions; for those who are stricken in body, mind, or estate; for those to whom the passing years bring anger and feebleness; and for those appointed to die. O God, send some word of yours to make a highway to all hearts that need your special touch of healing and grace, and draw nigh to us in the manifold ministry of your redeeming love. We pray in the name of Jesus Christ, our Lord and Savior. Amen.

Benediction

May the inspiration of God the Father, the encouragement of God the Son, and the enlightenment of God the Holy Spirit be yours now and forever. Amen.

The Day Of Pentecost

First Lesson: Acts 2:1-21
Theme: The Coming Of The Holy Spirit

Call To Worship

Leader: Bless the Lord, O my soul.
People: You are clothed with honor and majesty.
Leader: You make the winds your messengers,
People: fire and flame your ministers.
Leader: You send forth your Spirit, and all is made new.
People: May the glory of the Lord endure forever. Amen.

Invocation

Lord, may this day be a new Pentecost — a day in which you will pour out your Spirit and put a new heart within us; a day in which our faltering spirits will be revived, and our enthusiasm will be renewed; a day in which you will equip us for service, and send us out to change your world. In Jesus' name we pray. Amen.

Confession

O Lord, as we come to this time of worship, we acknowledge our weakness. We are easily distracted; we are often annoyed and grumpy; we bring with us the problems of home, work, and of school. So we ask that your holy and powerful Spirit will come to the aid of our weak spirits, enabling us to make this hour a truly meaningful and life-changing experience; through Jesus Christ our Lord. Amen.

Offertory Prayer

Lord, we pray that the Holy Spirit will accompany these gifts, giving wisdom to those who will distribute them, granting effectiveness to those whose ministries will be supported, and bringing salvation and a better life to those whose lives will be touched. Amen.

Hymns

"Holy Spirit, Truth Divine"
"Come, Holy Ghost, Our Hearts Inspire"
"O Spirit Of The Living God"

The Day Of Pentecost

Second Lesson: 1 Corinthians 12:3b-13
Theme: The Gift Of The Spirit

Call To Worship

Leader: Just as the body is one and has many members, and all the members of the body, though many, are one body, so it is with Christ.

People: In the one Spirit we are all baptized into one body, and we are all made to drink of one Spirit.

Leader: Now there are varieties of gifts, but the same Spirit.

People: To each is given the manifestation of the Spirit for the common good.

Invocation

Lord, we come together this morning to celebrate the birthday of the Church with the outpouring of your Holy Spirit. We give you thanks for all the gifts, great and small, that you have bestowed upon your children. Through our worship help us to see more clearly our function in the Church — your Body on earth — and together may we be a living witness to your love throughout all the earth; through Jesus Christ, who abides with you in the unity of the Holy Spirit, one God, forever. Amen.

Confession

Dear Lord, you have granted each of us our gifts and talents, but often we have failed to use them to your honor and glory. For this we ask your forgiveness, and pray that by the power of your Holy Spirit we may become more aware of our gifts and dedicate them to the service of your children, our brothers and sisters. Amen.

Offertory Prayer

Lord, we offer our gifts this morning to help spread the flame of the Holy Spirit, so that others may know that Christ is with them to guide, comfort, and fulfill them. Amen.

Hymns

"Take My Life, And Let It Be"
"We Are The Church"
"Of All The Spirit's Gifts To Me"

The Day Of Pentecost

Gospel Lesson: John 7:37-39
Theme: Pentecost

Call To Worship

Jesus said: "Out of the believer's heart shall flow rivers of living water." Come, everyone who thirsteth, and receive the promised Holy Spirit. Amen.

Invocation

O God, today we celebrate the time when you sent down your Holy Spirit upon the apostles and kindled the zeal and enthusiasm of Christ's followers. Mercifully grant that this morning the same Holy Spirit may come among us and renew our determination to be loyal disciples of Jesus who lives and reigns with you in the unity of the same Spirit, one God, world without end. Amen.

Confession

Gracious and Merciful God, we bow before you ready to receive your Holy Spirit. We acknowledge our unworthiness, but relying on your forgiveness we stand ready to seek a new life in Christ strengthened by the power of your Holy Spirit. Amen.

Offertory Prayer

Father, accompany these gifts by the power of your Spirit, so they may truly express the warmth of your love and the truth of your gospel. Amen.

Hymns

"Breathe On Me, Breath Of God"
"Spirit Of God, Descend Upon My Heart"
"Spirit Of The Living God"

The Day Of Pentecost

Psalter: Psalm 104:24-34, 35b

Words Of Assurance

By this we know that we abide in him and he in us, because he has given us of his own Spirit.

Pastoral Prayer

O Holy and Righteous God, you are the divine Spirit that was in Jesus Christ. You remain with us and continue the mighty deeds which he began. In the power of your Spirit you invite us to worship you and to receive your residential presence in our lives. We can know you in Spirit, just as truly as the disciples knew their Lord on the shores of Galilee, if we surrender ourselves to you.

Help us to be aware of how much we need your Holy Spirit in our lives day by day. We need your Spirit to help us believe the Good News of the gospel that saves us from our sins. We need your Holy Spirit to walk beside us as our counselor to guide us into all truth. We need the comfort and communion which the Spirit gives to those who faithfully walk with you. We need the continual witness of the Spirit that we are, indeed, your sons and daughters, still in the making. We need your Spirit to teach us to pray, to direct our daily choices, to inspire our creativity, to see visions of what is yet to be, to dream dreams that integrate in the present what has been in the past.

We pray that through this illuminating power of your Spirit we shall recognize and lay aside the personal pretenses, the masks that hide who we really are. We pray for the ability to live as authentic persons who accept responsibility for their own thoughts, behaviors, and feelings, and who love in deed as well as in word. Take from us anger and pride, the compulsiveness and greediness that so often set us against our brothers and sisters, our neighbors and our friends. Help us to win the struggle against such demonic tendencies, whether within ourselves or the structures of society that hurt and cripple so many children.

As at the Day of Pentecost, we pray that we may be transformed by your Spirit's coming upon us, taking away our fear, making us bold to face the enemies of Christ, and giving us power to present a convincing witness that in Jesus Christ you have reconciled the world to yourself. Enliven our concern for lost souls who stumble through the darkness of fear and hopelessness, often disoriented by shame and guilt, alienated, painfully alone, with none to love or care.

As we celebrate the birth of your Church on the Day of Pentecost, grant us a spirit of generous stewardship that we may maintain our church as a place where the gospel is faithfully preached, the sacraments regularly administered, and all grow toward mature adulthood to the measure of the stature of the fullness of Christ. We pray in Jesus' name. Amen.

Benediction

What Jesus said to his disciples, he also says to us: "Peace be with you, as the Father has sent me, even so I send you ... Receive the Holy Spirit." Amen.

The Holy Trinity

First Lesson: Genesis 1:1—2:4a
Theme: Creation

Call To Worship
To the God who created, let us sing praises. To the Son who reveals the infinite, let us bring open minds. To the Spirit who makes all things new, let us lift our souls in worship.

Invocation
Hear our prayers, O God, and receive our praises. Give us a sense of awe in your holy presence, and give us a new vision of what life can be. Fill us with your Spirit, and incline our hearts to be receptive to your Word. Amen.

Confession
Our Father, too often we see only the bad in the world around us, and complain about our misfortunes. Forgive us, we pray, and open our eyes to the beauty of your creation all around us, and open our minds and hearts to the reality of our blessings. Amen.

Offertory Prayer
Because the Father has provided the world and all its resources, because the Son has given us an example of sacrifice, and because the Spirit has inspired our desire to share, we give these gifts for the glory of the Triune God. Amen.

Hymns
"O God Who Shaped Creation"
"All Things Bright And Beautiful"
"All Creatures Of Our God And King"

The Holy Trinity

Second Lesson: 2 Corinthians 13:11-13
Theme: Live In Peace

Call To Worship

In a world filled with anger, we offer a message of love. In a world filled with tension, we offer a message of peace. Come, let us celebrate our unity in the Holy Spirit, whose living presence links us with each other and to God.

Invocation

By the power and grace of the Blessed Trinity, may we banish from our hearts whatever might endanger peace; may we be transformed into witnesses for truth; may we be inspired to overcome the barriers that divide us; may all people of the earth become as brothers and sisters. This we pray in the name of the Father, the Son, and the Holy Spirit. Amen.

Confession

Lord of life and love, quiet our souls in your presence with the stillness of a wise trust. Lift us above dark moods, and the shadow of sin, that we may find your will for our lives; through Jesus Christ our Lord. Amen.

Offertory Prayer

We are grateful, Father, that you have provided for all of our needs; and not only for our needs, but also for many of our wants. Receive these offerings as an expression of our thanks for your generosity. Amen.

Hymns

"This Is A Day Of New Beginnings"
"Let There Be Peace On Earth"
"Go Forth For God"

The Holy Trinity

Gospel Lesson: Matthew 28:16-20
Theme: Christ With Us Always

Call To Worship

Come, let us worship and bow down; let us honor the God who made us; let us praise the Savior who died for us; let us thank the Holy Spirit who empowers us. Come, let us worship the Triune God.

Invocation

O Lord, focus our eyes that we may see. Open our ears that we may hear. Sharpen our minds that we may understand. Sensitize our wills that we may respond. Through Jesus Christ our Lord. Amen.

Confession

Our Father, through this time of holy worship, enable us to see clearly what we have allowed ourselves to become. Then help us to see what, by your grace, we can some day become. Comfort us with the power of your presence, and fill us with the power of your Spirit so we can be more than conquerors through Christ our Lord. Amen.

Offertory Prayer

O Lord, we present these offerings as our partial response to your great commission to go and make disciples of all nations. Follow them with your blessing, we pray, and accept our rededication to our responsibilities as your disciples. Amen.

Hymns

"O Jesus, I Have Promised"
"Go, Make Of All Disciples"
"Be Thou My Vision"

The Holy Trinity

Psalter: Psalm 8

Words Of Assurance

In this take comfort: that the Trinity can best be understood as God in action — planning, working out, and applying divine forgiveness.

Pastoral Prayer

Almighty God, source of all life and love, we give you thanks and praise that we are not alone, that we live in the world you have made, and that you are always creating and sustaining the world by the power of your Word. We give you thanks that you have so made us that we can know you and love you, trust you and serve you. We give you thanks that you love the world so much that you gave your only Son so that everyone who has faith in him will not die but have eternal life.

Lord, catch us off guard today. Surprise us with some moment or memory of beauty or pain so that for at least a few seconds we may be startled into seeing that you are with us here and now, shining in silent splendor. Let us know that you are everywhere and always, that you are barely hidden beneath, beyond, and within the very life we live each day.

Today, O God, we pray that you will bring healing to our fragmented selves so that we may be whole, functioning sons and daughters of yours. You know the many conflicting ways we feel and act, how we are so often losers instead of winners, afraid to venture, busy going nowhere. We discount ourselves as persons of value and worth. We discount our own potentialities for leadership, to think bold new thoughts, to create new exciting ways of doing your work. We are divided in our loyalties. We say that you are our beloved God and Father, and yet we find ourselves worshiping at the shrines of wealth, power, and prestige. We intuitively know that we are spiritual persons. Yet we find ourselves overwhelmed with the urgencies of passion, diverted from spirit to flesh, from long-range commitments to short-term pleasures. O God, we need you to be the organizing, centering power to bring harmony, wholeness, and perspective to our beings. Be the coordinating chairman to call our many selves to order. Unite the two so long divided: heart and mind, body and spirit, calling and deed. Let us love you with total abandonment, knowing that we shall never be abandoned by you.

All this we pray in the name of Jesus Christ our Lord. Amen.

Benediction

May the inspiration of God the Father, the encouragement of God the Son, and the enlightenment of God the Holy Spirit be yours now and forever. Amen.

Corpus Christi

First Lesson: Deuteronomy 8:2-3, 14-16
Theme: Do Not Forget The Lord Your God

Call To Worship
Come, all you who hunger and thirst after righteousness. Come, remembering that we do not live by bread alone, but by every word that comes from the mouth of the Lord.

Invocation
Lord, we come before you with a sense of awe, because you are the designer, creator, and sustainer of all things. Yet we come before you with boldness, for you are a compassionate and forgiving God, and you have healed us through your Son. So we come also with expectations, seeking new insights into your will and a fresh outpouring of your Spirit. Amen.

Confession
Almighty God, you know our innermost thoughts. You have seen how busy we are in looking successful and attractive, calm and in control. Yet you know also the turmoil and hunger that is inside us. You know the fears we have about tomorrow. You know where we have failed, where we are ashamed. Come to us with healing power. Fill us with your Spirit, we pray. Amen.

Offertory Prayer
Lord, as we wander through the wilderness of life on our journey to the Promised Land, you have provided for our every need. In gratitude we return a portion of that which has been entrusted to us that it may be used to bring to others the message of your love and your abiding presence. Amen.

Hymns
"Let My People Seek Their Freedom"
"God Of Grace And God Of Glory"
"Come, Thou Fount Of Every Blessing"

Corpus Christi

Second Lesson: 1 Corinthians 10:16-17
Theme: Unity In Christ

Call To Worship
There is one God, Father and Creator of us all. God is made known to us through his Son, Jesus Christ our Lord, and is present with us in the Holy Spirit. Together we are his Church — the Body of Christ. Come let us worship!

Invocation
Gracious God, as we gather at your table this morning, we recognize that we are one with all those around the world who call upon your name. We praise you for our unity and common purpose. May we never forget that Christ died for us all, and through our worship may we be drawn closer to you and closer to your children everywhere. Amen.

Confession
Lord, even as we give thanks for that which binds us together, we humbly confess that we have not always been willing to accept others who share the name of Christ. Our doors have not always been open to those who differ from us in appearance and in thinking. Cleanse our minds and hearts of prejudice, we pray, and enable us to come to your table with genuine love and concern for all your children. Amen.

Offertory Prayer
Christ, as you have invested yourself in our world and in our lives by sacrificing yourself, so we also invest ourselves in our world and in the lives of others by an act of sacrificial giving. May the gifts be worthy of what Christ has done for us. Amen.

Hymns
"I Come With Joy"
"One Bread, One Body"
"Lord Of The Dance"

Corpus Christi

Gospel Lesson: John 6:51-58
Theme: The Bread From Heaven

Call To Worship

Leader: Sing to the Lord, all the earth!
People: Tell of his salvation from day to day.
Leader: Declare his glory among the nations,
People: his marvelous works among all the peoples!
Leader: For great is the Lord, and greatly to be praised,
People: and he is to be held in awe above all gods.

Invocation

As the sun rises in the east, bathing our world in the glory of a new day, we pray that the Son of Righteousness will rise in our hearts and fill our lives with the splendor of his glorious presence. Like the growing flower which turns upward to the sun, like the thirsty deer who seeks out the refreshing stream, like the empty pitcher which is carried to the faucet, we turn to you, O Lord, asking that our bodies, minds, and souls may be renewed and refreshed by your truth, your light, and your love, in Jesus' name we pray. Amen.

Confession

Father, as we open our minds and hearts to receive that living bread from heaven, give us grace to set aside jealousy, animosity, and ill feelings. Enable us to subdue our doubts, our fears, and our unbelief. Help us to remove all impediments, and free us to worship in Spirit and in Truth, through Jesus Christ our Lord. Amen.

Offertory Prayer

O Lord, enable us, by these offerings, to imitate the loving arms of Christ, who reached out and lifted those who were in despair. Amen.

Hymns

"Become To Us The Living Bread"
"Here, O My Lord, I See Thee"
"Break Thou The Bread Of Life"

Corpus Christi

Psalter: Psalm 62:5-12

Words Of Assurance

Jesus has shown us the God who is the Father welcoming the return of The Prodigal, the Shepherd who seeks the Lost Sheep, and who sent his Son into the world that through him we might have eternal life.

Pastoral Prayer

O God, the eternal light that enlightens all people, set our minds and imaginations free to grasp in some meaningful way how you draw near to us in worship to further the work of salvation which you began when we first believed. We are grateful for the confirming witness of your Spirit that we are, indeed, your sons and daughters, that you love us everlastingly, and that you have called us to be co-creators with you of a new and better world. Thank you for every daily evidence of your watchful care and for never abandoning us to our foolish ways and deceitful designs. Thank you that as we worship, you rip away our masks and let us see ourselves as we really are: sinners alienated from you and one another, all standing in need of repentance and your words of grace and reconciliation.

We pray that you will correct and strengthen the internal life of your Church that as a people we may bear a convincing witness to the world of your power to transform life in all its demonic depths. You know how prone we are to play games of hypocrisy with one another, saying one thing and meaning another, smiling to another's face and then landing a well-placed kick when he or she passes by. Forgive us, and grant us the gifts of patience and forbearance as we deal with one another.

Thank you for seeing through all our pretenses and hypocrisies and calling us to repentance. Forgive and correct us by your love and mercy, that we may worship only at the altar of your self-giving, the Cross of Christ that ever towers "o'er the wrecks of time." Then the members of your redeemed Church we shall be, both individually and collectively, the living temples in which your Spirit can live and work.

We pray in the name and in the spirit of Jesus Christ our Lord. Amen.

Benediction

May the God who lives within us in the person of the Holy Spirit, be experienced daily as your sustainer, savior, and friend; and may the blessing of God the Father, the Son, and the Holy Spirit be with you now and always. Amen.

Proper 4
Sunday between May 29 and June 4 inclusive

First Lesson: Genesis 6:11-22; 7:24; 8:14-19
Theme: Faith

Call To Worship
Rejoice! We gather as God's people to celebrate the One who brings us to newness of life. God calls us to be faithful, to put our trust in him. Let us seek God together, and honor the Most High with our prayer and praise.

Invocation
Lord of life and love, quiet our souls in your presence with the stillness of a wise trust. Lift us above the dark floods of life's storms that we may find your will for our lives; through Jesus Christ our Lord. Amen.

Confession
O God, we hear you calling us to action, but often it seems to be ridiculous, and we think we know what is best. Forgive our foolishness, and strengthen our faith that trusting you we may carry out your will. In Jesus' name we pray. Amen.

Offertory Prayer
Almighty God, even as in the days of Noah the world seems to be corrupt and full of violence. In faith we bring these gifts that the saving message of your love and righteousness may be spread abroad, that people everywhere may turn from their evil ways and learn to live in love and concern for one another. Amen.

Hymns
"O Zion, Haste"
"All Things Bright And Beautiful"
"Where He Leads Me"

Proper 4
Sunday between May 29 and June 4 inclusive

Second Lesson: Romans 1:16-17; 3:22b-28 (29-31)
Theme: We Live By Faith

Call To Worship
Faith is the assurance of things hoped for, the conviction of things not seen. Come, let us worship the God of our faith, looking to Jesus, the pioneer and perfecter of our faith.

Invocation
As we worship this morning, our Heavenly Father, we pray that your Spirit will be our strength, your Word will be our guide, your love will be our comfort, and your promise will be our hope. Amen.

Confession
Lord, who judges all the earth, we confess that we have fallen short of your expectations of us, and by our works we can never be justified. By faith alone we dare to stand before you and ask your forgiveness. Amen.

Offertory Prayer
O Lord, as we offer our gifts, we offer also our lives in renewed dedication to you. Help us make our offering fit for your use. Amen.

Hymns
"O Jesus, I Have Promised"
"Great Is Thy Faithfulness"
"Let Us Plead For Faith Alone"

Proper 4
Sunday between May 29 and June 4 inclusive

Gospel Lesson: Matthew 7:21-29
Theme: A Firm Foundation

Call To Worship
God is love and those who abide in love abide in God, and God abides in them. Come, let us enter his gates with thanksgiving, and his courts with praise! Give thanks to God, bless his name! For the Lord is good.

Invocation
Heavenly Father, guide us during this time of worship by your Word and by your Spirit, so that your light will show us the way, your truth will enlighten our minds, your love will warm our hearts, your wisdom will give us true freedom, and your compassion will inspire us to share with others. Amen.

Confession
O Lord, in our haste we have often laid the foundations of our faith in the sand, and when the storms of life have come, the waves of distress and discouragement have washed over us. Through the power of your Holy Spirit strengthen our resolve to build only on Christ the solid Rock of our faith. Amen.

Offertory Prayer
Lord, we give these gifts both in gratitude for what you have done in our lives, and faith in what you can do for others through these gifts. Amen.

Hymns
"It Is Well With My Soul"
"Faith Of Our Fathers"
"The Voice Of God Is Calling"

Proper 4
Sunday between May 29 and June 4 inclusive

Psalter: Psalm 46

Words Of Assurance

Those who are open to the truth of God will find it, and those who are open to the forgiveness of God will experience it.

Pastoral Prayer

Eternal Spirit, in whom is our strength for this world, and our hope for that which is to come, we would worship you with sincere and humble hearts. We find life's problems difficult, its temptations strong, and our own will and wisdom insufficient. Our hearts need you, your forgiveness and cleansing, your refreshing light, the resource of your presence, and the guidance of your continuing fellowship.

We come to you, O God of compassion and understanding, asking that you will help others and ourselves who are experiencing a time of discouragement.

Some have been defeated in competition, or in business, or in love. Some are suffering from long periods of depression. Some are simply weary because of the ongoing struggles of life. Some have lost the incentive for going on. Some are experiencing low physical energy, low mental energy, or low spiritual energy.

Take our hand, Lord, and lead us on. Encourage us with your smile. Open our eyes to see the reward you have planned for those who love you. Infuse us with the divine energy that only your Spirit can give. Assure us that we are still your children, and that you have a plan for our lives. Unleash our creative energies, and give us the exhilaration of even some small victory along the way.

Have mercy upon our stricken world, O God. You are the God of moral law who makes the way of the transgressor hard. Be also to us now the God of new vision and fresh hope. Show us the way, not back into our old denials of human brotherhood, but forward into a better day of our redemption.

Now, our Father, we pray that you will grant us the will and the wisdom to use in your service all the gifts and attributes with which you have endowed us. Help us to recognize that we serve you best when we serve each other without thought of self.

We give our thanks and make our requests in the name of him who touches us and makes us whole again, even Jesus Christ our Lord. Amen.

Benediction
The Lord bless you and keep you; the Lord make his face to shine upon you and be gracious to you; the Lord lift up his countenance upon you, and give you peace. Amen.

Proper 5
Sunday between June 5 and June 11 inclusive

First Lesson: Genesis 12:1-9
Theme: Called To Be A Blessing

Call To Worship

As the people of Almighty God, it is important for us to be here today, for we need this time of reflection and renewal, we need God's comfort and direction, and we need the support and friendship of God's people.

Invocation

Help us, Father, to shore up our faith and renew our dedication so that we may go forth this morning, as strong disciples, to spread your work and be a blessing to all we meet. In Jesus' name we pray. Amen.

Confession

Almighty God, we hear you calling us to go forth, but we hold back, wanting to know all the details of the journey that lies ahead. Through this time of worship, Father, may our faith be strengthened, and our willingness to respond in faith to your call be renewed. Amen.

Offertory Prayer

O Lord, take all that we have and all that we are and can hope to become, and press it into the service of what you would have us to be, for your mercy's sake. Amen.

Hymns

"Guide Me, O Thou Great Jehovah"
"Spirit Of The Living God"
"Standing On The Promises"

Proper 5
Sunday between June 5 and June 11 inclusive

Second Lesson: Romans 4:13-25
Theme: God's Promises Fulfilled Through Faith

Call To Worship

Leader: Do you believe that God is able to do as God has promised?
People: By faith we believe that God is faithful to what he has promised.
Leader: Then come, let us worship together the God in whom we trust.
People: We come, praying that we may grow even stronger in our faith as we give glory to God.

Invocation

Almighty God, our Heavenly Father, we pray that this day may be a day of awakening for those who are complacent, a day of inspiration for those who are disheartened, and a day of resurrection and new life for all. Amen.

Confession

Our Father, we humbly confess that often we keep our love and concern for others to ourselves. Forgive us, we pray, and unlock the door of our hearts that we may freely share your love for others, through Jesus Christ our Lord. Amen.

Offertory Prayer

Lord, may the work accomplished by these gifts, together with the testimony of our daily lives, bring glory to your name, strengthen your work on earth, and be a continuing witness to your love and grace. Amen.

Hymns

"Standing On The Promises"
"Let Us Plead For Faith Alone"
"The King Of Love My Shepherd Is"

Proper 5
Sunday between June 5 and June 11 inclusive

Gospel Lesson: Matthew 9:9-13, 18-26
Theme: Through Faith We Are Healed

Call To Worship
The steadfast love of the Lord never ceases. God's mercies never come to an end. They are new every morning; great is God's faithfulness.

Invocation
Lord, through this time we spend together, may our faith blossom, may our hope be born anew, and may our love be made real; through Jesus Christ our Lord. Amen.

Confession
Lord, we come looking for easy answers to our personal problems as well as those of the world. Enable us to put things in perspective, and forgive us for relying on our own resources rather than putting our faith in you. In Jesus' name we pray. Amen.

Offertory Prayer
Almighty God, as Christ through his costly ministry translated heavenly love into earthly compassion, so we, through our gifts, translate our heavenly ideals into earthly realities. Accept this offering of your people, and so follow it with your blessing that it will advance the kingdom of our Lord and Savior, Jesus Christ. Amen.

Hymns
"Come, Thou Fount Of Every Blessing"
"O Christ, The Healer"
"Heal Us, Emmanuel, Hear Our Prayer"

Proper 5
Sunday between May 29 and June 4 inclusive

Psalter: Psalm 33:1-12

Words Of Assurance
Jesus said: "Anyone who comes to me I will never drive away."

Pastoral Prayer
God of the close-at-hand and God of the far-away; God of things seen and unseen; God of our yesterdays and all our tomorrows — we live today because you live in us. You are the divine Spirit, the friendly presence that ever surrounds us, that renews our strength and removes our fear. With your strong right arm you lift us up when we stumble and fall. You are the captivating magnet that draws our gaze upward, to see beyond the mountaintops our eternal source of life and love, power and help. From the vista of eternity you whisper the reason of our being: to glorify you and to enjoy you forever. We are misfits in the universe until we surrender our wills to you, prodigals in a far country until we come to our senses and remember you. We are cowards until we are endued by your power; scattered in our attention until we see you high and lifted up; confused and puzzled until we know that you are like Jesus Christ who walked the shores of Galilee. How marvelous to know that at the center, the very heart of the universe, your majesty shines forth as unconquerable love. You are enthroned in glory and power, declared in the highest heavens, and made known in the deepest recesses of our beings. You are the burning fire that cleanses our hearts, that touches our lips and sets upon them the ancient gospel of peace. Blessed be your name forever and ever.

Behold us with mercy, O God, as we daily wrestle with unprecedented problems, as we cut our way through wilderness thickets of confusion. We wonder whether or not some promised land lies ahead. Let us hear what you are saying to us through the vicissitudes of life; times of personal transition, unemployment, underemployment, relationships that don't relate, floods of sensuous delight that lead to wastelands of regret and despair. Speak through our restlessness to call us to your greater rest. Let the heaviness of our burdens remind us that you are the great burden-bearer. Let our galling yoke of disobedience remind us of Jesus who offers a yoke that is easy and a burden that is light. Forgive us our slowness to learn, our hardness of heart, our stupid pride, our persistence in making ourselves right and others wrong, our stubborn unbelief. Take away our sluggish passivities. Energize us and thrust us forth into the on-moving stream of life that in our moment of death we may know that we have truly lived. Hear our prayers in the name of him who said: "I am come that you might have life and have it more abundantly," even Jesus Christ our Lord. Amen.

Benediction
Go forth in peace for your faith has made you whole; and the blessing of God the Father, Son, and Holy Spirit be yours. Amen.

Proper 6
Sunday between June 12 and June 18 inclusive

First Lesson: Genesis 18:1-15
Theme: Be Hospitable To God

Call To Worship
The Lord is gracious to us and looks upon us with love. The Lord
understands us and extends his hand of grace. The Lord hears our
prayers and is sympathetic to our needs. So come, welcome the Lord.
Open your hearts and minds to him with boldness. Worship the Lord
with joy, and serve the Lord with gladness.

Invocation
O Lord, as we come to worship today, we would welcome you.
We ask for the confidence of faith, that we may recognize you and
approach you without distraction or faltering. Grant us an assurance
of your presence and a certainty of your love; through Jesus Christ,
our Lord. Amen.

Confession
Lord, grant that we may overcome our disbelieving hearts and our
doubting minds. Like Sarah of old, we are often tempted to laugh at
your promises and consider your goals outrageous. By your Spirit
strengthen our faith and restore our confidence in your power. Through
Jesus Christ our Lord. Amen.

Offertory Prayer
Lord, we pray: "Your kingdom come, your will be done, on earth
as it is in heaven." Now as we lay our gifts before you, we say that
prayer again — not with our lips only, but with our actions. Hear our
prayer, O Lord. Amen.

Hymns
"O How I Love Jesus"
"There's A Wideness In God's Mercy"
"My God, I Love Thee"

Proper 6
Sunday between June 12 and June 18 inclusive

Second Lesson: Romans 5:1-8
Theme: Hope Does Not Disappoint

Call To Worship
Our hope is in the Lord who stands ready: to receive us in mercy, to restore us to wholeness, to give us a new vision of his will for our lives, and to send us on our way rejoicing. Come, let us worship the God of Hope.

Invocation
O Lord, we pray that this day may be a day of awakening for those who are complacent, a day of companionship for those who are lonely, a day of re-examination for those who are confident, a day of inspiration for those who are disheartened, a day of release for those who carry guilt, and a day of restored hope and trust in you for all of us. Amen.

Confession
Almighty God, ruler of us all: forgive our shortcomings as individuals, as a church, and as a nation; purify our hearts to see and love the truth; grant us wisdom and steadfastness for the facing of these days; and bring us at last to your kingdom whose foundations are mercy, justice, and goodwill, and whose builder and maker you are; through Jesus Christ our Lord. Amen.

Offertory Prayer
O Lord, enable us to see that the blessings we enjoy are meant to be shared for the good of all humankind and for the glory of your name. Bless now these gifts, we pray, and use them to spread the gospel of your love. Amen.

Hymns
"Jesus, The Very Thought Of Thee"
"I Stand Amazed"
"Come Ye Disconsolate"

Proper 6
Sunday between June 12 and June 18 inclusive

Gospel Lesson: Matthew 9:35—10:8
Theme: Proclaim The Good News

Call To Worship
The Lord has chosen us to be his disciples and to carry out his mission on earth. As we worship together let us open our hearts and minds that we might be better prepared to go forth and proclaim the Good News.

Invocation
We praise you, O God, as the one who out of weakness can bring strength, and out of despair can bring hope. From a slave people in the Middle East you brought the redeemer of the world. From an immigrant people who came to North America you have brought a powerful nation. From us who claim no earthly fame or power you can bring a transforming presence in our community and even our world. From this quiet hour you can send us out, equipped by your Word and Spirit. So let it be. Amen.

Confession
O Lord, we are privileged to worship without harassment; we are free to proclaim the truth without fear of being silenced; we are at liberty to go out and witness publicly to our faith. Forgive us for not using these freedoms responsibly. Through this time of worship enable us to be more faithful disciples. Amen.

Offertory Prayer
Heavenly Father, as citizens of your heavenly kingdom we recognize the benefits we enjoy and wish to share with others. Receive these gifts as we give them freely and gladly that the good news of your love may be made known throughout the world. Amen.

Hymns
"We've A Story To Tell To The Nations"
"Go Forth For God"
"Go Make Of All Disciples"

Proper 6
Sunday between June 12 and June 18 inclusive

Psalter: Psalm 116:1-2, 12-19

Words Of Assurance
The Lord is merciful and gracious, abounding in steadfast love. His compassion knows no bounds, and through the Holy Spirit he is able to use us — weak as we are — for his purposes.

Pastoral Prayer
Eternal Spirit, Lord of all worlds and Father of our souls, we worship you. As people never understood this earth until they looked away from it to the sun and stars, no more can we understand ourselves until we see ourselves in our relationship with you. Lead us up from our low levels and out from our narrow boundaries, that we may escape from our obsession with ourselves, and loving and serving something greater than ourselves, find what we are in you.

Grant us a new vision of the causes we would serve — justice in a generation full of wrong, unselfishness in a time when many suffer, peace in a day of violence. Show us that though we be little yet we can stand for the greatest truths. As a wayside spring, and not the great lakes only, represent water; as a candle is an ambassador of light even as the sun, so take us in our littleness and make us representatives of those things without which humankind cannot live.

Release us from narrowness into wide compassion and sympathy. We acknowledge our selfishness; we are meanly content when things go well with us. Yet we live in a time filled with destruction, when lives are broken and hearts are heavy, and bitter barriers of prejudice and jealousy divide humanity. Grant unto your servants so sincerely to worship you without pretense and sham that across all lines of division our hearts may today perform an act of all-inclusive goodwill. Give us victory over private prejudices and mean vindictiveness, O God, for we would take into our care every sort and condition of persons.

If hearts are here to whom such calls come in vain because they are too sorely hurt themselves, we ask your strength for them. Not for soft and easy lives do we pray, but for great resources. Some here

209

today are struggling against powerful temptations. Some feel the burden of grief and anxiety too heavy to be borne. We ask for stability, for inward reserves of spiritual power, that while the outward person is decaying the inward being may be renewed day by day. So in the worship of your sanctuary, may serenity, stability, and peace come to your people.

Send us out, we pray, to face this world with radiance. Make our faith contagious. May Christ's joy be ours, and his promise of abundant life be fulfilled in us. May we be among those who help bring humanity to its victory, when the kingdom of God's righteousness shall come. We ask it all in the Spirit of our Lord and Savior, Jesus Christ. Amen.

Benediction

You are God's creation, God's loving handiwork, the focus of his presence on earth. May his love for the world be made manifest through your life; and the blessing of God the Father, Son, and Holy Spirit be with you now and always. Amen.

Proper 7
Sunday between June 19 and June 25 inclusive

First Lesson: Genesis 21:8-21
Theme: Even In Our Distress, God Is There

Call To Worship
Leader: God is our refuge and strength,
People: a very present help in trouble.
Leader: Therefore we will not fear
People: though the earth should change, and the mountains shake.
Leader: God is in the midst of us.
People: The Lord of hosts is with us. Amen.

Invocation
As we gather in the quietness and beauty of this place, we are overwhelmed with a sense of thankful awe. We rejoice in the knowledge that you have made us, O God, for something great and eternal, and that daily you equip us for service. We bless you, Lord, for the assurance that we will never slip away from your care, and we anticipate the miracle of spiritual discovery. Amen.

Confession
O God, like the Psalmist of old, and our Lord upon the cross, we cry out, "My God, my God, why have you forsaken me? Why are you so far from helping me, from the words of my groaning?" By the power of your Holy Spirit cleanse us from all distrust and faithlessness. Restore in us the confidence of the Psalmist who was able to say you "did not despise or abhor the affliction of the afflicted, and (you) did not hide (your) face from me." Amen.

Offertory Prayer
O God, we know you call us for service, and you bless us in order that we may be a blessing for others. With that sense of high calling, we present our tithes and offerings. Amen.

Hymns
"Be Still, My Soul"
"God Will Take Care Of You"
"He Leadeth Me: O Blessed Thought"

211

Proper 7
Sunday between June 19 and June 25 inclusive

Second Lesson: Romans 6:1b-11
Theme: Alive To God In Christ

Call To Worship
God calls us from darkness into light, from ignorance into knowledge, from death into life, from selfishness into service. Come, let us respond to the God who has called us.

Invocation
Eternal God, from whom we have come, to whom we belong, and with whom we will one day dwell, who else in heaven and on earth shall receive our praise, and to whom else can we go in our time of need? Hear our prayers and our praises, and may we know we are totally yours. Amen.

Confession
Lord, we know that as your disciples we are supposed to walk in newness of life, but old habits and ways die hard. We need your forgiveness, and the power of your Holy Spirit that we may truly be alive to God. We pray in Jesus' name. Amen.

Offertory Prayer
Almighty God, because the earth is the Lord's we present these gifts. Because as stewards we are responsible for everything in our care, we present these gifts. Because you have called us to be your people, we present these gifts. Amen.

Hymns
"He Touched Me"
"Make Me A Captive, Lord"
"Victory In Jesus"

Proper 7
Sunday between June 19 and June 25 inclusive

Gospel Lesson: Matthew 10:24-39
Theme: The Cost Of Discipleship

Call To Worship

Our help is in the name of the Lord, who made heaven and earth. Seek the Lord while he may be found; call upon him while he is near. Let the wicked forsake their ways, and the unrighteous their thoughts; let them return to the Lord, and he will abundantly pardon.

Invocation

O God, who has taught us to keep all your heavenly commandments by loving you and our neighbor, grant us the spirit of peace and grace, that we may be both devoted to you with our whole heart, and united to each other with a pure will; through Jesus Christ our Lord. Amen.

Confession

Lord, we are prone to compromise our beliefs to protect ourselves from inconvenience. We keep quiet instead of bearing witness to our faith; we are more concerned with keeping peace in the family than proclaiming your message of love. Forgive us, we pray, and grant us the strength to take up our cross daily and follow you. Amen.

Offertory Prayer

Great God, whose grace and goodness are visible every day: accept the gifts which we bring as an expression of our love for you, so that through them we may have a part in spreading the word of your deeds and proclaiming your faithful love throughout the world; through Christ our Lord. Amen.

Hymns

"Take Up Thy Cross"
"O Jesus, I Have Promised"
"Jesus Calls Us"

213

Proper 7
Sunday between June 19 and June 25 inclusive

Psalter: Psalm 86:1-10, 16-17

Words Of Assurance
Happy are the eyes that see God's majesty, and the ears that hear his Word, and the hearts that believe his promises.

Pastoral Prayer
Holy Spirit of God, who at Pentecost descended with power upon Christ's disciples, and sent them out to preach the gospel and to found the Church, inspire us also to sustain what they began. O Most High, mean to us what you meant to them: the grace of our Lord Jesus Christ, the love of God, and the fellowship of the Holy Spirit. Enrich our souls with that threefold experience, that you may be to us the Almighty Creator, the Saving Character, and the Indwelling Comforter.

Eternal Spirit, mysterious beyond our understanding, yet shining clearly in all that is excellent and true, we deeply need your help. We are not sufficient unto ourselves. As we did not create ourselves, so we cannot sustain ourselves amid life's disappointments and griefs, strains and anxieties, storms and temptations. Here we would lay aside all pride and humbly acknowledge our urgent need. For light enough to walk by through dark days, for inner strength to carry heavy burdens, undertake courageous deeds, sustain personal sorrow, and render faithful service to our generation, we pray to you, O God. Spirit of the Eternal, make us more than ourselves, because we have you for our ally and reinforcement.

Baptize us with the grace of appreciation. Enlarge our capacities for joy. Forgive us that we miss so many opportunities to be glad and grateful. Open our hearts to happiness in simple things, to mirth that has no bitter springs and no sad aftermath. In the beauty of nature, in human friendship, in family life, in the joys of common tasks and familiar relationships, may we find satisfaction, that we may live not only with integrity but with radiance.

We thank you, Lord, for the heritage which is ours in Christ, and for the great tradition that your Church has handed down to us. Make us worthy of our inheritance. Let us not because of any infidelity or lack of character hurt it by our mishandling. We pray for another Pentecost, another outpouring of your Spirit on your Church.

All this we pray in the name of Jesus Christ, our Lord and Savior. Amen.

Benediction

You came as disciples to learn, and as believers to worship. Now go forth as apostles to share, and as servants to help; and the blessing of God the Father, the Son, and the Holy Spirit go with you. Amen.

Proper 8
Sunday between June 26 and July 2 inclusive

First Lesson: Genesis 22:1-14
Theme: The Lord Will Provide

Call To Worship
Our God is a mighty God! Let us honor and bow down before him. Our God is a holy God! Let us stand in awe before him. Our God is a living God! Let us rejoice and take courage.

Invocation
Lord, we acknowledge that you are the creator and sustainer of all things; that in you we live and move and have our being; and that you are our hope for this world and the next. We come before you, then, praising you for your glory, thanking you for your goodness, and anticipating your blessing. Amen.

Confession
Father, we come as guests unworthy of your invitation. We have disobeyed your will. We have neglected our duties. We have faltered in our faith. We have quarreled with each other. We have neglected the means of grace. Nevertheless, we have received your invitation, so we have responded in faith and ask that you will receive us in mercy. Amen.

Offertory Prayer
O God, you have blessed us in so many ways. May we never take our blessings for granted. Help us to remember that privilege always implies responsibility. Accept these offerings as tokens of our responsibility to serve others in your name. Amen.

Hymns
"To God Be The Glory"
"He Leadeth Me: O Blessed Thought"
"All My Hope Is Firmly Grounded"

Proper 8
Sunday between June 26 and July 2 inclusive

Second Lesson: Romans 6:12-23
Theme: Wages Versus Gift

Call To Worship
Present yourselves to God as those who have been brought from death to life — present yourselves as instruments of righteousness.

Come, let us worship the God who has given us the free gift of eternal life in Christ Jesus our Lord.

Invocation
We give thanks, Heavenly Father, for this day of rest and recreation. May it help to ease the tensions of the past week. May it help free us from the shackles of sin that bind us. May it restore our energy for the week which lies ahead; and may it revitalize our Christian commitment to be instruments of your mercy in our world. Amen.

Confession
Lord, we know that you have freed us from being slaves to sin, but of our own free will we still wander from the pathway you have shown to be the "right way." Forgive our weakness, we pray, and through your Holy Spirit help us to make the right choices. In Jesus' name we pray. Amen.

Offertory Prayer
Blessed are you, O God, to whom we submit our souls and bodies as well as our gifts. Receive these symbols of our devotion as they represent our labor and our beliefs in your kingdom. Amen.

Hymns
"Glorious Things Of Thee Are Spoken"
"My Faith Looks Up To Thee"
"To God Be The Glory"

Proper 8
Sunday between June 26 and July 2 inclusive

Gospel Lesson: Matthew 10:40-42
Theme: Rewards

Call To Worship
In the name of Christ, I bid you welcome. In the name of Christ, God welcomes you. In the name of Christ, we welcome the strangers in our midst. In the name of Christ, we must all welcome one another.

Invocation
O Lord, Jesus Christ, make us conscious now of your healing mercies. Touch our eyes that we may see you; open our ears that we may hear your voice; enter our hearts that we may know your love. Overshadow our souls and bodies with your presence, that we may partake of your strength, your love, and your healing life so that we may go forth from this time of worship to witness to the world your great love. Amen.

Confession
Almighty God, we confess that we have not loved you with all our hearts and minds and souls and strengths, nor have we loved our neighbors as ourselves. Forgive us, we pray, and by the power of your Spirit enable us to show forth your love as we welcome those we meet this week. Amen.

Offertory Prayer
Lord, we bring these gifts not to receive rewards or recognition, but that they might do good. This is our way of reaching out with the love of Christ to our neighbors near and far. Amen.

Hymns
"Where Cross The Crowded Ways Of Life"
"O Master, Let Me Walk With Thee"
"This Is My Song"

Proper 8
Sunday between June 26 and July 2 inclusive

Psalter: Psalm 13

Words Of Assurance

Have confidence in the Lord, for he can heal the brokenhearted, restore the alienated, reunite the estranged, and forgive the wayward.

Pastoral Prayer

Eternal Spirit, who at first did brood over chaos and bring order from it, brood, we beseech you, over our souls. For our lives are disordered and amid the pressures of this world lost their meaning, direction, and aim. We need deep faith to undergird us, high hopes to allure us, profound resources to strengthen us. Brood, we beseech you, over your waiting and worshiping people; draw our lives together and make them whole.

Give us grace, Lord, to look deeply inward. From the immediate and external turn our eyes within. For the world is too much with us and we forget that while we have bodies we are souls. So minister to our inner life that we may have strength to rise above its temptations, to stand strong in the midst of its dismaying troubles, and to keep faith, courage, and honor high even when the world seems against us, that we may prosper even as our souls prosper.

Give us grace to look not only inward but upward. O God, let not the uplook of our spirits fail us in a day when the outlook is so dismaying. Let not God be lost to us. May our eyes steadfastly look up to you, and our lives be disciplined and directed by our devotion to the Highest.

Give us grace to look not only inward and upward but outward. Let our brothers and sisters come into the scope and horizon of our prayers. Let us bear our own troubles that we may be better able to help them in theirs. If we are in prosperity — and most of us are, O Lord — shame us from our selfish ease that we may remember those in frailty and need. Let our worship here result in an overflow of our generosity and affection.

All this we pray in the name of Jesus Christ our Lord. Amen.

Benediction

Become doers of God's Word and not listeners only, for those who persevere in what they have learned will be greatly blessed in what they do; and the grace of the Lord Jesus Christ, the love of God, and the fellowship of the Holy Spirit be with you always. Amen.

Proper 9
Sunday between July 3 and July 9 inclusive

First Lesson: Genesis 24:34-38, 42-49, 58-67
Theme: Love And Marriage

Call To Worship
Leader: Incline your ear, O Lord, and answer me,
People: for I am poor and needy.
Leader: You are my God; be gracious to me, O Lord,
People: for to you do I cry all day long.
Leader: Teach me your way, O Lord,
People: that I may walk in your truth.
Leader: I give thanks to you, O Lord, my God, with my whole heart,
People: and I will glorify your name forever.

Invocation
O Lord, all about us there are broken relationships. We come before you this day to be reminded of your love for us, and how we must return that love to keep our relationship strong. We come also to be reminded that this is also true in the covenantal relationship of marriage. We pray that this truth may shine forth in our lives and in our witness to others. Amen.

Confession
Lord, we know that love is kind, patient, forgiving, generous; and yet because we want our own way we fail to demonstrate our love. The result is that relationships are damaged or shattered. Help us, we pray, to mend our ways, to seek forgiveness, and to do what we can to reconcile with you and with those we have betrayed. Amen.

Offertory Prayer
O Lord, you know the very thoughts of our hearts and intentions of our minds. May these, as well as our gifts, be acceptable in your sight. In Jesus' name we pray. Amen.

Hymns
"Holy God, We Praise Thy Name"
"Dear Jesus, In Whose Life I See"
"God, Whose Love Is Reigning O'er Us"

221

Proper 9
Sunday between July 3 and July 9 inclusive

Second Lesson: Romans 7:15-25a
Theme: Inner Conflict

Call To Worship

This is the day the Lord has made: it is a day for singing and praying! It is a day for forgiving and reconciling! It is a day for resolving and renewing! It is a day for celebrating and rejoicing! Let us take this day which God has made and fill it with good things!

Invocation

Almighty God, whose voice is kind and whose leadership is sure, grant guidance to us for we are wandering; speak gently to us for we are hurting; and bring peace to us for we are restless; through Jesus Christ our Lord. Amen.

Confession

Lord, we do not understand our own actions. We know what is right, but then we go ahead and do the very thing we hate. Free us, we pray, from being captive to sin for we know it is only through Jesus Christ that we will be rescued from the weakness of our own wills. Amen.

Offertory Prayer

Father, we bring these gifts as evidence that your Word is alive in us, nourished by your Spirit, stirring with new life, budding with the promise of a generous harvest. Amen.

Hymns

"What A Friend We Have In Jesus"
"Dear Jesus, In Whose Life I See"
"We Shall Overcome"

Proper 9
Sunday between July 3 and July 9 inclusive

Gospel Lesson: Matthew 11:16-19, 25-30
Theme: Bring Your Burdens To The Lord

Call To Worship

Hear the invitation of Jesus as we bring to this service our needs and our burdens: "Come to me, all you that are weary and are carrying heavy burdens, and I will give you rest. Take my yoke upon you, and learn from me, for I am gentle and humble in heart, and you will find rest for your souls."

Invocation

Our Father in heaven, whose mercies are new every morning, we ask for a special measure of grace for this day. We ask that burdens may be lifted, that bodies may be healed, that the lonely may find companionship, that seekers may find truth, that achievers may find satisfaction, and that the anxious may find peace; through Jesus Christ our Lord. Amen.

Confession

Forgive our foolish ways, Almighty God, for we stumble and fall, time and again, as we seek to carry the burdens of life under our own power. We are weighed down with sorrow and guilt, distraught by the many demands placed upon us, and we never cease to worry. Open our hearts that we may hear you call and respond by bringing our burdens to you in faith and trust. Amen.

Offertory Prayer

We give, Lord, because we believe. We believe in the power of the Word. We believe in the power of prayer. We believe in the power of sacrificial gifts. And so we present these offerings that others, too, may believe. Amen.

Hymns

"Stand By Me"
"Precious Lord, Take My Hand"
"Leave It There"

Proper 9
Sunday between July 3 and July 9 inclusive

Psalter: Psalm 72:1-17

Words Of Assurance
Jesus said: "Anyone who comes to me I will never drive away."

Pastoral Prayer
Holy and Eternal God, out of the storms of the world we come into this quiet place to worship you, our abiding refuge. Thanks be to you for silence which enfolds strength and tranquility leading us to things deep and true. Meet with us here in the inner place of our spirits and refresh us with your living presence.

We find that life is often difficult Lord. It seems that a storm is usually either coming or going, and that the periods of sunshine are all too brief.

Help us when we are disappointed, to accept it without bitterness. Help us, when we are insulted, to reject the temptation to respond in kind. Help us, when we are in pain, to endure it with patience. Help us, when we are worried, to experience your peace. Help us when we fail, to have the perseverance to begin over again. Help us, when we are defeated, to accept it without excuse.

We thank you this morning, O God, for giving us space — space to grow and toddle and fall, space to dance and dream, space to be alone, space to make connections, space to run toward another or to walk away, space to be and do, to love and to laugh, to risk and become.

Thank you, God, for all who share our space: spouses, parents and children, brothers and sisters, friends and neighbors, adversaries and competitors, critics and supporters.

Thank you, God, for filling the space with: music and art, good work to do, purpose and passion.

Open us up to exploration of all the space you have given us, and open us to the task of being gracious stewards and hosts in that space.

With grateful and expectant hearts we pray in Jesus' name. Amen.

Benediction

Whatever has been the benefit of your presence here, keep it not to yourself, but share with others your faith, your trust, and your hope; and the blessing of God the Father, Son, and Holy Spirit be with you always. Amen.

Proper 10
Sunday between July 10 and July 16 inclusive

First Lesson: Genesis 25:19-34
Theme: Patience

Call To Worship

Leader: I waited patiently for the Lord.
People: He inclined to me and heard my cry.
Leader: He set my feet upon a rock,
People: making my steps secure.
Leader: He put a new song in my mouth,
People: a song of praise to our God.

Invocation

O Lord, our God, who has given your Word as a lamp to our feet and a light to our path, open our eyes to the truth, show us clearly your chosen direction, then incline our wills to walk in it. Amen.

Confession

Lord, we live in an age that demands instant gratification, immediate results. We don't like to be put on hold, nor told we have to wait. We find it hard to tolerate delays. Open our eyes to a new understanding of your ways. Help us seek first your kingdom, and increase our faith in your promise that when we do, everything else will be supplied according to our needs. Amen.

Offertory Prayer

Our Father, we present these gifts as an act of faith, knowing that you will receive them in love and use them in power. Amen.

Hymns

"Not So In Haste, My Heart"
"All My Hope Is Firmly Grounded"
"Hymn Of Promise"

Proper 10
Sunday between July 10 and July 16 inclusive

Second Lesson: Romans 8:1-11
Theme: Life In The Spirit

Call To Worship
May our worship be as God requires: in Spirit and in Truth. May our spirits find a kinship with God's Spirit, and may our minds be receptive to the clear truth of God's Word.

Invocation
Our Father, we open our hearts to you this day, and pray that your Spirit will come and dwell with us. Perform great things in us, O God. Expose us to the light of your Truth. Warm us in the glow of your love. Hold us up by the arm of your strength, and send us away with a resolve to express your presence in our lives. Amen.

Confession
We are determined, O God, to set our minds on things of the Spirit, and to live our lives according to the Spirit. However, we fail to show forth the mind of Christ, and too often we do not let the Holy Spirit control our actions. Forgive us, Lord, and give new life to our mortal bodies, through Jesus Christ our Lord. Amen.

Offertory Prayer
God, we know that you bless us in order that we in turn may be a blessing for others. Accept these gifts and bless them that they may be a blessing to others. Amen.

Hymns
"O Love That Wilt Not Let Me Go"
"Spirit Of God, Descend Upon My Heart"
"Amazing Grace"

Proper 10
Sunday between July 10 and July 16 inclusive

Gospel Lesson: Matthew 13:1-9, 18-23
Theme: Parable Of The Sower

Call To Worship
As we come together to worship God and hear the Word, let us come with receptive hearts that we may hear the Word and understand it. Then may we go forth prepared to yield an abundant harvest.

Invocation
O God, let not the good seed which is your Word be snatched away by the evil one, or fall upon a surface baked hard by cynicism, or be choked out by the busyness of a hectic lifestyle. Instead, may it take root in soil which has been well prepared by your Spirit, and may it spring up into lives which are both beautiful and fruitful; through Jesus Christ our Lord. Amen.

Confession
Lord, like the seed which falls on rocky ground we have often received your Word with great joy, but when trouble has arisen we have fallen away. Weeds have grown in our spiritual gardens, and the cares of the world and the lure of wealth have choked your Word. Send forth your Holy Spirit to prepare us to receive your Word that we might bear good fruit for your kingdom. Amen.

Offertory Prayer
Lord, as we present these gifts as part of our harvest, help us not to grow weary in well-doing, knowing that in due season we shall reap, if we do not lost heart. Amen.

Hymns
"Morning Has Broken"
"God Of Grace And God Of Glory"
"Open My Eyes That I May See"

Proper 10
Sunday between July 10 and July 16 inclusive

Psalter: Psalm 25

Words Of Assurance

Blessed are your eyes, for they see, and your ears, for they hear.

Pastoral Prayer

Everlasting God, whose living Spirit has brought all things into being, we glory in the wonder of your creation. Your mind has given order to the universe; we bless you for your truths and laws, often hidden in unfathomable ways. You have revealed your love in Jesus Christ; and we praise you for your immeasurable goodness in your continual redemption. We come to you, our Father, needing your guidance and sustaining, your judgment and comfort.

You who have fearfully and wondrously made all things, direct the eyes of our understanding to see the work of your hands in the beauty, form, and bounty of nature. Since all mysteries and knowledge have been known to you from the beginning of the world, inspire us with a reverent spirit as we discover and explore. Make us mindful that children and flowers, stars and atoms, and all that has life and form were fashioned as good in your sight.

Holy God, who places each generation of humanity into a new garden of blessings and freedom, forgive us for our self-will and disobedience in the use of your gifts. While fruit-laden boughs reflect your lovingkindness, we have often wasted or withheld food while many hungered. Cleanse and restore the image of yourself within us. Make us as your children, bound together with all who seek to know your will for all the earth.

O Christ, who spoke at mountainside and field, grant us a new awareness of your presence as the summer's majesty and splendor, rest and gladness, surround us. Give to those who are filled with anxieties for tomorrow sufficient strength for today. Keep us from evading tasks with useless dreaming. Guide us in work, play, and companionship into ways which cause us to return to your altar with joy and thankfulness. Lead the heavy-laden by your Spirit into green pastures and refreshing streams.

Grant grace unto us and to your Church everywhere to declare the gospel of your glorious life and kingdom. So may people know and believe that you are Lord and Redeemer of all, to the glory of the Father and our Lord Jesus Christ. Amen.

Benediction

What you have heard with your ears, may you believe in your hearts; and what you believe in your hearts may you practice in your lives; and the blessing of God the Father, Son, and Holy Spirit be upon you now and always. Amen.

Proper 11
Sunday between July 17 and 23 inclusive

First Lesson: Genesis 28:10-19a
Theme: How Awesome!

Call To Worship
How awesome! God is present with us. Surely the Lord is in this place, for this is none other than the house of God.

Invocation
We pray, Father, that as we gather here, nothing will hinder our worship. Help us to overcome distractions, preoccupation, and wanderings of mind. May we have the grace to set aside jealousy, animosity, and ill feelings. Enable us to subdue our doubts, our fears, and our unbelief. Then, Lord, may we have a real sense of your presence, and hear again your promise to be with us always. Amen.

Confession
Father God, we confess that we have failed to be obedient children: we have not done your will; we have broken your law; we have rebelled against your love; we have not loved our neighbors; we have not heard the cry of the needy. Forgive us, we pray. Free us for joyful obedience; through Jesus Christ our Lord. Amen.

Offertory Prayer
O Holy One, receive us and our gifts as we dedicate them and ourselves to you for your consecration. Amen.

Hymns
"Holy God, We Praise Thy Name"
"We Are Climbing Jacob's Ladder"
"Nearer, My God To Thee"

Proper 11
Sunday between July 17 and 23 inclusive

Second Lesson: Romans 8:12-25
Theme: Children Of God

Call To Worship
Leader: Come to God, the Father of us all.
People: We come, as children of the Almighty.
Leader: Come to Christ, our brother by adoption.
People: We come as joint heirs with Christ.
Leader: Come, as people of hope.
People: We come, waiting with patience for what we do not see.

Invocation
Almighty God, we come to claim our inheritance as joint heirs with Christ. We live by hope that being led by your Spirit we will live lives worthy of your children. We thank you for your revelation in Jesus Christ, in whose name we pray. Amen.

Confession
O God, our Eternal Parent, like spoiled children we complain about the sufferings of this present time without considering the blessings of living under your care. Revive the hope that is in us, and grant us the patience to wait for it, we pray in Jesus' name. Amen.

Offertory Prayer
Our Father, we present these gifts as an act of faith, knowing that you will receive them in love and use them in power, investing them in the lives of eternal souls and bringing about your divine purpose. Amen.

Hymns
"Come, Thou Almighty King"
"My Jesus I Love Thee"
"This Is My Father's World"

Proper 11
Sunday between July 17 and July 23 inclusive

Gospel Lesson: Matthew 13:24-30, 36-43
Theme: Parable Of The Weeds And The Wheat

Call To Worship
God has given us life. God has given us the good earth. God has given us people to love. God has given us Jesus Christ. What more can we ask? Come, let us worship the Lord our God!

Invocation
Almighty God, give us pure hearts, that we may see you. Give us open minds that we may hear you. Give us willing hands that we may serve you. Give us happy spirits that we may praise you. Through Jesus Christ our Lord. Amen.

Confession
Lord, we know that while we are in the world we will always be confronted with all kinds of sin and evildoers. Lead us not into temptation, and grant us wisdom, courage, and strength to resist the evil, that the day may come when we will shine like the sun in your kingdom. Amen.

Offertory Prayer
Lord, we present these gifts because we believe in a cause much greater than our own; we believe in a kingdom far greater than any earthly nation; and we believe in a divine will which desires peace and salvation for all. Amen.

Hymns
"Come, Ye Thankful People, Come"
"Where He Leads Me"
"O Spirit Of The Living God"

Proper 11
Sunday between July 17 and July 23 inclusive

Psalter: Psalm 139:1-12, 23-24

Words Of Assurance
There is no place where God cannot be with us. Wherever we go he will lead us and hold us fast. Amen.

Pastoral Prayer
Eternal Spirit, so high above us that we cannot comprehend you, and yet so deep within us that we cannot escape you, make yourself real to us now. In a shaken world we seek stability; in a noisy world we need inner peace; in a fearful world we want courage; and in a world of rising and falling empires we crave a vision of your eternal kingdom whose sun never sets.

Seek us out, every one, in the special circumstances and needs that each soul faces. Young and old we come, the merry-hearted and the bereaved, families together here and solitary souls lonely and far from home. Some of us are tempted to be proud of the world's prizes and some are crestfallen because of failure; some are strong in body and others are striving to keep the inward self renewed while the outward self perishes. O Sun of our help and strength, be to us like the sun indeed and shine into every window.

While you do comfort us, kindle also within us sincere penitence. Let some austere word of righteousness be spoken to our consciences today; save us from ignoble excuses, our cheap defenses, our unworthy self-deceits. Give us grace to be honest with ourselves, that we may rightly judge our dealing with the personality you have entrusted to us, with the friends and family that surround us, with the opportunities you have put before us, and with the stewardship committed to us.

With thankful and yet with burdened hearts we pray for your Church. Make it, we pray, a loyal servant of your cause. Grant unto all of us joined together in this fellowship, vision and dedication, wisdom, generosity, and devotion that we, a company of Christ's disciples, may exhibit his Spirit, further his work, and be faithful servants of his kingdom. Send us out strong in the Lord and in the power of his might; we pray in the name of Jesus Christ our Lord and Savior. Amen.

Benediction

Go out and be a blessing in your world. Return no one evil for evil. Weep with those who weep. Be happy with those who rejoice. Feed the hungry and clothe the poor. Seek justice for the oppressed; and the blessing of God the Father, Son, and Holy Spirit will be yours. Amen.

Proper 12
Sunday between July 24 and July 30 inclusive

First Lesson: Genesis 29:15-28
Theme: Paying The Price

Call To Worship
Leader: We will bless the Lord at all times.
People: His praise shall continually be in our mouths.
Leader: O magnify the Lord with me,
People: and let us exalt his name together.

Invocation
As we gather in this house of worship, challenge us, O God, with your truth and inspire us with your love. Then as we return to our worlds of work and learning and living, enlighten us with your wisdom and empower us with your strength. Amen.

Confession
O God, help us to seek forgiveness and be open to forgiving others. Often we are confronted by those who would deceive or trick us, and our first reaction is to seek revenge. Help us to remember that forgiving and being forgiven changes us forever, and in that spirit may we find the strength to dispel thoughts of revenge and ill will. Amen.

Offertory Prayer
Almighty God, we present these gifts as symbols of our devotion, and as expressions of our determination not to grow weary in doing what is right. Amen.

Hymns
"If Thou But Suffer God To Guide Thee"
"There Is A Balm In Gilead"
"Take Up Thy Cross"

Proper 12
Sunday between July 24 and July 30 inclusive

Second Lesson: Romans 8:26-39
Theme: More Than Conquerors

Call To Worship
Let us call on the Lord and give thanks! Let us sing to God and tell of God's wonderful works! Let us rejoice and give glory to God!

Invocation
As children, who from time to time throughout the day come to their parents to be reassured of their love, so we as children come to you, Heavenly Father, to be reassured of our place in your family, and to be encouraged in our mutual care for each other. Amen.

Confession
Praise be to you, O God, for in life's darkest moments when we think that we are all alone and there is no hope, we can turn to you knowing that in Christ, our constant companion, we are more than conquerors. Amen.

Offertory Prayer
Our Father, in order to share the love of Christ, in order to follow the example of Christ, we present these gifts in the name of Christ. Amen.

Hymns
"We'll Understand It Better By And By"
"I Need Thee Every Hour"
"Victory In Jesus"

Proper 12
Sunday between July 24 and July 30 inclusive

Gospel Lesson: Matthew 13:31-33, 44-52
Theme: What Is The Kingdom Of God Like?

Call To Worship
Leader: Come, let us sing to the Lord.
People: Let us make a joyful noise to the rock of our salvation.
Leader: Let us come before his presence with thanksgiving.
People: For the Lord is a great God, and a great King above all gods.

Invocation
Guide us, O Lord, by your Word and Spirit, that in your Light we may see light, in your Truth we may become truly free, and in your will we may experience peace, through Jesus Christ our Lord. Amen.

Confession
Almighty God, we pray that your kingdom may come, but we feel so inadequate to help in its realization. Come to us again with the reminder that like the mustard seed and the yeast you can use our small talents for large purposes; through Jesus Christ our Lord. Amen.

Offertory Prayer
Father in heaven, we know that it is not the size of our gifts that count, but the spirit in which they are given. Accept these gifts we pray, and our complete devotion to you and your kingdom. Amen.

Hymns
"The Kingdom Of God"
"We've A Story To Tell To The Nations"
"How Great Thou Art"

Proper 12
Sunday between July 24 and July 30 inclusive

Psalter: Psalm 105:1-11, 45b

Words Of Assurance
Neither death, nor life ... nor anything else in all creation, will be able to separate us from the love of God in Christ Jesus our Lord. Amen.

Pastoral Prayer
Father, thank you for today: fresh with the sparkling dew, bright with the splendor of a new day, and alive with the vitality of your perennial Spirit. May we receive this day thoughtfully, graciously, and tenderly. Thank you for the joy of good health; for the enthusiasm of youth; for the wisdom of mature years; for the insatiable thirst for the good, the true, and the beautiful; for this season of refreshment to restore body, mind, and spirit; for your Word through which life's meaning is revealed and we are nurtured; for vacations that refresh and help to restore a proper perspective to year-round tasks; for your love persevering through disappointment, loneliness, failure, and frustration; for the promise of a new heaven and a new earth in the presence of the disintegration of the present order.

Oh, to be your person in all the relationships of our every day — as Jesus was. This is our calling! Do not give up on us, O God; call us again and again. In life or in death may we be faithful to our high calling to be your children.

In our hurry and flurry may we not neglect to wait upon you to get our signals straight. May we wait, lest our words pose as your words and our actions as your acts. For as the heavens are high above the earth, so are your thoughts higher than our thoughts and your ways than our ways. May we be still and know that you are God, for in quietness and confidence is our strength.

May your good work begun in us continue and be brought to fruition through the victory that you offer in Christ, we pray in Jesus' name. Amen.

Benediction

You are the Lord's own, his hands and feet on earth, temples of his Spirit, so you may share his life and blessings with others. Go now in peace, and the blessing of God the Father, the Son, and the Holy Spirit go with you. Amen.

Proper 13
Sunday between July 31 and August 6 inclusive

First Lesson: Genesis 32:22-31
Theme: Encountering God

Call To Worship
Seek ye the Lord while he may be found. Call upon him while he is near. Seek and you shall find; knock and the door shall be opened unto you.

Invocation
Lord, we remember the promise that if we will ask we will receive, and that if we knock the door will be opened. So we ask that you will enlighten our minds and warm our hearts. We ask that you will give us new courage in facing whatever difficulties may lie ahead in the days before us. We ask that you will stand by us in this hour and in all the hours of our lives. Yes, Lord, we ask your blessing upon us. Amen.

Confession
Lord, we cannot depart from you without your blessing. Forgive us, if that seems bold, for we know how undeserving we are. Nevertheless, we know that without your love, your guidance, your strength we are nothing. So we cry out again: O Lord, bless us, we pray. Amen.

Offertory Prayer
Lord, as you have blessed us we would be a blessing to others. In that spirit we present our offerings for your blessing. Amen.

Hymns
"Blessed Assurance"
"Come, O Thou Traveler Unknown"
"Lord, Dismiss Us With Thy Blessing"

Proper 13
Sunday between July 31 and August 6 inclusive

Second Lesson: Romans 9:1-5
Theme: For Whom Are The Promises Of God?

Call To Worship
Leader: O Lord, our Lord, how majestic is your name in all the earth!
People: When I look at the heavens, the work of your fingers, the moon and the stars which you have established,
Leader: what are people, that you are mindful of us, and the family of humankind, that you care about us?
People: You have made us a little less than yourself, and have crowned us with glory and honor.
All: O Lord, our Lord, how majestic is your name in all the earth!

Invocation
Almighty God, we thank you for your Son, Jesus Christ, who came that your love might be made known to all peoples everywhere, and that they might find their rightful place in the family of God. Be near to us in our worship, that we might go forth from this place to bear our witness to this gospel. In Jesus' name, we pray. Amen.

Confession
Lord, it is with anguish and sorrow that we confess we have failed to recognize as our brothers and sisters those children of yours who are different from us. Some are a different nationality or ethnic background; others are of different races; some attend different houses of worship. Open our eyes, Lord, to the truth that all are your children and members of your household. Amen.

Offertory Prayer
Lord, we present these gifts because we believe in a kingdom far greater than any earthly nation; and we believe in a divine will which desires peace and salvation for all. Amen.

Hymns

"Hope Of The World"
"Majesty, Worship His Majesty"
"Standing On The Promises"

Proper 13
Sunday between July 31 and August 6 inclusive

Gospel Lesson: Matthew 14:13-21
Theme: Caring For The Needs Of Others

Call To Worship
Come, brothers and sisters in the faith, let us gather with God who cares for us as a father, who comforts us as a mother, who walks with us as a brother or sister, and who listens as a friend.

Invocation
Almighty God, we praise you for the many opportunities that are presented to us to serve you by caring for the needs of others. Open our eyes that we may see our Lord in every needy person we are called to help, and grant us the wisdom not to miss any opportunity of serving you. Amen.

Confession
Lord, we have failed to respond to the needs of others, and in our failure we have missed opportunities to minister to you. Forgive us, we pray, and the next time keep us from passing by unheeding, on the other side. Amen.

Offertory Prayer
We approach you, Lord, as one who can take common things and common people, consecrate them by your love, and make them holy! We ask you now to do just that with these our gifts. Amen.

Hymns
"Where Cross The Crowded Ways Of Life"
"O Young And Fearless Prophet"
"Here I Am, Lord"

Proper 13
Sunday between July 31 and August 6 inclusive

Psalter: Psalm 17:1-7, 15

Words Of Assurance

When Jesus saw that the multitude was hungry he multiplied the loaves and fishes so that all might be satisfied. Even so we can count on God to care for us.

Pastoral Prayer

O Lord God Almighty, you know the thoughts of all people; you search our hearts, our inmost beings. You have called us to your presence though we are unworthy. Turn not your face from us, but wipe away all our transgressions. Wash away the defilements of our souls, and thoroughly sanctify us, so that while we pray you to grant forgiveness of sins to others, we ourselves may not be cast away. Send the grace of your Holy Spirit upon us: make us worthy to stand before your holy presence.

Our God, great both in love and in power, now as always we give you our thanks and praise. How can we speak aright of all that you are and all that you have done? Our minds cannot contain what you have created. How can we comprehend you, the Creator of all? And yet you do not stay distant from us; you draw near to us in Jesus Christ and claim us for yourself. In him you show us what you are and what we may become. In him you promise us your kingdom and make known its secrets. We praise you! Lord our God, all that we have and will have comes from you. To you we give our thanks and praise.

To you we also bring our prayers and petitions. Your goodness encourages us to bring before you the needs of the world you have made, of your Church and of our loved ones.

We pray, therefore, for those who are racked by hunger while we waste our food and feed ourselves too well. Do not let our consciences rest until the good things of this earth are justly shared by all.

We remember before you those who suffer from armed conflict while others profit from their troubles. Bring peace in our time, we pray, and speed the work of those who struggle for peace.

Hear us also, O God, as we offer our prayers for your Church. Make it faithful in preaching, in praise, and in action.

Hear all our prayers, O God, both those spoken aloud and those whispered in our hearts. Look with favor upon those that accord with your will and advance the cause of your kingdom. May that kingdom come in us and throughout the world, we pray through Jesus Christ our Lord. Amen.

Benediction

May God grant you the ability for every task you undertake, the courage for every challenge you meet, and the strength for every cross you bear; and the blessing of God the Father, the Son, and the Holy Spirit be yours now and forever. Amen.

Proper 14
Sunday between August 7 and August 13 inclusive

First Lesson: Genesis 37:1-4, 12-28
Theme: Jealousy

Call To Worship
Worthy is the Lord to be praised, for he has created the atom and the galaxy and placed the planets in their orbits. He has painted the rainbow and the butterfly wing, and given birds their songs. He has created all the peoples of the earth, and has called them to mercy and justice. Worthy is the Lord to be praised!

Invocation
Lord, we ask that you will help us to prepare our souls as we settle down for this time of worship. Give us a sense of awe before your holiness. Open our eyes to see the light of your truth. Give us compassion and love for our fellow worshipers, and shut out any distractions which threaten to dilute the beauty of this hour. Amen.

Confession
Lord, how often we have felt threatened by the love and attention showered upon those close to us. Our jealousy often knows no bounds. Forgive our self-pity, we pray, and help us to understand there is enough love for all. Teach us how to love, how to rejoice in the good fortune of others, and keep us from envy, rivalry, jealousy, and ill will. In Jesus' name we pray. Amen.

Offertory Prayer
O God, let us live as one in Christ, sharing our need and our abundance, until all may know the love of Christ Jesus, in whose name we pray. Amen.

Hymns
"Let There Be Peace On Earth"
"Breathe On Me, Breath Of God"
"Help Us Accept Each Other"

Proper 14
Sunday between August 7 and August 13 inclusive

Second Lesson: Romans 10:5-15
Theme: Salvation Is For All

Call To Worship

Everyone who calls upon the name of the Lord shall be saved. Come, let us worship together. Let us call upon the name of the Lord, our Redeemer. Let us sing praises to the God of our salvation, and offer up our prayers of thanksgiving.

Invocation

O Eternal God, speak to each of us the word that we need, and let your Word abide with us until it has wrought in us your holy will. Cleanse, quicken, and refresh our hearts; direct and increase our faith. Grant that we, by our worship at this time, may be enabled to see you more clearly, to love you more fully, and to serve you more perfectly; through Jesus Christ our Lord. Amen.

Confession

Lord, we hear the words: "Faith comes from what is heard; and what is heard comes through the word of Jesus Christ." Yes, and we nod our heads in assent when we hear: "How are they to believe in one of whom they have never heard? And how are they to hear without someone to proclaim him?" But we have been slow to respond to the call to be one of those messengers. Send your Spirit upon us, Lord, that we may be counted among your faithful messengers of the Good News. Amen.

Offertory Prayer

O Lord, as we open our treasures and present our offerings, we pray that you will use them to proclaim the good news that we have received and desire for all people everywhere to hear and believe. In Jesus' name. Amen.

Hymns

"Pass It On"
"How Shall They Hear The Word Of God"
"We've A Story To Tell To The Nations"

248

Proper 14
Sunday between August 7 and August 13 inclusive

Gospel Lesson: Matthew 14:22-33
Theme: When The Storms Overtake Us

Call To Worship

Seek the Lord with expectancy and hope; and when you find him he will be your happiness and you will worship and serve him the rest of your life.

Invocation

O Lord, we often walk with our eyes downcast, looking down to the path immediately before us, dismayed by the ruts and the obstacles, cursing the heat and the dust.

Through the experience of worship, may we see life in a new perspective. Give us a new challenge, new hope, and a new vision. No matter what the circumstance, may we gain a sense of your presence with us. Amen.

Confession

Lord, like Peter of old we respond to your call to come to you, but then the going gets rough, the storms of life threaten to overcome us, and we begin to sink. Strengthen our faith, we pray, and grant us the courage to follow you believing in our deeds as well as in our words that you can truly save us. Amen.

Offertory Prayer

When we were in despair, you lifted us. When we were lost, you sought us out. When we were worn out, you refreshed us. Now, O Lord, we use this opportunity to express our thanks and to pass on our privileges to others. Amen.

Hymns

"Trust And Obey"
"He Leadeth Me, O Blessed Thought"
"Stand By Me"

Proper 14
Sunday between August 7 and August 13 inclusive

Psalter: Psalm 105:1-6, 16-22, 45b

Words Of Assurance
Jesus said: "Take heart, do not be afraid." You of little faith, why do you doubt?

Pastoral Prayer
Eternal Spirit, to whom we belong and in whom we live, we worship you, seeking a fresh consciousness of your reality and your penetrating presence. Too often, like creatures of the sea, we question whether there is any water; like birds upon the wing, we ask whether there is air. For, lo, in you we live and move and have our being; yet we spin long arguments about your existence and labor our debates about your attributes. This day we would not debate, but experience you. We would not argue, but would know.

O God, help us never to lose our vision of you. You are the center and the circumference. You bind together all that is worthy and meaningful in life. Steady our faith in you. If some of us here today have been shattered by doubt, hurt by disbelief, until life has been drained of its worth, restore to us such a vision of you that we may believe triumphantly again.

Beget in us a new love for people. Forgive us that so often we are fatigued by them, worn out by their multitude and the irritation of their demands. Give us grace to see beneath the surface into the hearts of persons; to sympathize more deeply with the needs of human lives; to love better the things that are unlovely; to mend more helpfully the things that are amiss.

Beget in us a new hatred of sin. Forgive us that we ever by familiarity become accustomed to wickedness until we first tolerate and then embrace it. O God, by as much as we love people, may we hate the things that ruin people, despoil them of their loveliness and hope, and wreck them like shattered hulks upon the shore. Give us again indignation against things that are base and vile.

Now gather all of us into your everlasting arms, and according to the diversity of our need be the multiplicity of your supplies, O God of grace and truth. We ask it in the name of Jesus Christ, your Son our Lord. Amen.

Benediction

May God, through his Son Jesus Christ, restore and renew daily his life within you, giving you the courage you need in the face of life's unpredictables, and granting victory over all that would threaten you; and the blessing of God the Father, Son, and Holy Spirit abide with you now and always. Amen.

Proper 15
Sunday between August 14 and August 20 inclusive

First Lesson: Genesis 45:1-15
Theme: Reconciliation

Call To Worship

How very good and pleasant it is when kindred live together in unity! Come, let us worship the head of the human family, the God and Father of us all!

Invocation

Heavenly Father, as we have gathered in this holy place in the presence of each other and of the Risen Lord, we ask that your light will bring understanding in every mind; that your grace will bring peace in every heart; and that your vision for saving our troubled world will ignite every imagination. Amen.

Confession

Father Almighty, as we stand in the presence of our brothers and sisters in Christ we are ashamed, for we have often failed to recognize them as your children. We cringe at the thought of how we have treated them. We have sold them into slavery, we have abused them, we have discriminated against them. We come now seeking their forgiveness and yours, O God, as we ask your help in bringing about reconciliation within the family of God. Amen.

Offertory Prayer

Lord, we offer our gifts in gratitude for the love of Christ. Bless both the gifts and the givers, and grant that both may be used effectively in serving you. Amen.

Hymns

"Depth Of Mercy"
"This Is A Day Of New Beginnings"
"Help Us Accept Each Other"

Proper 15
Sunday between August 14 and August 20 inclusive

Second Lesson: Romans 11:1-2a, 29-32
Theme: Irrevocable Love

Call To Worship
If you are sorrowing, come and be comforted. If you are discouraged, come and find hope. If you are happy, come and sing praises. For the love of God is irrevocable, and he stands knocking at your door awaiting your welcome.

Invocation
Almighty God, as we gather in expectation and hope, we pray that you will forgive us by your grace, comfort us by your promises, inspire us by your Spirit, encourage us by your people, and challenge us by your Word. Amen.

Confession
Almighty and Everlasting God, you are always more ready to hear than we are to pray, and to give more than we either desire or deserve. Pour upon us the abundance of your mercy, forgiving us those things of which our conscience is afraid, and giving us those good things for which we are not worthy to ask, except through the merit of your Son, Jesus Christ our Lord. Amen.

Offertory Prayer
Our Father, we present these gifts as an act of faith, knowing that you will receive them in love and use them in power, investing them in the lives of eternal souls and bringing about your divine purposes. Amen.

Hymns
"Jesus Is All The World To Me"
"Love Divine, All Loves Excelling"
"I Love To Tell The Story"

Proper 15
Sunday between August 14 and August 20 inclusive

Gospel Lesson: Matthew 15:(10-20) 21-28
Theme: What Does Your Heart Say?

Call To Worship

Thankful for God's presence with us, knowing that God loves us and cares for us, believing in the power of prayer, and anticipating that we will be strengthened for the challenge of the week ahead, let us worship the Lord our God.

Invocation

Lord, out of your great love for us, you have given us this world — the only world we have. Help us to discover, moment by moment, your presence in it. Help us to see it, listen to it, live in it as the divinely created school of learning how to love. Amen.

Confession

O Christ, to whom all authority is given both in heaven and earth: transform our wills and our understanding, cleanse our hearts and enlighten our minds, that our thoughts and desires being made obedient to your pure and holy law, we may grow up in all things unto you, and present ourselves a living sacrifice, to the praise and glory of your holy name. Amen.

Offertory Prayer

O Lord, as we present these gifts we pray that they may be pleasing to you for they are given out of the love and gratitude in our hearts for all your good gifts. Use them, we pray, for the good of your kingdom that others may know of your bountiful mercy. Amen.

Hymns

"Tell Out, My Soul"
"Lord, Speak To Me"
"O For A Thousand Tongues To Sing"

Proper 15
Sunday between August 14 and August 20 inclusive

Psalter: Psalm 133

Words Of Assurance
Just as God's words are challenging, demanding, and exacting, God's forgiveness is comforting, strengthening, and life-enriching.

Pastoral Prayer
Eternal God, the Shepherd of our souls, out of the noise of the world, its turbulence and its truculence, we come with reverence to worship you. Refresh in us the spirit of wonder and awe. From things that humans have made, we come into your sanctuary to think of what you have made. Deepen in us the wonder of the stars, the glory of the sun, the march of the seasons, the procession of day and night. O God, from everlasting to everlasting, whose years never fail, mystery upon mystery is this life of ours, its background, its sustenance, and its destiny. In reverence and wonder we worship you!

Give us a fresh vision, we beseech you, of the Highest. Let Christ dawn upon us anew this day. Make everything that is excellent in life real to us. Break upon our dull sight with the vision of the ineffable and the beautiful, that we may delight in life again and be thankful. Too easily we learn to despise life. We would learn to love it again this morning, to see that it is good, and to cry once more with all our hearts, "Serve the Lord with gladness."

We come before you, O God, with deep regret for the wrongs that we have done. Many an opportunity we have wasted, and we have made a sad tale of what might have been a glorious story. We have left our friends sad when they should have been happy, depressed when they might have been elevated, dull when they might have been illumined. For all that has been wrong in us we repent and acknowledge the reality of our human sin that lies like a shadow across the face of the earth. Make more poignant within us the sense of our iniquities, personal and social. Send us out with firmer purpose and high resolve, with penitence and power.

We seek in you, O Lord, depth and strength of character to handle the joys and adversities of the days ahead. We ask you for no more comfortable time. We know our destiny lies with hardship, but we pray for houses built upon solid foundations of enduring rock, that will not fall when the rains descend and the floods come and the winds blow. Let not prosperity spoil us or adversity shake us, but let joy be our opportunity. Let trouble evoke the best in us, that we may be worthy, even though afar off, to be disciples of the Christ who took into his life both the lilies of the field and the cross on Calvary.

Grant us zest in living that no grimness of the times can take away, and resilience of heart that no fear can destroy. So help us to bear living witness to the triumphant grace of Jesus Christ in whose name we pray. Amen.

Benediction

May your faith be strong. May your mind be at peace. May your soul be filled with faith and hope; and the blessing of God the Father, Son, and Holy Spirit be yours now and always. Amen.

Proper 16
Sunday between August 21 and August 27 inclusive

First Lesson: Exodus 1:8—2:10
Theme: Overcoming Adversity

Call To Worship

Leader: Out of the depths I cry to you, O Lord.
People: Lord, hear my voice! Let your ears be attentive to the voice of my supplication!
Leader: I wait for the Lord, my soul waits,
People: and in his word I hope.
Leader: O Israel, hope in the Lord!
People: For with the Lord there is steadfast love.

Invocation

Gracious God, our Heavenly Father, you are our guide in life's journey, our shelter in life's storms, our inspiration in life's challenges, and our partner in life's victories. We come now to give you thanks and lift up our praises to your almighty power. Replenish our faith and grant us renewed courage for the facing of life's adversities, we pray in Jesus' name. Amen.

Confession

O Lord God, when the forces of evil would enlist our support and attempt to use us to further their cause, be our strength for we are weak. When we keep silent in the face of wrong, open our lips for we often lack the courage. By the power of your Holy Spirit enable us to be used by you to further your kingdom's goals in the face of adversity; we pray in Jesus' name. Amen.

Offertory Prayer

Lord, we offer our gifts in gratitude for the love of Christ. Bless both the gifts and the givers, and grant that both may be used effectively in serving you. Amen.

Hymns

"Am I A Soldier Of The Cross"
"Praise, My Soul, The King Of Heaven"
"Go Forth For God"

Proper 16
Sunday between August 21 and August 27 inclusive

Second Lesson: Romans 12:1-8
Theme: Unity In Diversity

Call To Worship
The Lord says: "Come, all you who labor and are overburdened."
He doesn't say: "Come, all you Americans, or Methodists, or all you
who look and act alike," but, "Come all!" Let us worship the God who
welcomes us all, and may we find unity in our diversity.

Invocation
Holy Spirit, as you gave messages to the churches as recorded in
the Holy Scriptures, so we ask that you will speak today to this congregation and to all congregations as they gather for worship around
the world. Whatever their native tongue, may your people speak the
language of peace. Whatever their national origin, may your people
live and worship together in harmony. Whatever their status in life,
may they experience your blessings and your grace. Amen.

Confession
Father, we pray for the rewards of your kingdom, but we shirk our
responsibilities here on earth. It is easy to listen to your commandments, but they seem so difficult to live by. Teach us, Lord, that your
life of love is only hard if we try to adapt your way to our life, instead
of our life to your way. Teach us, Lord, that the rewards of your kingdom begin now for those who carry out their responsibilities. Amen.

Offertory Prayer
Lord God, as we present our gifts of thanksgiving, we pray that
through them and us we may be instrumental in breaking through the
barriers that divide us as we extend a hand that shares and heals. In
Jesus' name, we pray. Amen.

Hymns
"Forward Through The Ages"
"We Are The Church"
"For The Healing Of The Nations"

Proper 16
Sunday between August 21 and August 27 inclusive

Gospel Lesson: Matthew 16:13-20
Theme: On This Rock

Call To Worship
Nations have flourished and fallen; ideologies have blossomed and withered; rulers have conquered and been conquered. But the Church of Christ is built on a rock, and neither time, nor enemies, nor hell itself can destroy it. Come, let us worship the Lord of the Church.

Invocation
Lord, we thank you for this time of worship, for the Church which has nurtured us, and for the struggle and triumph of the life of faith. Reveal again to us the beautiful truths of the divine way, and equip us to walk that path in confidence and peace. Amen.

Confession
O God, when the world asks, "Who is this Jesus?" we mumble words about a man from Galilee who lived long ago. We should be proudly proclaiming him as the living Christ, and showing his power by the lives we live. Send your Spirit upon us that we may bear witness to the Son of God, and thus become one of the building blocks of your kingdom. Amen.

Offertory Prayer
Bless our gifts, O Lord, and through them let us show forth your glory. Amen.

Hymns
"Hail To The Lord's Anointed"
"All Hail The Power Of Jesus' Name"
"The Church's One Foundation"

Proper 16
Sunday between August 21 and August 27 inclusive

Psalter: Psalm 124

Words Of Assurance

Thus says the Lord: "If my people who are called by my name humble themselves and pray and seek my face, and turn from their wicked ways, then I will hear from heaven, and will forgive their sin and heal their land."

Pastoral Prayer

O Lord, into your hands we commit ourselves this day. Give to each one of us a watchful, humble, and diligent spirit, that we may seek in all things to know your will, and when we know it may we perform it perfectly and gladly, to the honor and glory of your holy name.

O Lord, our Christ, may we have your mind and your spirit. Make us instruments of your peace: where there is hatred, let us sow love; where there is injury, pardon; where there is discord, union; where there is doubt, faith; where there is despair, hope; where there is darkness, light; and where there is sadness, joy.

O Divine Master, grant that we may not so much seek to be consoled, as to console; to be understood, as to understand; to be loved, as to love; for it is in giving that we receive; it is in pardoning that we are pardoned; and it is in dying that we are born to eternal life.

Grant us, O Lord, in all our duties your help, in all our perplexities your counsel, in all our dangers your protection, and in all sorrows your peace.

O Lord Jesus Christ, who bids your Church to bring all persons to yourself and to make all humanity one family in you, make clear to each one of us our part in the task. Fire our minds with a vision of a more perfect society here on earth in which justice and right, peace and brotherhood shall reign according to your will. Help us each one, O Lord, to do our part, that your will may be done on earth as it is in heaven. We pray in Jesus' name. Amen.

Benediction

May the Lord grant you convictions for the sake of truth. May he grant you toleration for the sake of love. And may he grant you wisdom to exercise each in its proper place; in the name of the Father, the Son, and the Holy Spirit. Amen.

Proper 17
Sunday between August 28 and September 3 inclusive

First Lesson: Exodus 3:1-15
Theme: God Is Calling

Call To Worship

Leader: Make a joyful noise to the Lord, all you people!
People: We will serve the Lord with gladness!
Leader: Come into his presence with singing. Know that the Lord is God!
People: It is he that made us, and we are his!

Invocation

Almighty God, help us to behold your presence in the blazing glory of nature wherever we go. As we draw near to you on the holy ground of this place of worship help us to hear your call and to respond in faith. Amen.

Confession

Lord, how often we respond to calls to serve you with lame excuses about our own inadequacies. We always seem to be looking for a way to avoid your call. Remind us, Lord, that we do not rely on our own strength or wisdom, but your promise to be with us in every endeavor. In Jesus' name. Amen.

Offertory Prayer

You have blessed us, God of creation, far beyond most of the peoples of the earth. Help us never to take our blessings for granted, and help us also to remember that privilege always inspires responsibility. Amen.

Hymns

"I Am Thine, O Lord"
"The Voice Of God Is Calling"
"O Young And Fearless Prophet"

Proper 17
Sunday between August 28 and September 3 inclusive

Second Lesson: Romans 12:9-21
Theme: Marks Of The True Christian

Call To Worship
Thus says the Lord: "Let those who boast boast in this, that they understand and know me, that I am the Lord." As we come together to worship this morning let it be a time when we get to know the Lord better. Let us listen for the marks of a true Christian, and determine to live more Christ-like lives. Come, let us worship together!

Invocation
We thank you, O God, that through our shared worship we can bear each other's burdens and share each other's joys. By our presence here, we acknowledge that we are mutually dependent. Without each other, our faith becomes weak and our journey in life becomes a lonely trek in the wilderness. Consecrate, then, this time that we spend together, to our mutual upbuilding and our common love. Amen.

Confession
Heavenly Father, when we look at the marks of a true Christian as set forth in Paul's letter to the Romans, we realize how far we fall short, how inadequate are our lives. Humbly, we ask your forgiveness, and pray that in this time of worship your Holy Spirit will renew and strengthen our determination to love you more fully and serve you more adequately, through Jesus Christ our Lord. Amen.

Offertory Prayer
Heavenly Father, we present these gifts as a partial response to the Apostle Paul's plea for Christians to contribute to the needs of the saints and extend hospitality. Bless these gifts, we pray, that through your Church they may be used to carry our your will. Amen.

Hymns
"A Charge To Keep I Have"
"Take Time To Be Holy"
"I Want A Principle Within"

263

Proper 17
Sunday between August 28 and September 3 inclusive

Gospel Lesson: Matthew 16:21-28
Theme: The Cross And Self-Denial

Call To Worship
Jesus told his disciples that those who would choose to be his followers must deny themselves and take up their cross and follow him. May this time of worship be an opportunity to re-examine our commitment to follow Jesus!

Invocation
Almighty God, author of eternal light, illumine our hearts by the light of your grace, that our lips may praise you, that our lives may bless you, that our worship may glorify you; through Jesus Christ our Lord. Amen.

Confession
O Holy God, we are often astonished by your power and presence in our lives, but we are rarely transformed. We frequently hear your Word, but we seldom listen. We love to talk, but are afraid to act. Grant us the vision to see through the wonders of the everyday to the wonders of your kingdom. Guide us to a faith in action. In the name of Christ our Lord. Amen.

Offertory Prayer
Eternal God, from whom we have received all things, we return these gifts as symbols of our sacrifice and of our work. Intensify our sacrifice and consecrate our work, so that your will may be done on earth as it is in heaven. Amen.

Hymns
"Must Jesus Bear The Cross Alone"
"Jesus Calls Us"
"Take Up Thy Cross"

Proper 17
Sunday between August 28 and September 3 inclusive

Psalter: Psalm 105:1-6, 23-26, 45c

Words Of Assurance
When the Lord sends us as his messengers into the world he assures us that he will be with us. Amen.

Pastoral Prayer
O Lord, our God, only you are eternal, and it is only to you that we can turn when everything else fails. All of our human wonders are as castles in the sand when compared to you. We praise you for your power as it has worked for our good, for your grace reaching new to us each day, for your love expressed in Jesus Christ our Savior.

Look upon us, O Lord, in our conceits and in our distresses. Cause us to become more constant in our devotion, more fervent in our prayers, more determined to walk in the steps of your Son.

To that intent, dear God, point us to the needs that cry for our presence, our hands, and our money.

Make us so disturbed at the thought of poverty and injustice that we will strain our resources for the help of others. Reach in pity to those for whom life has lost its taste, and give new hope to the bereaved, new courage to the endangered, new assurance to the anxious, new trust and confidence to those who find the road covered with the unknown.

As we are strangers and pilgrims, Lord, go with us in every path and to every place, that assured of your presence we may live more fully for the loving service of one another, like him whom we acknowledge as our Savior, even Jesus Christ. Amen.

Benediction
May there be granted to you courage for every challenge, wisdom for every decision, strength for every temptation, and joy for every triumph; and the blessing of God the Father, Son, and Holy Spirit be with you always. Amen.

Proper 18
Sunday between September 4 and September 10 inclusive

First Lesson: Exodus 12:1-14
Theme: The Community Of Faith

Call To Worship
Let us come before the Lord our God, calling upon him in our difficulties, celebrating with him in our victories, counseling with him in our perplexities, for he is God of both mercy and power.

Invocation
Lord, we are gathered here as part of your family to celebrate your saving grace. As you freed the Israelites of old from the bondage of Egypt, so have you liberated us from the shackles of sin by the sacrifice of your Son, Jesus Christ. Thanks be to you, O God. May we never let your love be forgotten as we gather our families in the community of faith to worship your holy presence. Amen.

Confession
Almighty God, we come into your presence conscious of our weakness. When we are puffed up, bring us back to reality. When our spirits are low, speak words of encouragement. When we are angry, help us to forgive. When we are wandering, lead us in the right path. When we are puzzled, reveal yourself to us. We pray in Jesus' name. Amen.

Offertory Prayer
Heavenly Father, we present our offerings not as meaningless formalities or repetitious habits, but as genuine acts of love and heartfelt sacrifice. Amen.

Hymns
"Draw Us In The Spirit's Tether"
"All Praise To Our Redeeming Lord"
"Here, O Lord, Your Servants Gather"

Proper 18
Sunday between September 4 and September 10 inclusive

Second Lesson: Romans 13:8-14
Theme: Love One Another

Call To Worship
God answers the prayers we cannot utter. God understands the thoughts for which there is no language. God receives the praise we cannot articulate. God meets the needs for which there is no name. Come, let us worship Almighty God!

Invocation
Lord, remove any barriers that are here this morning: any barriers of suspicion or hard feelings which may separate us from each other; any barriers of unbelief or disinterest which may separate us from you. Overcome, Father, these and other hindrances which keep us from loving you and one another, and unite us by your Spirit as we come together in praise. Amen.

Confession
Lord, we bow before you in contrition, for quarreling and jealousy have filled our lives as individuals, as families, as churches, and as nations. Send your Spirit upon us that we may awaken to the fact that life cannot go on like this without dire consequences, and enable us to love as Jesus taught us. Amen.

Offertory Prayer
O Lord, we present these offerings that they may be lights to show forth your love through our love for our neighbors. Amen.

Hymns
"Awake, O Sleeper"
"Pass It On"
"Rise Up, O Men Of God"

Proper 18
Sunday between September 4 and September 10 inclusive

Gospel Lesson: Matthew 18:15-20
Theme: Two Or Three Together

Call To Worship
Jesus said: "Where two or three are gathered in my name, I am there among them." Come, let us be awed by his presence. Let us be shaped by his standards. Let us be enlightened by his wisdom. Let us be mobilized by his Spirit.

Invocation
Be present in our midst, O Lord, in this time of worship. Hear our prayers as prayers from those who have sometimes found it hard to speak to you, not knowing what to say nor how to say it. Hear our songs as songs from those who have sometimes found it hard to sing our praise of you. And when we leave here, send us out enriched by your presence among us, for the sake of Jesus Christ our Lord. Amen.

Confession
Lord, some of us are here with smiles on our faces even though we are hurting inside. Some of us are here to show our neighbors that we are religious, even though we don't feel very religious. Some of us are trying to create an impression with externals even though they mean very little. As we come into your special presence, we know that our souls are naked before you, that all pretense is stripped away, and that you know us for what we really are. Receive us, Lord, by your grace, and help us to worship you in sincerity and truth. Amen.

Offertory Prayer
Receive, O Lord, this fruit of our labor as an evidence of our devotion. Bless the gifts and encourage our commitment, through Jesus Christ our Lord. Amen.

Hymns
"Surely The Presence Of The Lord"
"We Meet You, O Christ"
"God Is Here"

Proper 18
Sunday between September 4 and September 10 inclusive

Psalter: Psalm 149

Words Of Assurance
For as the heavens are high above the earth, so great is God's love toward those who fear him; as far as the east is from the west, so far does he remove our transgressions from us. Amen.

Pastoral Prayer
Almighty God, Lord of life and Father of our Lord Jesus Christ, we are aware of your majesty and your mystery, your holiness and your glory. We thank you that you are God above and beyond us. But we are also aware of your coming to us and your being with us, of your taking our part and your sharing our humanity. We thank you that you accept and love us, that you discipline and correct us, that you provide for us and lead us, that you call us into your family and send us out into life to serve in your name. We thank you for the Church, the Body of Christ, and the Family of the Faithful. We are grateful for all those who share with us all the good that is ours in Christ: for those who pray for us and those whom we remember in our prayers; for those who stretch our minds and for those who make us laugh; for those who weep with us and those who let us weep with them; for those who are easy to love and for those who test our capacity to love; for those who freely give and for those who graciously receive what we seek to offer them. We thank you that in Christ we find the faith which binds us to you, the hope which sustains us, and the love which gives meaning to life both now and forever.

O God, you hear us before we speak, and you answer beyond our expectations. Therefore, we are bold to make our intercessions before you. We pray for your creation that it may be set free from the bondage of decay, pollution, and exploitation by humankind. We pray for the world which you love and redeem. Hasten the day when the mystery of your will and purpose to unite all things in Christ shall be fulfilled. Guide the leaders of the nations who make momentous decisions which affect the lives of millions. Grant that those decisions may be made under your sovereign lordship even when those who make them do not recognize that lordship. Bless, O Lord, those who seek to be ambassadors of reconciliation among nations, within the Church, in families, and between friends estranged. Be with those who need your healing grace for bodies or for minds. Comfort those who mourn because of loss or failure. Strengthen those who feel over-burdened, and restore meaning to those who see no sense in the routine of living.

Hear these our prayers, O Lord, for we make them in the name and for the sake of Christ who is our Advocate. Amen.

Benediction

Go in peace. Be diligent in your work, true to your friends, kind to your enemies, helpful to the unfortunate, and loyal to your God; and the blessing of God the Father, the Son, and the Holy Spirit be yours. Amen.

Proper 19
Sunday between September 11 and September 17 inclusive

First Lesson: Exodus 14:19-31
Theme: Trust

Call To Worship
Leader: Let us turn to the Lord our God with humility,
People: for the contrite heart he will not turn away.
Leader: Let us turn to God with sincerity,
People: for he calls us to worship in Spirit and in Truth.
Leader: Let us turn to God with confidence,
People: for he cares for us with a steadfast love.

Invocation
Almighty God, as we hear again the story of the miraculous crossing of the Red Sea as Moses, trusting in your promises, led the Israelites to freedom from the Egyptians, may our time of prayer and worship open our souls to your Spirit, and free us to rejoice in the freedom we enjoy as we put our trust in Jesus Christ, our Lord. Amen.

Confession
Lord, like so many others we want to see a sign, a miracle, before we wholly trust in your power. Forgive our foolishness, increase our faith, and through your Spirit strengthen our determination to put our trust in you and follow where you lead us. In Jesus' name we pray. Amen.

Offertory Prayer
Almighty God, as we pray, so we give, that your kingdom may come, and your will be done on earth as it is in heaven. Amen.

Hymns
"Guide Me, O Thou Great Jehovah"
"Trust And Obey"
"'Tis So Sweet To Trust In Jesus"

Proper 19
Sunday between September 11 and September 17 inclusive

Second Lesson: Romans 14:1-12
Theme: Judge Not

Call To Worship
Christ calls all to come and worship, to come and serve this day. Christ calls all, the sure of faith and those who doubt, those singing for joy and those bowed down with sorrow. Christ calls all, whatever their worship customs, he calls all of us to be one body in love and witness. Let us worship the Christ who calls!

Invocation
Almighty and Most Merciful God, we call upon your gracious favor to awaken in all of us the will to learn Christ's way and the courage to embody Christ's example. Keep us from judging others, and from believing that "our way" is the only way faithfully to follow you. Grant that with humility of heart, we may ever look unto you, the fountain of all wisdom, power, truth, and righteousness, through Jesus Christ our Lord. Amen.

Confession
God of grace, we confess that we have sometimes been too quick to proclaim you sovereign in our lives and too slow to live as your disciples. We have been quick to judge others, and slow to see our own shortcomings. Instead of seeking the unity you desire we have often been exclusive in our family of faith. Forgive us, Lord, and by the power of your Holy Spirit enable us to mend our ways. Amen.

Offertory Prayer
O God, by giving these offerings we communicate the message that we really care, that we honor you as the Lord of our lives and that we love the cause for which you lived and died. Amen.

Hymns
"Have Thine Own Way, Lord"
"O Spirit Of The Living God"
"Help Us Accept Each Other"

272

Proper 19
Sunday between September 11 and September 17 inclusive

Gospel Lesson: Matthew 18:21-35
Theme: Forgiveness

Call To Worship

The Lord has called us, his Church to be the salt of the earth, preserving what is good in our decaying society. He has called us to be lights in this world, providing direction and guidance amid human confusion. Let us neither be ashamed of our discipleship, nor hide our lights. Come, let us praise the Lord!

Invocation

O God, we praise you for your strong and relentless love, and we respond by coming to you in faith. We know that by your love we can count on your forgiveness for our sins of omission as well as commission. Through this time of worship help us to see again our need to forgive those who trespass against us, and to show forth the same mercy and love we expect from you. Amen.

Confession

Almighty God, in whose love there is mercy, we come together to be renewed in life as we are forgiven. We confess our sin and seek to be open to you and to one another. We know life goes bad when we ignore the claims of love, but we continue to isolate ourselves and run away from your loving care. Bring us back once again, O God, and renew our spirits by your love. Amen.

Offertory Prayer

Father, with these gifts we reach across the barriers of time, of social status, of creed, of language, of color, and of economic position, proclaiming our mutual caring as children of the one God and Father of us all. Amen.

Hymns

"Holy, Holy, Holy! Lord God Almighty"
"Forgive Our Sins As We Forgive"
"There's A Wideness In God's Mercy"

Proper 19
Sunday between September 11 and September 17 inclusive

Psalter: Exodus 15:1b-11, 20-21

Words Of Assurance
Here is the good news: "Christ Jesus came into the world to save sinners."
— To forgive you in your failure,
— to accept you as you are,
— to make you what you were meant to be.

Pastoral Prayer
Eternal God, high above our imaginations, whose judgments are a great deep, we worship you. We seek you in the sanctuary that we may be saved from ourselves. Small creatures are we, too much absorbed by trivial busyness; our lives, we confess, are filled with temporal details. Today in this place of worship, in awe before your eternity and greatness, we would gain altitude and horizon. Carry us out of ourselves into interests larger than ourselves. Let saints and scientists speak to us the memories of history and the thoughts of seers, that, so seeing ourselves as citizens of a great world, we may be greater because of it.

Save us from our weak self-pity. Our complaints rise before you, as have the lamentations of our ancestors before us. You understand how heavily life bears on us when the waves and billows go over us, and so we pray save us from our self-pity. Give us deep resources of interior strength that we may face life with adequacy, may rise above the difficulties that confront us and carry off a victory in spite of them; that thus life may grow strong from within and be triumphant without; that we may rejoice and be glad in it, difficult though it is. We know, Lord, that with your help, once again we can sing that we are more than conquerors through Christ who loves us.

Save us from weak excuses. Give us the honesty to face our sins. We acknowledge that we practice subterfuge and will not be candid concerning our failures. Grant that in this place of prayer, we may see the evils that we do harming not only ourselves but those for whom we care the most. Create in us clean hearts, O God.

Inspire all of us, we pray, to be equal to our great opportunities, responsible in the use of our freedom, sensitive in our relationships, and as generous as our Lord in the giving of ourselves.

All this we pray in the name of the One who came to reveal your reign, to heal this creation, and to show forth your love, even Jesus Christ, our Lord. Amen.

Benediction

Go forth in peace, walking in harmony with God who has created you, and walking in harmony with those who travel with you; and the blessing of God the Father, Son, and Holy Spirit go with you. Amen.

Proper 20
Sunday between September 18 and September 24 inclusive

First Lesson: Exodus 16:2-15
Theme: Our Daily Bread

Call To Worship
The Lord says, "Come." Come, drink the water of life for the refreshment that truly satisfies. Come, eat the bread of life, for the satisfaction of your great yearnings. Come, share the wine of the Spirit, for the intoxication that gives lasting joy.

Invocation
Merciful God, we come to you this morning hungering for that "Bread of Life" which alone can truly satisfy us. We pray that you will take our apathy, our coldness of heart, our discouragement, and transform them by your spirit into enthusiasm, into hope, and into sacrificial love, through Jesus Christ our Lord. Amen.

Confession
Lord, in our greedy society we find ourselves behaving like everyone else. We constantly want more. We are not satisfied with what we have. Forgive us, we pray, and teach us again the lesson of seeking "our daily bread," and the dangers of storing up worldly goods "where moth and rust corrupt." We pray in Jesus' name. Amen.

Offertory Prayer
O Lord, accept that which we offer you and increase its power to feed the hungry, comfort the destitute, and proclaim your Word as an instrument of grace in our world. Amen.

Hymns
"Great Is Thy Faithfulness"
"God Will Take Care Of You"
"Father, We Thank You"

Proper 20
Sunday between September 18 and September 24 inclusive

Second Lesson: Philippians 1:21-30
Theme: Living The Fruitful Life

Call To Worship

Leader: Praise God with shouts of joy, all people.
People: God comes to us in love to renew and redeem.
Leader: Hear God's Word calling you to life, claiming you in love.
People: We come to give thanks to God and praise the name of the Lord.

Invocation

God of grace, you have entrusted us with the message of your power, justice, and love. Awaken in us the commitment to grow in all that is good so we might declare to the world the great things you have done. Through your Holy Spirit strengthen us that we might not be intimidated by opponents, and be ready to suffer for Christ if necessary. In Jesus' name, we pray. Amen.

Confession

Lord, we have not always lived our life in a manner worthy of the gospel of Christ. With renewed determination to be worthy disciples send us forth to love in ways that will bear much fruit for the kingdom. Amen.

Offertory Prayer

Lord, we strive to live in a manner that will be worthy of the gospel of Christ, and so we bring these gifts that through them we may bear witness to the world that through the gift of your Son all who believe in him may have eternal life. Amen.

Hymns

"Near To The Heart Of God"
"Precious Lord, Take My Hand"
"O Master, Let Me Walk With Thee"

Proper 20
Sunday between September 18 and September 24 inclusive

Gospel Lesson: Matthew 20:1-16
Theme: Workers For God

Call To Worship

Come, let us worship God. Let us be awed by his presence. Let us be shaped by his standards. Let us be enlightened by his wisdom. Let us be mobilized by his Spirit.

Invocation

O Lord, come among us that we may pray and not lose heart. We are abandoned and alone without you. Come among us that in our persistence our hope for your kingdom will be renewed, our faith in your mercy will be refreshed, our love of you and your creation will be rekindled. This we pray in the name of the One who is Lord of all, even Jesus Christ. Amen.

Confession

Gracious God, how often we have been more concerned about the rewards given to our fellow laborers in your field than we have been about our own faithfulness. Cleanse us from all feelings of envy and covetousness, and help us to find our satisfaction and joy in serving you faithfully. Amen.

Offertory Prayer

Lord, we present these gifts, our sacrifice of praise and thanksgiving, and pray that we may have the grace not only to give generously, but to give well: without expecting recognition, without trying to buy control over people or projects, and without feeling like martyrs for our sacrifice. Amen.

Hymns

"Dear Jesus, In Whose Life I See"
"In Christ There Is No East Or West"
"The Voice Of God Is Calling"

Proper 20
Sunday between September 18 and September 24 inclusive

Psalter: Psalm 78:1-4, 9-20, 32b-38a

Words Of Assurance
Since God has forgiven us, let us in turn forgive both ourselves and each other, for Jesus' sake. Amen.

Pastoral Prayer
O Creator of Wisdom, we offer you our praise and thanksgiving this morning for the treasure of knowledge and the gift of understanding. Cause us to seek your wisdom as fine gold, and search for it with enthusiasm as for hidden treasures.

We praise you, O Word of God, for the community that gathers to listen together, to seek your wisdom together. Keep our ears open, however, to those who do not gather with us lest we not hear in full the word you have spoken. Rest upon our hearts that we may be more than hearers of the word, but also doers of your Word in our world.

O Spirit of Truth, we pray especially this day for our efforts as a church to educate our children, our youth, and adults. Be with us in our endeavors, strengthen our prayers, guide our understanding that our efforts may enrich and embolden our discipleship. Lead us into a discipleship that acts as well as learns. Let us not be content with knowledge of you that does not call us to join in your work of mending a broken creation.

Now, as at all times, listen to the cries of our hearts, the longings of your people, and come among us. All this we pray in the name of that great Teacher, even Jesus Christ our Lord. Amen.

Benediction
May God grant you the ability for every task you undertake, the courage for every challenge you meet, and the strength for every cross you carry; and the blessing of God the Father, Son, and Holy Spirit be yours. Amen.

279

Proper 21
Sunday between September 25 and October 1 inclusive

First Lesson: Exodus 17:1-7
Theme: Is The Lord Among Us Or Not?

Call To Worship
Come, hear the teachings of our Lord. Listen to the glorious deeds of the Lord. Do not hide them from your children. Tell the coming generations the wonders that the Lord has done.

Invocation
God of all beauty, who makes the sun to rise in splendor, and in glory set, and the stars to march in quiet radiance across the sky, open our eyes until we see your beauty on the face of the earth, that we may more fully know you, and may love all beauty because it speaks to us of you; through Jesus Christ our Lord. Amen.

Confession
Lord, when the difficulties of life overtake us, and we feel so all alone, grant us a new sense of your presence and faith that enables us to trust you to guide us through life's wilderness. Amen.

Offertory Prayer
Lord, we present these offerings that we may be partners with you in responding to the needs of the world both for food and water for the hungry of body, and word of your love and saving grace for those who hunger and thirst after righteousness. Amen.

Hymns
"Ye Servants Of God"
"There's Within My Heart A Melody"
"God Of The Ages"

Proper 21
Sunday between September 25 and October 1 inclusive

Second Lesson: Philippians 2:1-13
Theme: Shining As Lights In The World

Call To Worship
Jesus said: "I am the light of the world; he who follows me will not walk in darkness, but will have the light of life." As we come together this morning in worship let us recharge our spiritual batteries that we may go forth to let our lights shine before the world, that they may see our good works and give glory to our Father in heaven.

Invocation
As we gather in worship, challenge us, O God, with your truth, and inspire us with your love. Then as we go out again into the world empower us with your strength that our lives may shine as your lights for a dark world. Amen.

Confession
Our Father, our lights flicker and threaten to go out because we fail to recharge our batteries through prayer and worship. We live in a crooked and perverse generation, and we need to shine for you like stars in the world. Send your Holy Spirit upon us that we may truly let our lights shine, that people may see our good works and give glory to you. Amen.

Offertory Prayer
Bless these gifts, O Lord, and through them let us show forth your glory. Amen.

Hymns
"Close To Thee"
"This Little Light Of Mine"
"O How I Love Jesus"

Proper 21
Sunday between September 25 and October 1 inclusive

Gospel Lesson: Matthew 21:23-32
Theme: Testing Our Profession Of Faith By Our Deeds

Call To Worship
Come, let us sing praises to the Lord. For the Lord is our strength and our salvation. His presence is among us, and his Spirit empowers us to be his people.

Invocation
O Lord, come among us that we may pray and not lose heart. We are abandoned and alone without you. Come among us that in our persistence our hope for your kingdom will be renewed, our faith in your mercy will be refreshed, our love of you and your creation will be rekindled. This we pray in the name of the One who is Judge and Lord of all, even Jesus Christ. Amen.

Confession
O Lord, we have been quick to profess our faith in you and to declare our intention of following you. Then when the opportunity to serve you has arisen we have looked the other way; we have failed to respond to your call to love our neighbors and even our enemies. Create in us pure hearts, O God, and help us to serve you not only with our lips but with our very lives. Amen.

Offertory Prayer
Eternal God, giver of every good and perfect gift, who seeks above all our gifts to give yourself to us, grant that with these token gifts, we may more fully give ourselves in joyous obedience and service; through Jesus Christ our Lord. Amen.

Hymns
"I Want A Principle Within"
"The Voice Of God Is Calling"
"O Jesus, I Have Promised"

Proper 21
Sunday between September 25 and October 1 inclusive

Psalter: Psalm 78:1-4, 12-16

Words Of Assurance
Trust in the Lord, and do good, and he will give you the desires of your heart. The Lord is gracious and merciful, slow to anger and abounding in steadfast love.

Pastoral Prayer
It is so hard for us to think of you, our Father, so hard for us to feel your presence as we do the presence of a friend whom we can see and touch and hear. You are so high, so lifted up, so pure and wonderful in all your ways that you seem almost past our understanding altogether.

Yet we know that you are closer to us than breathing, and nearer than hands and feet. Even when we doubt you, we know that it is you who gives us the strength to doubt. So once again, in fellowship with those who share our vows and hopes with us, we bow before you. Pulling back as best we can the thoughts that wander far away from you, we fix our minds on you and pray that you will heal our hearts and make them whole. For we are so worried, Lord, so anxious, so fretful. We are hurried, yet we have eternity. We are afraid, yet we have you. We wish we knew your will for us, yet in Christ you give us the very knowledge which we seek and say we do not have.

Come now to this portion of your people, we pray. Descend upon this congregation. In the heart of each of us be not an idea only, a theory, a thought, a hope, or a dream. Be a Being met and known. Persuade us into praying, and out of our prayers bring forth that knowledge which the world can neither give nor take away, that confidence which has no fear of life or death, that peace which passes understanding and is not moved by any awfulness which humans conceive or undertake.

What we can do to make the world more nearly as you intended it, reveal to us, our Father, and what we comprehend of your will for us, grant us to obey. Lead us until our daily work becomes an instrument for high and holy things. Transform our homes that they may be the seedbeds of your purpose. Chasten our souls until they know the joy of sacrifice. And bring us in the end to love you with all our hearts and to serve you with all our strength.

We lift our prayers in the name and for the sake of Jesus Christ our Lord. Amen.

Benediction

What you have heard with your ears, may you believe in your hearts; and what you believe in your hearts may you practice in your lives; and the blessing of God the Father, the Son, and the Holy Spirit be upon you now and always. Amen.

Proper 22
Sunday between October 2 and October 8 inclusive

First Lesson: Exodus 20:1-4, 7-9, 12-20
Theme: The Ten Commandments

Call To Worship

Come, let us worship the Lord, our God. Remember this is the sabbath day and keep it holy. Let us give thanks to the Lord our God who has given us a moral code to live by.

Invocation

O God, by whom the meek are guided in judgment, and light rises up in darkness for the godly, grant us, in all doubts and uncertainties, the grace to ask what you would have us to do, that the Spirit of wisdom may save us from all false choices. In your light may we see light, and in your straight path may we not stumble; through Jesus Christ our Lord. Amen.

Confession

Almighty God, we have your commandments to guide us but still we have choices to make all the day long. In our foolishness so often we know what is right, but we still select the wrong. Strengthen us in our resolve to live according to your laws, and by the power of your Holy Spirit help us to make the right choices. Amen.

Offertory Prayer

Lord, help us never to view our services as a drudgery or our gifts as a sacrifice. Help us instead always to give and serve in enthusiastic response to your presence in our lives. Amen.

Hymns

"O Worship The King"
"I Am Thine, O Lord"
"I Need Thee Every Hour"

Proper 22
Sunday between October 2 and October 8 inclusive

Second Lesson: Philippians 3:4b-14
Theme: Forget The Past — Press On Toward The Goal!

Call To Worship
Come, we that love the Lord, and let our joys be known. The true worshiper will worship in spirit and in truth. Amen.

Invocation
O Lord, through this time we spend together, may our faith blossom, may our hope be born anew, and may our love be made real, through Jesus Christ our Lord. Amen.

Confession
Merciful God, we are weighed down by so many concerns and worries that we find it difficult to press on toward the goal for the prize of the heavenly call of God in Christ Jesus. Free us from our burdens, Lord, and enable us to press on. Through Jesus Christ our Lord. Amen.

Offertory Prayer
Almighty God, these tokens of our work are small, pitiful symbols of the love we have for you. Receive them and transform them into ministries of love in the name of Jesus Christ our Lord. Amen.

Hymns
"More Love To Thee, O Christ"
"Lead On, O King Eternal"
"We Are Climbing Jacob's Ladder"

Proper 22
Sunday between October 2 and October 8 inclusive

Gospel Lesson: Matthew 21:33-46
Theme: Unfaithful Stewards

Call To Worship
God calls us together as his children to reassure us of his love, to encourage our care for each other, to remind us of our responsibilities, and to send us out as people who bear his name. Come, let us worship him!

Invocation
O God of wisdom and knowledge, illumine us by your Spirit and by your Word. From the Scriptures may we learn your instructions and by your Holy Spirit may we be inclined to follow these instructions to live a good and holy life. Amen.

Confession
O God, we know that your Son came into the world to save us from our sins, but too often we have accepted him with our lips, only to deny him with our actions. Strengthen us by the power of your Holy Spirit, that our words and deeds may be one. In Jesus' name, we pray. Amen.

Offertory Prayer
Our Father, we know that no matter how much we give in this offering we cannot earn your favor. So we now accept your grace with gratitude, and ask that you accept these gifts as tokens of our love and appreciation, through Jesus Christ our Lord. Amen.

Hymns
"Christ Is Made The Sure Foundation"
"Jesus Shall Reign"
"Stand Up, Stand Up For Jesus"

Proper 22
Sunday between October 2 and October 8 inclusive

Psalter: Psalm 19

Words Of Assurance

Be assured of this: that the Christ who taught forgiveness and exemplified it during his earthly ministry, continues to practice it today through the ministry of the Holy Spirit.

Pastoral Prayer

O Lord, our God, in whose presence we stand, in whose care our restless lives are held, to whose mercy we turn again and again, the voice of your Spirit calls us. It sounds in our inmost being like a haunting melody, and reminds us of the beautiful music for which we were created. Although we are conscious of the blaring discord we have actually made, yet your voice still calls us, and the deep yearning within us responds.

Eternal God, we come to you in prayer as to a trusted friend. You see us as we are, and though it seems impossible to believe, accept us as we are. Your judgments are those that would fashion us after your image. The spiritual vistas of your creation invite us to lift our eyes and souls to you. We know full well we have fallen short of your purposes, but we thank you that you have not forsaken us, but instead revealed Jesus as the way for you to gain entry again into our hearts.

We thank you for our blessings that we are inclined to take for granted: our health, our families, our life's work, our friends. Teach us again that these are to be treasured and nurtured as we live each day fully. We thank you for the joys that we have experienced this week, and the power of your Holy Spirit that strengthened us in times of difficulties.

Help us, O Lord, to be your people in the world. Challenge us today to witness here, where we live, as a faith community. May the attractive power of our lives made holy invite others to seek your Word for their lives. We offer this prayer in the name and for the sake of Jesus Christ our Lord. Amen.

288

Benediction

Go forth in peace, for you have been forgiven. Go forth in power, for you have been renewed. Go forth in joy, for you have been loved; and the blessing of God the Father, the Son, and the Holy Spirit go with you. Amen.

Proper 23
Sunday between October 9 and October 15 inclusive

First Lesson: Exodus 32:1-14
Theme: Another Chance

Call To Worship
Come, let us worship the Lord. Let us give thanks to God, for God has been good to us, and we are God's people. The Lord's name be praised!

Invocation
O Lord, our God, so often when our prayers are not answered the way we want or as quickly as we expect we are tempted to forsake you, like the Israelites of old. We thank you for being God of a second chance. Grant us in all our doubts and uncertainties, the grace to ask what you would have us to do, that the spirit of wisdom may save us from all false choices, and that in your straight path we may not stumble; through Jesus Christ our Lord. Amen.

Confession
Almighty God, you have given us life, but we have not lived. We have been called to freedom, but we have found the burden heavy, the anxiety painful. In fear and pride we have turned from you, O God, to live in self-deceit and to serve other lords. We admit our willfulness and our weakness in denying you. Cleanse us from our sins, Father, and create in us clean hearts that we may follow you faithfully all your days. Amen.

Offertory Prayer
Lord, we come to you with thankful and grateful hearts because we know that you never stop loving us no matter how wayward we become. Accept these offerings as an expression of our gratitude and use them that others may know of your great love. Amen.

Hymns
"Depth Of Mercy"
"Forgive Our Sins As We Forgive"
"There's A Wideness In God's Mercy"

Proper 23
Sunday between October 9 and October 15 inclusive

Second Lesson: Philippians 4:1-9
Theme: Rejoice In The Lord, Always

Call To Worship
Hear these words from Paul's letter to the Philippians: "Rejoice in the Lord always; again I will say, Rejoice ... the Lord is near."

As we come together in worship may we remember that the Lord is indeed near, and let us rejoice by singing praises to his name.

Invocation
God, to whom belong adoration and praise, prepare us, through the active presence of your Spirit, to come before you worthily, and to ask of you rightly; enlighten our understanding; purify our every desire; quicken our wills into instant obedience to your Word; strengthen every right purpose; direct this time of worship to the magnifying of your name, and to the enduring good of us your children and servants; through Jesus Christ our Lord. Amen.

Confession
Lord, it is so easy to become lazy in our prayer life and lax in our worship. We need to be restored in our devotion and to have a fresh sense of your active presence in our lives. Come now and sensitize us, prod us, and urge us on to a more holy life. Amen.

Offertory Prayer
Almighty God, we know that without love, our charity is as a noisy gong or a clanging cymbal. We present these offerings in a spirit of love and rejoicing for your many blessings, and pray that they may make a sweet symphony of praise to you, O Lord. Amen.

Hymns
"O For A Heart To Praise My God"
"Take Time To Be Holy"
"Lord, I Want To Be A Christian"

Proper 23
Sunday between October 9 and October 15 inclusive

Gospel Lesson: Matthew 22:1-14
Theme: God Calls Us

Call To Worship

Christ our Lord invites us to come and feast with him. He invites all who love him and who earnestly repent of their sins. He welcomes all who seek to live in peace with one another. Come, let us accept the invitation and come into his presence with praise and thanksgiving.

Invocation

Almighty God, you have created us in your own image, and have called us your children. We come therefore as part of your family to give you thanks, to hear your Word, and to seek your will for us. Make us aware of your presence, and make us attentive to your voice. We pray in Jesus' name. Amen.

Confession

O Lord, shed your light upon the dark places of our hearts. Instill within us a worship that is sincere, a faith that is unwavering, a hope that is certain, and a love that is vibrant. Amen.

Offertory Prayer

O Great God, we bring these gifts as symbols of our whole selves, proclaiming in this one act your Lordship over all the universe. Use these tokens to bring all of creation into the bond of love we know and celebrate in your kingdom; world without end. Amen.

Hymns

"Where Cross The Crowded Ways Of Life"
"I Am Thine, O Lord"
"Softly And Tenderly Jesus Is Calling"

Proper 23
Sunday between October 9 and October 15 inclusive

Psalter: Psalm 106:1-6, 19-23

Words Of Assurance

Ask and it will be given you; seek and you will find; knock and it will be opened to you. For everyone who asks receives, and he who seeks finds, and to him who knocks it will be opened.

Pastoral Prayer

O Spirit of God, eternal source of all creative energy, the divine power that transforms our potentialities into actualities, draw near to us as the Holy Spirit which was in Jesus Christ. We are afraid of raw energy and power, for it is unguided and untamed, like the lightning which hurls its thunderbolts across the skies. We distrust power and energy that we cannot control or turn off and on at will. When we think of you, O God, as all-powerful, we draw back in awesome dread of what your power can do. We see so much in the world that doesn't make sense. We long for a world of equality where every person will have an opportunity to develop his or her potential for creativity, health, happiness, and fulfillment. Instead, we find that the strong devour the weak, the rich consume ill-gotten gains wrested from the hands of the poor, and the courts of justice are desecrated as influential persons of wealth seek to buy freedom from the consequences of their evil deeds. This is the kind of naked, raw power that we see in the world, God, and we are suspicious of how you use your all-powerfulness, when we see these things happening. We wonder if you cannot do a better job in running the universe to which we belong.

Yet, who are we to blame or question you when we refuse to acknowledge or to use the powers we have to change ourselves or the small part of the world for which we are responsible? It is we who choose to create the individual worlds in which we live and not you. We choose whether to be honest or courageous or loving. We choose whether to be warm, open, and trusting, or cold, closed, and suspicious. We continually go down the same disappointing roads, never learning from our mistakes, always blaming somebody else for the failure and defeat which clutches our lives. The world which we loudly deplore is the world which we ourselves have helped to create, and we can blame no one else. Lord, forgive our past failures and weakness, and grant us new strength and determination to pattern our lives after your Son, Jesus Christ.

Hear our prayers in the name of him who died and rose again and shares forever the power of your glory, even Jesus Christ our Lord. Amen.

Benediction

Rejoice always, for you are God's own people. May your lives daily be filled with his grace, mercy, and peace. The blessing of God the Father, the Son, and the Holy Spirit be with you always. Amen.

Proper 24
Sunday between October 16 and October 22 inclusive

First Lesson: Exodus 33:12-23
Theme: God's Invisible Presence

Call To Worship

Leader: We are the people of God.
People: It is good to remember that!
Leader: God has promised to be with us.
People: We can depend on that!
Leader: Come, let us worship our God with joy and thanksgiving!

Invocation

Help us, Father, as we gather here, to catch a new glimpse of your majesty, to gain a new insight into your will, to attain a new awareness of our place in your plan, and to find a new usefulness for ourselves in your world; through Jesus Christ our Lord. Amen.

Confession

O God, now present with us, and whose love never fails, we confess that often our love and response to you is so inadequate. You give us so many gifts, so many opportunities, so many gentle nudges to care for ourselves and others, and so often we fail to notice or listen. Teach us to be open to your love for us. Help us to respond to you with all that we are, heart and soul and mind. As you love us, help us to love others. In Christ's name. Amen.

Offertory Prayer

Lord, we present these offerings in gratitude for we have received much from your hand. We present these offerings in love, for we have a deep concern for others. We present these offerings in faith, for we know that you can work mightily through them. Amen.

Hymns

"Glorious Things Of Thee Are Spoken"
"Immortal, Invisible, God Only Wise"
"God Of The Ages"

Proper 24
Sunday between October 16 and October 22 inclusive

Second Lesson: 1 Thessalonians 1:1-10
Theme: An Example To Others

Call To Worship

Thanks be to God for all of you! May the inspiration and renewal of this time of worship together come to you not only in word, but also in power and in the Holy Spirit, and with full conviction.

Invocation

Comfort us, Lord, with your Word and Spirit. Challenge our pre-conceptions, test our principles, disturb our prejudices, and question our priorities, so that through the pain of self-examination may come the joy of discovery and growth. Amen.

Confession

Almighty God, hear our struggle to know your will among our doubts. And when we leave here, send us out enriched by your presence among us. In Jesus' name we pray. Amen.

Offertory Prayer

O Lord, receive these offerings from your people, and receive here our lives for your service. You created and formed us, and you may need to re-create and reform us before we can become the servants that you would have us to be, but we are yours. Amen.

Hymns

"God Of Grace And God Of Glory"
"Sing Praise To God Who Reigns Above"
"For The Healing Of The Nations"

Proper 24
Sunday between October 16 and October 22 inclusive

Gospel Lesson: Matthew 22:15-22
Theme: Give God His Due

Call To Worship

Leader: We are God's people.
People: We live in God's world.
Leader: We have come to God's house to honor God's name,
People: and to prepare ourselves for God's work.
Leader: Come, let us praise him!

Invocation

Almighty God, we pray this morning for enlightenment, because some of us are confused by the conflicting voices of our world, each claiming the truth. We pray for faith, because some of us become disillusioned by the inconsistencies of profession and practice. We pray for peace, because some of us are anxious and worried over the increasing violence of society, and the escalating tensions between nations. We pray for love, because all of us need to follow more consistently the example of Jesus Christ, our Lord. Amen.

Confession

Lord, we are often confused and torn by our loyalty to you and the demands of society. When we are faced with a conflict between the two, help us by the power of your Holy Spirit to remain loyal to you and to have the courage to be guided by your principle of love. Amen.

Offertory Prayer

Our Father, employ these gifts and us for your glory, for the welfare of your people everywhere, and for the spiritual enhancement of our lives. Amen.

Hymns

"I Love Thy Kingdom, Lord"
"Sing Praise To God Who Reigns Above"
"Jesus Calls Us"

Proper 24
Sunday between October 16 and October 22 inclusive

Psalter: Psalm 99

Words Of Assurance

Hear the Good News: Christ Jesus came into the world to save sinners, to forgive you in your failures, to accept you as you are, to set you free from evil's power, and make you what you were meant to be.

Pastoral Prayer

God of grace, we celebrate today that in the cross and resurrection of Jesus, you have begun something new with us. You have broken the grip of sin and selfishness, you have showered us with undeserved forgiveness. Your Spirit moves among us — in our homes and in our communities, in our nation and in distant places — impatient to conquer evil and renew creation. Catch us up in your plan, O God. Heal us by your grace and make us agents of your mercy.

As at the day of Pentecost, we pray that we may be transformed by your Spirit's coming upon us, taking away our fears, making us bold to face the enemies of Christ, and giving us power to present a convincing witness that in Jesus Christ you have reconciled the world to yourself. Give unto us a personal story to tell and lips that proclaim it with joy and certainty. Enliven our concerns for lost souls who stumble through the darkness of fear and hopelessness, often disoriented by shame and guilt, alienated, painfully alone, with none to love and care.

We remember with gratitude, O God, all messengers of your Word who through stormy seas and perilous paths brought the gospel to our land. Without this precious heritage we could not this hour rejoice in the gift of your life and love. Bestow upon us strength and courage that our faith and deeds may become consistent witness to all who watch our ways. May those who do not love you be persuaded by your truth and those who do not know you, find in Christ life's deepest thirst satisfied. Impart to us the worldwide vision of the Spirit which belongs to your disciples.

We pray in the holy name of Jesus Christ our Lord. Amen.

Benediction

Rejoice always, for you are God's own people. May your lives daily be filled with his grace, mercy, and peace; and the blessing of God the Father, Son, and Holy Spirit be with you always. Amen.

Proper 25
Sunday between October 23 and October 29 inclusive

First Lesson: Deuteronomy 34:1-12
Theme: Leadership

Call To Worship
Earthly leaders come and go, but we can always depend upon the God of our Salvation to raise up new leaders through whom he will show us the way ahead. Come, let us worship Almighty God — the same yesterday, today, and forever.

Invocation
Lord, we owe much to those who have gone before us, leading us ever onward toward the land of promise. We thank you for the example they have given us in mentoring others to take over the leadership when they must relinquish it. Empower our leaders by your Holy Spirit, and may we be faithful followers. Amen.

Confession
We confess that we are disappointed when we do not see the fruition of our dreams. Often we are reluctant to have others assume positions of leadership, and find ourselves being critical of their methods. O Lord, give us a deeper understanding of what it means to work in unity for the building up of your kingdom, and grant us the humility and patience we need to be faithful disciples. Amen.

Offertory Prayer
O Lord, so often do we ask for your blessings, and so seldom do we thank you for them. Receive our thanks as we express it both in word and in this act of sacrifice. Amen.

Hymns
"Lead On, O King Eternal"
"Dear Lord, Lead Me Day By Day"
"Lord Whose Love Through Humble Service"

Proper 25
Sunday between October 23 and October 29 inclusive

Second Lesson: 1 Thessalonians 2:1-8
Theme: Courage To Declare The Gospel

Call To Worship

Rejoice, people of God! Bow your heads before the One who is our wisdom and our strength. Rejoice, people of God! Celebrate the life within you, and Christ's presence in our midst! Come, be touched and cleansed by the power of God's Spirit.

Invocation

Most Holy God, we await the touch of your Spirit with eagerness. We ask that you enter the lives of each one of us today, refreshing and renewing and healing with the power of your loving Spirit, that we may live with purpose and enthusiasm and courage after the manner of Jesus Christ our Lord. Help us to care so deeply for one another and for your children everywhere that we will be determined to share not only the gospel of God, but also our selves. Amen.

Confession

O Lord, cleanse us from all manner of deceit and improper motives as we attempt to share your gospel with others. Let us not use flattery or seek praise as we present ourselves as your disciples. In all things may our aim be to please you, O God, through Jesus Christ our Lord. Amen.

Offertory Prayer

Lord, we are anxious to share not only the gospel but our very selves with your children throughout the world who have not accepted your love. Bless these gifts, we pray, as symbols of the giving of our selves for the work of your kingdom. Amen.

Hymns

"'Tis So Sweet To Trust In Jesus"
"O For A Heart To Praise My God"
"A Charge To Keep I Have"

Proper 25
Sunday between October 23 and October 29 inclusive

Gospel Lesson: Matthew 22:34-46
Theme: The Greatest Commandment

Call To Worship
As we gather to worship, let us have eyes open to see, ears alert to hear, minds ready to understand, and hearts prepared to love. Come, let us worship together!

Invocation
Almighty God, as we hear again how Jesus set forth the Greatest Commandment, we pray that in this time of worship we may come to a clearer understanding of all that is implied in this wonderful declaration of love. Make us strong and warm our hearts that we may go forth from this holy place determined to show forth our love for you and our neighbor in all that we do and say. Amen.

Confession
Our Father, we confess that we have not always loved you with all our heart, mind, soul, and strength. Nor have we loved our neighbors as ourselves. Forgive us, we pray, and create in us more loving hearts that we may be faithful to your commandments. Amen.

Offertory Prayer
O Lord, through these gifts we wish to show our love for you. Bless them, we pray, that they may now be used to show our love of neighbors near and far. In Jesus' name we pray. Amen.

Hymns
"Love Divine, All Loves Excelling"
"The Voice Of God Is Calling"
"O Young And Fearless Prophet"

Proper 25
Sunday between October 23 and October 29 inclusive

Psalter: Psalm 90:1-6, 13-17

Words Of Assurance

May the Father surround you with loving kindness, bathing your soul and body in mercy, and restoring you to wholeness and peace. Amen.

Pastoral Prayer

Our Father, in some ways it has been a good week for us. Some of us have accomplished our work, have been loved by our family and supported by our friends, have escaped dangers, and enjoyed a measure of well-being. In other ways it has been difficult for us. Some of us have suffered financial setbacks, or have been involved in personal disputes, or have become emotionally tired or physically weak. We need this time together, and we need this sense of your special presence. We ask that our strength will be renewed, our vision will be restored, and we will once again bask in the peace of your presence.

We know, Father, that you have given us many opportunities to be of real help to people, and all too often we have allowed these opportunities to sift through our fingers. We sensed that someone wanted to talk about a serious problem, but we kept the conversation on a superficial level. We knew that someone needed our companionship, but we felt we couldn't afford the time. We didn't want to get involved. We thought only of our own convenience and our own welfare. Forgive us, Father, for our complacency and our coldness, and help us to embody the loving concern of Jesus Christ.

Realizing that we are sometimes negative in our thinking and critical in our opinions of others, we ask that you will heal our attitudes. Help us to greet each new day with anticipation, expecting the best. Remind us to try to understand others before condemning or criticizing them. Help us to be sensitive to the feelings of others, and not to look down on them because they have different likes and dislikes than we have. Help us to be open to suggestion and correction. May others detect in us the quiet hope of Christian confidence, and may they see in us a reflection of the compassion of Jesus Christ.

We ask these things in Christ's name. Amen.

Benediction

May the Lord walk before you to guide you, hover over you to protect you, and live within you to strengthen you; and the blessing of God the Father, the Son, and the Holy Spirit be yours. Amen.

Proper 26
Sunday between October 30 and November 5 inclusive

First Lesson: Joshua 3:7-17
Theme: Partnership With God

Call To Worship
Let us remember that God is our refuge and strength, our light and our hope. Let us become aware of God's presence in this place and in our lives. Let us listen with open minds and hearts to the word God wishes to share.

Invocation
Almighty God, we read that Joshua assured the Israelites that the Lord was among them, and we come together this day thankful that we too can be sure of your presence with us. We are grateful that you bring calm to our troubled days, and our fearful hearts are filled with your peace. In this time of worship may we hear your Word for our lives, and by your Holy Spirit send us forth with the courage to carry out your wishes. In Jesus' name we pray. Amen.

Confession
Almighty God, our self-reliance, our stubbornness and arrogance have often led us astray. Help us in this hour to recognize your presence among us, to respond to the touch of your hand, to be attuned to the sound of your still, small voice, to shake the scales of blindness from our eyes, and to submit our lives to the desire of your will. Amen.

Offertory Prayer
Lord, we are committed to you and your kingdom, and we strive to keep ever before us the vows we made to support the work of your Church with our prayers, our presence, our service, and our gifts. In recognition of this responsibility we present these offerings and ask your blessing upon them. Amen.

Hymns
"Leaning On The Everlasting Arms"
"I Want Jesus To Walk With Me"
"Jesus Savior, Pilot Me"

Proper 26
Sunday between October 30 and November 5 inclusive

Second Lesson: 1 Thessalonians 2:9-13
Theme: God's Work In Us

Call To Worship
It is said that they will know we are Christians by our love. We come together this morning that we might be renewed and refreshed in order to go back into the world as more loving disciples. Come, let us worship!

Invocation
O Holy Spirit of God, abide with us: inspire all our thoughts, pervade our imaginations, suggest all our decisions, order all our doings. Be with us in our silence and in our speech, in our haste and in our leisure, in company and in solitude, in the freshness of the morning and in the weariness of the evening. Give us grace at all times humbly to rejoice in your mysterious companionship; through Jesus Christ our Lord. Amen.

Confession
Lord, we hear you pleading with us to lead lives worthy of you and your kingdom, but when we look at what we have done and what we have left undone we realize how unworthy we are. Forgive us, by your grace, and empower us through your Spirit to lead better lives. Amen.

Offertory Prayer
Because we love you with heart, mind, and soul, we bring these offerings and worship you with our gifts, our Father. Because we love our neighbors as ourselves, we make this sacrifice and dedicate ourselves to the task that is yet unfinished. Amen.

Hymns
"Ye Servants Of God"
"I Am Thine, O Lord"
"I Want A Principle Within"

Proper 26
Sunday between October 30 and November 5 inclusive

Gospel Lesson: Matthew 23:1-12
Theme: Practice What You Preach

Call To Worship
Leader: O give thanks to the Lord, for he is good.
People: For his steadfast love endures forever.
Leader: Let the redeemed of the Lord all say:
People: His steadfast love endures forever.

Invocation
Our Father in heaven, who through your Son, Jesus Christ, not only taught us how to live, but showed us the way of sacrificial, self-giving service, we come to give you thanks and praise your holy name. Through your Holy Spirit enable us to take to heart the call to humble servanthood. Amen.

Confession
Lord, we live in a time when self-esteem is highly praised, and success is touted as a worthy goal. When we find it difficult to behave humbly and to take on the role of servanthood be our strength and redeemer. Amen.

Offertory Prayer
Lord, it is easy to say in words that we love. It is more difficult to say it with our deeds. Receive these gifts as tangible expressions of our love. We pray in Jesus' name. Amen.

Hymns
"Christ, Whose Glory Fills The Skies"
"Be Thou My Vision"
"More Love To Thee, O Christ"

Proper 26
Sunday between October 30 and November 5 inclusive

Psalter: Psalm 107:1-7, 33-37

Words Of Assurance
Trust in the Lord, and do good, and he will give you the desires of your heart. Amen.

Pastoral Prayer
Let us be still! Let us be receptive and open! Let us be eager and believing! Let us be humble! Let us be ready for God to do a miracle in our lives! Let us pray:

We are grateful, Lord, for this house of worship. We enjoy its comfort, we enjoy its music, but most of all we enjoy the opportunity of meeting with you, our God, with our brothers and sisters in the faith, and with those who have come to share the warmth of this hour.

As we come before you to confess our wrongdoings, we know that we have no excuse or defense. You have given us light on the way, but we have often closed our eyes. You have offered us help, but we have often preferred to take care of things by ourselves. You have given us warnings by your Word and life's happenstances, but we have continued in our accustomed ways. You have given us standards to follow, but we have preferred the easier standards of our society. Pardon us, Lord God, not only for our shortcomings, but also for our failure to use the resources you have given us.

Loving Heavenly Father, realizing that we are sometimes negative in our thinking and critical in our opinion of others, we ask that you will heal our attitudes. Hasten the day of your kingdom, Lord, that all humankind may see it together and find relief from the burdens of living. In the meantime, help us to be followers of Christ, who taught us how to live as if the kingdom were here, sharing what we have with other persons and loving one another for no reason at all, except that you first loved us and Christ died for us to redeem us from emptiness and loneliness. In his name we pray. Amen.

Benediction
Go forth in peace. No! That is too easy. Go forth as peace. Be the healing presence wherever you go, and God will go with you. In the name of the Father and the Son and the Holy Spirit. Amen.

Proper 27
Sunday between November 6 and November 12 inclusive

First Lesson: Joshua 24:1-3a, 14-25
Theme: We Will Serve The Lord

Call To Worship

Leader: As we come before the Lord, to offer our praise and thanks-giving, choose you this day whom you will serve.

People: Far be it from us that we should forsake the Lord to serve other gods. The Lord our God we will serve and him we will obey.

Invocation

Almighty God, we give you thanks and praise for guiding us thus far along life's journey. We come now seeking your blessing and renewing our covenant for ourselves and for our families that we will serve you and you only. Amen.

Confession

Deliver us, Lord, from the idolatry which seeks to create a god who does not challenge us; from the pride which causes us to be critical of our friends and neighbors; from the stubbornness which closes our ears to new truths; and from the coldness which pulls away from the loving arms of the Savior. In Jesus' name we pray. Amen.

Offertory Prayer

O Lord, we give these gifts to you in thanksgiving for all you give to us. May the gifts be made holy and used to serve you as you would desire. We pray in Christ's name. Amen.

Hymns

"Breathe On Me, Breath Of God"
"I Am Thine, O Lord"
"O For A Thousand Tongues To Sing"

Proper 27
Sunday between November 6 and November 12 inclusive

Second Lesson: 1 Thessalonians 4:13-18
Theme: Encourage One Another

Call To Worship
Let us remember that God is our hope and our salvation. He is our refuge and strength. Let us become aware of God's presence in this place and in our lives. Come, let us worship the God of our hope, creator of heaven and earth.

Invocation
O God, make the door of this house wide enough to receive all who need human love and fellowship, but narrow enough to shut out all envy, pride, and strife. Make its threshold smooth enough to be no stumbling block to children, nor to straying feet, but rugged enough to turn back the tempter's power. God, make the door of this house the gateway to your eternal kingdom. Amen.

Confession
O Lord, in the quietness of this hour, help us to release our fears and anxieties. Enable us to leave behind our jealousies and our hurt feelings. Remove from our minds the petty concerns that distract us. Help us to focus on that which is holy and which is full of hope; then send us forth with a new vision and a new commitment. Amen.

Offertory Prayer
Lord, because we wish to share the good news that we have come to know, to experience, and to enjoy, we present our tithes and offerings and ask your blessing on them. Amen.

Hymns
"There's A Wideness In God's Mercy"
"Now Thank We All Our God"
"It Is Well With My Soul"

Proper 27
Sunday between November 6 and November 12 inclusive

Gospel Lesson: Matthew 25:1-13
Theme: Be Prepared

Call To Worship

Leader: I heard the voice of Jesus say, "Come unto me and rest."
People: I replied, "Later, Lord. I'm too busy now."
Leader: I heard the voice of Jesus say, "Behold, I freely give the living water; thirsty one, stoop down and drink and live."
People: I replied, "Not now, Lord, I'm not thirsty."
Leader: Come, let us worship together, and prepare our hearts and minds to receive our Lord.

Invocation

Lord, we come to you weary, worn, and sad, knowing we will find in you a resting place. We come thirsty for the living water that will revive our souls. For we would bathe in your light until our traveling days are done. Amen.

Confession

Forgive our impatience, Lord, for we live in an age of instant gratification. We ask questions and we expect immediate answers. We expect our prayers to serve as magic lanterns that will produce your presence like Aladdin's genie. Prepare our hearts and minds to wait patiently for you, O God, knowing that you will come to us in your time, and keep us ever ready and prepared to welcome you and serve you. Amen.

Offertory Prayer

O Lord, receive our offerings, not as boasts, not as bribes, but as sincere and silent expressions of our faith and as positive proof of our love. Amen.

Hymns

"O Day Of God, Draw Nigh"
"Marching To Zion"
"When We All Get To Heaven"

Proper 27
Sunday between November 6 and November 12 inclusive

Psalter: Psalm 78:1-7

Words Of Assurance
Have confidence in the Lord, who can forgive your sins, restore your sense of values, and give you eternal life. Amen.

Pastoral Prayer
O Lord, you have promised that, if with all our hearts we truly seek you, we shall surely find you. With all our hearts we seek you now. Loose us from whatever worries and distractions have pursued us here, that we may focus all our power to think, to will, to do — on you. We are frail children of time and fate, here today, tomorrow gone — weak men and women dependent on your patience. But we believe we are also your children, heirs of the eternal, fitted for communion with you, with spirits as lasting as your own. In this high faith we lift our prayer to you.

We thank you for your goodness to us. May we try more consistently to deserve it. We thank you for treating us better than we deserve. Help us to treat each other in the same way.

We need your forgiveness, Lord. We have done things we ought not to have done. We cannot plead ignorance. We knew what was right and did what we knew was wrong. We ask you to forgive us what we can hardly forgive ourselves. We have left undone things we might have done and done well. Impel us to stir up the gift that is in us, to take whatever talent you have entrusted to us and use it to the full. We need your cleansing. Deeds unkind, words untrue, thoughts unclean — the stain of these is on us all. When we contrast our moral shabbiness with your holiness, we are ashamed. Create in us a clean mind, a clean imagination. What in us is dark, illumine. What is low, raise and support. We need your reinforcement. We do not ask to escape sorrows which are a part of life. We ask only assurance that in your divine economy nothing good is lost.

Now come close to us one by one. Be real to each one gathered here, and may there come peace out of anxiety, steadfastness out of turmoil, forgiveness out of guilt, strength out of weakness, faith instead of fear. We ask it in the spirit of Jesus Christ our Lord and Savior. Amen.

Benediction

May the mighty God bless and keep you forever. May he give you his strength in every endeavor. May his Spirit always guide and uphold you, and may his love forever enfold you. Go in peace, and the blessing of God the Father, the Son, and the Holy Spirit go with you. Amen.

Proper 28
Sunday between November 13 and November 19 inclusive

First Lesson: Judges 4:1-7
Theme: Deborah — The Judge

Call To Worship
Much in life is mysterious. Many things that happen to us are beyond explanation. To life's deepest questions there don't seem to be easy answers. Nevertheless, we come here in faith: faith that God cares, faith that there is an ultimate answer, faith that with God's help we will not only survive but flourish. Come, let us worship together.

Invocation
O Lord, if we have come with troubled minds, give us the confidence of true faith. If we have come with wavering allegiance, give us the strength of moral courage. If we have come with depleted spirits, give us the inspiration of a new vision. We ask it in Jesus' name.

Confession
Hear our prayer, O Lord, and be sensitive to the sorrow of our hearts, for we have strayed from your path, we have followed the impulses of our wills, we have neglected your commands. Cleanse us, O God, restore us to your good graces, and enable us to live for you with joy. Remind us once again, that when you show us the way to go, you also promise to go with us. Amen.

Offertory Prayer
O Lord, we know that by means of our gifts we can transcend the limits of time and space, reaching to the utmost parts of the globe and extending our influence far beyond our own short lifetime. For our infinite possibilities through these gifts we now give thanks. Amen.

Hymns
"Holy God, We Praise Thy Name"
"God Hath Spoken By The Prophets"
"O God, Our Help In Ages Past"

Proper 28
Sunday between November 13 and November 19 inclusive

Second Lesson: 1 Thessalonians 5:1-11
Theme: Children Of Light

Call To Worship

Leader: Brothers and sisters, do you dwell in darkness?
People: No, we are children of light.
Leader: As children of light what is your task?
People: To encourage one another and build each other up.
Leader: Come, then, let us worship together as children of the day, awaiting the coming of the Lord into our hearts.

Invocation

Our Father, may we experience today a brush with eternity. Raise us above the mundane and the commonplace. Stir up visions in our minds. Plant noble desires in our hearts, and inspire great hopes in our souls; through Jesus Christ our Lord. Amen.

Confession

Lord, we know that we should love one another and strive to build each other up, but we find it easier to be critical and to find fault. Help us not to be passive bystanders waiting for the coming of your kingdom, but active participants in your work here on earth. To that end renew our determination to show forth your love in all our relationships. Amen.

Offertory Prayer

O Lord, we present these gifts as an expression of our love for you and for our neighbors near and far. Amen.

Hymns

"O Day Of God, Draw Nigh"
"I Know Whom I Have Believed"
"There's Within My Heart A Melody"

Proper 28
Sunday between November 13 and November 19 inclusive

Gospel Lesson: Matthew 25:14-30
Theme: Trustworthy Stewards

Call To Worship
God has given each of us talents to be invested in the building of his kingdom on earth. As we gather to give thanks and praise to God, let us also ask ourselves if we have been trustworthy stewards of that which God has given us.

Invocation
O Lord, as we gather here, we are aware of how exceptionally blessed we are, and how fortunate we are to be entrusted with your Word and your world. It is our prayer that during this time of worship we may become increasingly aware that our ownership is neither absolute nor eternal, and that we must some day give to you a full account of what we have done with what you have given us. Amen.

Confession
Lord, often when we are called upon to invest ourselves in the life of your Church, or in our community, yes, and in our homes too, we make excuses: we don't have time, we're not good enough, we don't know how. Help us in this time of worship to learn from the parable of the talents that, whatever our gifts, we are to invest them faithfully in the building of your kingdom. Amen.

Offertory Prayer
O God, our Father, as we present these gifts we remember that we are responsible for all that we do, all that we are, and for all that we have. Amen.

Hymns
"What Does The Lord Require?"
"Must Jesus Bear The Cross Alone?"
"A Charge To Keep I Have"

Proper 28
Sunday between November 13 and November 19 inclusive

Psalter: Psalm 76

Words Of Assurance
The Lord is gracious and merciful, slow to anger and abounding in steadfast love. Amen.

Pastoral Prayer
O Lord, our God, who judges all things, and whose love is like a consuming fire, may our approach to you ever be filled with awe and wonder. May our hearts hunger and thirst toward a holiness and justice which is angered by all that would threaten, demean, or diminish your creation. Your fierce love has shown forth to us in Jesus Christ. Transform us daily to be like him. Give us love enough to speak the truth, and concern enough not to be conformed to the world to which we are called to be agents of change.

We come before you asking you to release our tight hold on our own lives that we might be held by you. Enter our lives with your Spirit. Where our defenses are hardened, break us. Shatter the false gods we have placed before you, exposing them as the lifeless, helpless idols they are. Destroy our anxiety over career and family. Release our grasp on things; and work the hardest work of all: open our hold on ourselves that we might no longer be constricted by our pettiness, but might be available to your will and filled by your overwhelming Presence.

We pray for the mind of Jesus. May our judgments be like his. May we live in his passions, prayers, and loves. We pray for the privilege of being ambassadors for Christ and bridges to a wounded world. Never let us forget the wounds we carry, nor the imperfections with which we speak. Give us compassion for the needy, and indignation where justice does not prevail. May we be links in the chain which binds men and women to your love. All this we pray in Jesus' name. Amen.

Benediction
May the comfort of God's presence, the instruction of his Word, and the power of his Spirit, be with you all your days. In the name of the Father, and the Son, and of the Holy Spirit. Amen.

Proper 29 (Christ The King)
Sunday between November 20 and November 26 inclusive

First Lesson: Ezekiel 34:11-16, 20-24
Theme: The Good Shepherd

Call To Worship
Our God is a Good Shepherd. Our King is a loving Shepherd. Our Ruler is a caring Shepherd. Come, let us worship the Good Shepherd, Christ the King!

Invocation
We need to be reminded, Lord, that there is a power on earth higher than ourselves, that there is a plan which is greater than our intentions for tomorrow, and that there is a future which none of us can predict.

So it is good for us to stand in the midst of mystery, to sense the awesome power of your presence, and to acknowledge your authority in our lives. Amen.

Confession
Merciful God, all we like sheep have gone astray, but we thank you for the assurance of your love and the promise of your Word that as our Good Shepherd you will seek us out and bring back to your green pastures those who have strayed. Amen.

Offertory Prayer
Lord, take all that we have, take all that we are, take all that we hope to become, and consecrate them to the glory of your name, the fulfillment of your purpose in life, and the healing of our world. Amen.

Hymns
"The King Of Love, My Shepherd Is"
"Rejoice, Ye Pure In Heart"
"Where He Leads Me"

Proper 29 (Christ The King)
Sunday between November 20 and November 26 inclusive

Second Lesson: Ephesians 1:15-23
Theme: Spirit Of Wisdom

Call To Worship
It is good for us, from time to time, to lift our eyes from the confusion and despair of our world, to catch a glimpse of the glory of God, to acknowledge the kingship of Jesus Christ, to stand in awe before the might of his power, and to feel the stirring of his Spirit within us. Come, let us worship our God and King!

Invocation
O God, our Father, we pray for a spirit of wisdom that our hearts may be enlightened and through the eyes of faith we will recognize Christ our Savior as Christ our King who, with God and the Holy Spirit, has put all things under his feet, and established his Church as his body to carry out his work on earth. Amen.

Confession
Gracious God, as we struggle with all the problems with which life confronts us, when we call upon you for help we are surprised by your power and your greatness. As we come to know you better day by day reveal to us the greatness of Christ's power, and the hope that is ours in his reign. Amen.

Offertory Prayer
O Christ, our King, receive this offering as an expression of our honor and praise, and for the strengthening of your sovereign rule on earth. Amen.

Hymns
"Praise My Soul, The King Of Heaven"
"Crown Him With Many Crowns"
"Rejoice, The Lord Is King"

Proper 29 (Christ The King)
Sunday between November 20 and November 26 inclusive

Gospel Lesson: Matthew 25:31-46
Theme: Ministering To The King

Call To Worship
Leader: I will extol you my God and King;
People: and bless your name for ever and ever!
Leader: Great is the Lord, and greatly to be praised;
People: and God's greatness is unsearchable!

Invocation
Lord, we come to praise you as our God and King. In this time of worship open our hearts and minds to the ways in which you present yourself to us as those who need to be ministered to. May our praise not be with our lips alone, but in the response we give to those who need our love and care. Amen.

Confession
The outstretched hand, the cry for help, the lonely look of desperation, and we are tempted to turn aside and look the other way. You, O Lord, are our King and Savior, and you have taught us that when we minister to the needs of those around us we are in truth ministering unto you. Sharpen our keenness of vision, that we might see you in these strangers that cross our paths, and responding to their needs we may know that we have indeed seen the Lord. Amen.

Offertory Prayer
Gracious God, we present these gifts that they may be used by you through your Church to feed the hungry, visit those in prison, clothe the naked, and make your love and concern known to all those in need. Amen.

Hymns
"Sing Praise To God Who Reigns Above"
"Jesus Shall Reign"
"Rejoice, The Lord Is King"

Proper 29 (Christ The King)
Sunday between November 20 and November 26 inclusive

Psalter: Psalm 100

Words Of Assurance

God is faithful and has called us into fellowship with his Son, Jesus Christ. Amen.

Pastoral Prayer

Almighty God, our Creator and Sustainer, when we consider the glories of all your creation, we stand in awe and wonder. It is difficult to grasp the full meaning of our having been created in your image, and yet through your Son, Jesus Christ, we have come to know you as Father, and to accept our loving welcome into your family. We give you thanks for having sent us the Good Shepherd to guide us along our path. We know the way, but so often we stray as we neglect the hungry, the naked, the sick and imprisoned.

Send your Holy Spirit upon us that we may be found worthy of your kingdom and that we might help care for all your sheep, not for our own good, but as our way of giving thanks and the glory you are due. We pray in the name and in the spirit of Jesus Christ, our Lord. Amen.

Benediction

Receive the blessing of God and go forth in peace, knowing that you have been chosen by God for faithful service in this life and for eternal joy in the life to come; and the blessing of God the Father, the Son, and the Holy Spirit be upon you. Amen.

Pentecost 27 (Lutheran)

First Lesson: Jeremiah 26:1-6
Theme: Listen To The Lord: Speak For The Lord

Call To Worship
As we wait with anticipation for the visit or a letter from a friend, for the voice of a loved one on the phone, for the breaking of day after a dark and lonely night, so let us wait for the Lord, straining to hear the sound of his voice, eager to feel the stirrings of the Spirit, and longing to experience the joy of his presence.

Invocation
O Eternal God, who by your grace in Christ Jesus has made us citizens of heaven, grant to us the light and power of your Holy Spirit, that we may clearly see and willingly accept our responsibilities as citizens of heaven here on earth. We know that you often send unlikely messengers to unusual places to carry your message to turn from sin to your ways. Help us to be open to your call, and send us where you will to witness to your love. Amen.

Confession
Lord, we expect people to listen when we proclaim your will by word and deed, and we feel defeated and frustrated when they don't. Help us to hear your message to Jeremiah when you said: "It may be that they will listen." Grant us that kind of understanding and patience as we go forth in your name. Amen.

Offertory Prayer
Lord, to build your Church, to proclaim your love, and to nurture your people, we present these offerings. Amen.

Hymns
"Near To The Heart Of God"
"If Thou But Suffer God To Guide Thee"
"Go Forth For God"

Pentecost 27 (Lutheran)

Second Lesson: 1 Thessalonians 3:7-13
Theme: Stand Firm In The Faith

Call To Worship

God is here! Let us celebrate his presence. With God's help we can make our whole life a celebration.

God is here! Let us pledge our love to him. In love, let us give our lives to him, to do with as he pleases.

Invocation

Almighty God, our Heavenly Father: receive us in this hour as we offer ourselves anew to you in body, soul, and spirit. Let not this time of worship pass except it leaves its benediction with us. Give to us the peace which passes all understanding. Speak to us your Truth, that we may glorify you; through Jesus Christ our Lord. Amen.

Confession

Lord, we thank you for the faith of our parents, our forefathers and mothers, and all those who in days gone by have stood firm in their beliefs. We would be just as loyal, but times are different and we don't seem to be as successful in passing on our faith to the next generation. Strengthen us, O God, that by word and deed we may make known your saving grace and the power of your love. Amen.

Offertory Prayer

Father, you have been most generous in your care for us. Receive these gifts, we pray, as tangible expressions of our gratitude, and use them for the upbuilding of your kingdom. Amen.

Hymns

"Faith Of Our Fathers"
"Stand Up, Stand Up For Jesus"
"A Charge To Keep I Have"

Pentecost 27 (Lutheran)

Gospel Lesson: Matthew 24:1-14
Theme: Endurance

Call To Worship

Our soul waits for the Lord; yea our heart is glad in him, because we trust in his holy name.

Come, let us give thanks to the God of our salvation, and sing praises to his name.

Invocation

Lord, we are always seeking quick answers and clear instructions about our place in your kingdom. Make us aware of false prophets who would lead us astray. In this lawless world keep us faithful to your Word, and keep our love from growing cold. Amen.

Confession

Heavenly Father, it is so easy to forget about you in daily life, and to disregard the spiritual dimensions of our being. Forgive us for our failures, we pray, and help us in this time of worship to touch base with heaven, to see time in the perspective of eternity, and to see our finiteness in relation to your infinity. Draw near to each one gathered here, we pray in Jesus' name. Amen.

Offertory Prayer

O Lord, we humbly ask that these gifts may be used effectively in your service so that the world's pain may be eased a little; through Jesus Christ our Lord. Amen.

Hymns

"O God, Our Help In Ages Past"
"I Need Thee Every Hour"
"O Jesus, I Have Promised"

Pentecost 27 (Lutheran)

Psalter: Psalm 78:1-4, 9-20, 32b-38a

Words Of Assurance
Jesus said: "As the Father has loved me, so have I loved you; abide in my love."

Pastoral Prayer
O God, our Father in heaven, we give you thanks for this opportunity to come together in this holy place, as Christian people, and to draw near to you in spirit and in truth. We thank you for Jesus Christ, your Son, our Lord, the one who has shown us that you are indeed the God of great love and compassion. We thank you for him who is our way to you, who gives us life that is abundant and beyond death, who is the truth that frees us from that which is false and hateful and unloving.

Our Father, we are different in so many ways. We are all individuals, with our own particular backgrounds and our own peculiar needs. Yet Father, we recognize how much alike we are in so many ways. We know that we are all sinners; that we have fallen short of the mark you have set for us; that we have been selfish, proud, lazy, and disobedient. We have been fearful with despair when we should have rejoiced in the still, small voice that comes from you to those who will listen with their whole hearts.

We are all alike in our great need of you: we need to know of your love for us, the love of the Father for his wayward children. We need your forgiveness; we need your companionship and strength as we walk and travel through this earthly life. We need you, O God, to give us purpose, to give us direction, to take us out of our confusion, to make some deep sense out of our days, to give us understanding and hope, even in times of trouble and sorrow and death. And, O God, we are all so much alike because we need each other in so many ways.

O Lord, we pray this day that truly you will so cleanse us and so abide with us that we may indeed be, in your sight, a glorious church. May it never be rightly said of us that we are an indifferent, complaining, divided, or hypocritical people. May it be, instead, that with humility and determination we shall all work together to walk in the footsteps of our Master, giving unto you all the glory, all the praise, all the honor; through Jesus Christ our Lord. Amen.

Benediction

Rejoice always, for you are God's own people. May your lives daily be filled with his grace, mercy, and peace. The blessing of God the Father, Son, and Holy Spirit go with you. Amen.

Reformation Sunday

First Lesson: Jeremiah 31:31-34
Theme: A New Covenant

Call To Worship
While our God never changes, our world does. God may be the same today, yesterday, and forever, but we are called to confront new challenges. Today, as we come to worship, we also come to celebrate the Reformation of the Church of Jesus Christ our Lord.

Invocation
Almighty God, we pray for your holy Church. Where it is in error, put your law within it; where it is in need of change, reform it; where it is divided, show it the way to unity. Renew in us all a great desire for the coming of your kingdom. We pray in the name of Jesus Christ our Lord. Amen.

Confession
O Lord, as part of the Church of Jesus Christ we know that we are the body of Christ to carry on his ministry here on earth. We know, too, that for a body to function properly all parts must work together. Send your Holy Spirit upon us that we may reach out in Christian love to all parts of the Body of Christ, that together we may work in unity for the coming of your kingdom. Amen.

Offertory Prayer
O Lord, we give these gifts to you in thanksgiving for all you give to us. May the gifts be made holy and used to serve you as you would desire. In Christ's name. Amen.

Hymns
"A Mighty Fortress Is Our God"
"Many Gifts, One Spirit"
"The Church's One Foundation"

Reformation Sunday

Second Lesson: Romans 3:19-28
Theme: Justified By Faith

Call To Worship
We cannot buy God's love. We cannot win God's favor by our good deeds. God's grace is a gift freely given to all who have faith in Jesus Christ. Come, let us worship the God of our salvation.

Invocation
Lord, we are the ones who need reformation. Without love our worship is a mere formality, and so we come to you seeking the confidence of your abiding love as an example of how we should live. Strengthen our faith, we pray, for we know that it is only through faith that we shall be able to reach out and accept the gift of your salvation. Amen.

Confession
Yes, all have sinned, O God, and that includes us. We have fallen short of what you would have us to be and do. We have truly failed in living the Christian life. Thanks be to you, O God, for the gift of your Son, Jesus Christ, through whom we are given another chance, a new life, a new beginning. Praise be to you, O God. Amen.

Offertory Prayer
Lord, we know that money cannot buy your love, but we bring these gifts as an expression of our love for you, and for our neighbors around the world. Amen.

Hymns
"There Is A Balm In Gilead"
"All My Hope Is Firmly Grounded"
"Savior, Like A Shepherd Lead Us"

Reformation Sunday

Gospel Lesson: John 8:31-36
Theme: True Disciples

Call To Worship

Jesus has promised that if we remain faithful to his Word we will truly be his disciples, and we will know the Truth, and the Truth will make us free.

Come, let us worship our liberating God made known to us in Jesus Christ.

Invocation

Lord, we prize our freedom, and often boast that we are free to do as we please. In this time of worship help us to see that such freedom makes us slaves of sin. Lead us to the true freedom found in Jesus Christ, which will make us part of your family. Amen.

Confession

We have not been true to our discipleship, Lord, and by our own strength we find it impossible to be faithful witnesses of Christ to our world. Come to us in our weakness, renew in us the vision of your kingdom on earth as it is in heaven, and by your Holy Spirit make it possible for us to be true disciples of Jesus Christ our Lord and Savior. Amen.

Offertory Prayer

Heavenly Father, use these gifts, we pray, to give sight to the blind, food to the hungry, education to the deprived, and the Word of promise and hope to those who are without Christ. Amen.

Hymns

"We Shall Overcome"
"I Know Whom I Have Believed"
"God Of Grace And God Of Glory"

Reformation Sunday

Psalter: Psalm 124

Words Of Assurance

Now hear the Good News: Christ Jesus comes into this world to save sinners. That means he forgives our failures, he loves us as we are, and he offers us the freedom to live in him. Amen.

Pastoral Prayer

Infinite God, our Father, we thank you that, in an age so filled with anxieties, fears, and mistrust, we may witness to those eternal truths that are central to our Protestant heritage and faith. We express our thankfulness for the traditions and deeper meanings at the heart of the Reformation, and for the freedom that makes it possible for us to give expression to them.

Teach us to love one another. May we see the good in every person. We know that in your sight there are no racial differences and that every person of every race is a beloved child of yours. Forgive us for the barriers we have erected that separate us one from another. Bring us closer together in unity, understanding, and love. Then, our Father, may we be forgiven for the hurts we have inflicted on others, as we forgive the hurts that have been ours.

Bless us, our Father, as we witness to the faith that is in us, a faith that sets us free as it binds us to you. Accept our Protestant witness growing out of a biblical faith related to you, to Christ, and to our brothers and sisters. Send us forth from the worship of this day committed to serve you more fully, as Christian workers, functioning effectively in the life of our church, community, and world. We ask this in the spirit of Jesus Christ, our Lord. Amen.

Benediction

Those who obey God's Word will be truly free, and will be blessed in all they do. Go in peace, and the blessing of God the Father, Son, and Holy Spirit go with you. Amen.

All Saints' Sunday

First Lesson: Revelation 7:9-17
Theme: Salvation

Call To Worship

Today as we gather to give thanks and praise to Almighty God we especially lift our voices and praise in thanksgiving for all those who have gone before us to be at home with our Heavenly Father. Come, let us worship and join with others around the world in giving blessing and glory, thanksgiving and honor to our God, forever and ever.

Invocation

O God, as we gather here to worship we are aware of being surrounded by a great cloud of witnesses, those who have gone before: heroes of the faith, martyrs for the cause, keepers of the Book. May we be worthy, Lord, to walk in their steps, and may we carry forward the cause they have so nobly advanced. Amen.

Confession

Lord, as we lift our prayers of thanksgiving for all the saints who have gone before us, we are often negligent in thanking you for all the saints that surround our daily lives and help us in so many ways. Thanks be to you, O God, for all the saints! Amen.

Offertory Prayer

O Lord, we place before you the sign of our faith, the fruits of our labor, the evidence of our devotion, and the witness of our commitment. Amen.

Hymns

"How Great Thou Art"
"Ye Servants Of God"
"Come, Let Us Join Our Friends Above"

All Saints' Sunday

Second Lesson: 1 John 3:1-3
Theme: Children Of God

Call To Worship
With the Word as our illumination, with the Spirit as our inspiration, with the Savior as our redemption, and with the Saints as our example, we gather in confidence to worship the Lord our God.

Invocation
Our Heavenly Father, we, your children, gather to give thanks for your loving care. We praise you for the great heritage which is ours, left for us by all your children who have gone before us and now abide with you in eternity. We glorify your holy name for the assurance that we are surrounded by this great host, and we lift our voices with them in praise to you. Amen.

Confession
Heavenly Father, as we journey along life's way keep us ever mindful of all your other children that surround us: the saints on earth as well as the saints in heaven. Where we can minister to them, open our eyes to the opportunity, and grant us the warm heart to respond. Amen.

Offertory Prayer
Lord, as we remember those who have gone before — those who sacrificed so we could hear the Word of life, those who gave their resources so we could have a house of worship, those who gave of themselves so we could receive Christ — we present these gifts of thanksgiving and praise. Amen.

Hymns
"Lord, I Want To Be A Christian"
"For All The Saints"
"Children Of The Heavenly Father"

All Saints' Sunday

Gospel Lesson: Matthew 5:1-12
Theme: The Cost Of Blessings

Call To Worship

We come together as a community of faith to rejoice in a love beyond comparison. We come to remember all those who have died in the faith and give thanks for the examples of Christian living they set for us. Come, let us worship!

Invocation

O Lord, our God, loosen our tongues to praise, unclog our ears to hear, clear our minds to understand, inspire our wills to follow, and cleanse our hearts to worship, so this hour may be a holy time and a life-changing experience. Amen.

Confession

Lord, we come to you seeking your blessing, and yet we fail to live up to the admonitions set forth in your Word. Forgive our shortcomings, we pray, and by your Holy Spirit enable us to do your will that we too might be counted among the Saints whom we honor today. Amen.

Offertory Prayer

We present to you, O God, our offerings as we rededicate our lives to you. Help us to serve you faithfully in this life so that we may praise you joyfully in the life to come. Amen.

Hymns

"I Sing A Song Of The Saints Of God"
"Shall We Gather At The River"
"For All The Saints"
"Faith Of Our Fathers"

All Saints' Sunday

Psalter: Psalm 34

Words Of Assurance

Jesus said: "I am the resurrection and the life; he who believes in me, though he were to die, yet shall he live, and whosoever lives and believes in me shall never die."

Pastoral Prayer

Almighty God, our Heavenly Father, we thank you for all who have lived to honor you and now enjoy the ineffable bliss of your eternal home. All about us are evidences of their devotion to you and to us who tarry yet a while. They confessed their faith in you — and you helped them to build enduring shrines and temples for worship of you. They confessed their faith in you — and you were their one true light as they fought the powers of darkness. They confessed their faith in you — and you empowered them to watch and pray and count their gain but loss.

We pray, O God, that you will bestow upon us the faith of your saints. If we have failed to attribute our blessings to you, forgive us. If we have not worshiped you aright, forgive us. If we have not confessed you before the world, forgive us. Turn us to you, O God, and let us see your radiant self. Suffer us to follow in the footsteps of these your saints, that we may wear with them the victor's crown of gold.

Open our eyes that we may see your glorious kingdom. Because we trust in you may our arms be strong and our hearts be brave. May we hear the distant triumph song and know that the end of sorrow shall be near your throne. Let our awareness of the communion of saints, both living and departed, strengthen our faith and inspire us to more faithful Christ-like living. We pray in Jesus' name. Amen.

Benediction

Since we are surrounded by so great a cloud of witnesses, let us run with patience the race that is set before us, looking unto Jesus, the author and finisher of our faith; and the blessing of God, Creator, Redeemer, and Sustainer be with you. Amen.

Day Of Thanksgiving

First Lesson: Deuteronomy 8:7-18
Theme: Thanksgiving

Call To Worship

Leader: Come, let us sing for joy to the Lord.

People: For the Lord is the great God, the great King above all gods.

Leader: Come, let us bow down in worship, let us kneel before the Lord our Maker.

People: For he is our God and we are the people of his pasture, the flock under his care.

Invocation

God of seedtime and harvest, summer and winter, light and darkness, we are grateful that in the cycles of your mercy you have again brought us to this time of Thanksgiving. Accept now our praise for the continuing evidence of your power and love.

In the abundance of your countless gifts give us your grace to fill others' lives with love, that we may more nearly be worthy of all you have given us. We ask it in the name of Jesus, our Savior. Amen.

Confession

Gracious God, we humbly seek your forgiving mercy, for despite the warnings your Word has given to your children we have been guilty of exalting ourselves, of claiming that we have gotten so many things by our own power and might. Yes, in our prosperity we have often forgotten that it is you, O Lord, who gives us power and strength and wisdom. Cleanse our hearts of all unworthy thoughts that we may truly give you thanks and praise. Amen.

Offertory Prayer

Blessed are you, O God, Creator and Redeemer of the whole world. From you we receive the gifts of life, and by your grace we have gifts to offer you. Accept our offerings and our lives in praise and thanksgiving, through Jesus Christ our Lord. Amen.

Hymns

"All Things Bright And Beautiful"
"Joyful, Joyful, We Adore Thee"
"Now Thank We All Our God"

Day Of Thanksgiving

Second Lesson: 2 Corinthians 9:6-15
Theme: Thanks-By-Giving

Call To Worship

We come today to rejoice in the many blessings God has given us. We come to give thanks for the abundance of God's blessings bestowed upon us. We come to remember that out of our abundance we are to share joyously and generously, that Christ's work may be carried out here on earth.

Invocation

Lord, help us to realize that there is no "Thanks-taking" day or "Thanks-getting" day. "Thanks-giving" is the tune of angels, and if we forget the language of Thanksgiving we will never be on speaking terms with happiness. Thanks-giving isn't meant for just one day, but for always; and so we give you thanks for all your blessings today, tomorrow, and forever. Bless us, we pray, so that as we have received so may we give. Amen.

Confession

Lord, we have been quick to thank you for your many blessings, but we have been slow in remembering that you have provided in abundance in order that we might share abundantly in every good work. Quicken our concern for others, and enable us to share joyfully in the work of your kingdom. Amen.

Offertory Prayer

Gracious God, you have poured upon us every blessing imaginable, and more. Put your Spirit in our hearts, that this offering may be a sign of our new life in Christ. Guide and transform what we offer, that our gifts may bring abundant blessings to others. Amen.

Hymns

"Come, Ye Thankful People, Come"
"Praise To The Lord, The Almighty"
"Forth In Thy Name, O Lord"

Day Of Thanksgiving

Gospel Lesson: Luke 17:11-19
Theme: Gratitude

Call To Worship

Leader: Make a joyful noise to the Lord!
People: Come into his presence with singing!
Leader: Enter his gates with thanksgiving!
People: Give thanks to him, bless his name!
Leader: For the Lord is good; his steadfast love endures forever.
People: And his faithfulness to all generations.

Invocation

Most Gracious God, by whose appointment the seasons come and go, and who makes the fruits of the earth to provide for the needs of your children: we offer you our thanksgiving that you have brought us through the circuit of another year, and that according to your promise seedtime and harvest have not failed. Remembering your bounty we offer you the sacrifice of our thanksgiving, and pray that you will feed our souls with the Bread of Life; through Jesus Christ our Lord. Amen.

Confession

Almighty God, you know how many of us receive your blessings, and how few of us give you thanks and praise. Forgive us, Lord, and make our hearts more sensitive to your bountiful mercies. Especially when you bless us through the ministries of others, help us to be more grateful, more thankful. In Jesus' name we pray. Amen.

Offertory Prayer

O Lord Christ, who taught that it is more blessed to give than to receive, and whose personal example was one of self-denial and sacrifice, inspire us to be generous and loving, seeking the welfare of others for your sake. In that spirit accept these gifts we pray. Amen.

Hymns

"We Gather Together"
"Now Thank We All Our God"
"For The Beauty Of The Earth"

Day Of Thanksgiving

Psalter: Psalm 65

Words Of Assurance

Have confidence in the Lord, who can forgive your sins, restore your sense of values, and give you eternal life.

Pastoral Prayer

O Lord, our Heavenly Father, from whom comes every good and perfect gift, and under whose loving care we abide always, we bow before you as a fellowship of kindred minds to thank you now, our God, with hearts and hands and voices.

We praise you that you have surrounded us with your infinite goodness, that you have continually poured forth your benefits age after age, and that of your faithfulness there is no end.

For the beauty of the earth, and the bounty it produces for our physical needs, for the order and constancy of nature which brings day and night, summer and winter, seedtime and harvest — for all your gifts of mercy, we are thankful.

For the power of love that binds us together as families and inspires us to establish our homes, to clothe our children, and to provide food for their growth, and for the resources of mind and strength that enable us to do this, we give you hearty thanks.

For our work that calls us, for our country founded on your precepts of liberty and justice, for our schools that lift us above the plane of ignorance, and for the countless organizations whose purposes are for the welfare and happiness of humankind — these too have all come forth because of your love for us as your children — we express our profound thanks.

Above all, O God, we praise you for your Son, Jesus Christ, who lives within our hearts; for your Holy Spirit, who renews, comforts and inspires our souls; for your Word that reveals truth to our minds; and for your Church whose prophets, saints, martyrs and ministers have helped us remain steadfast in our faith. For all these channels through which our spiritual needs are met, we raise our voices in humble thanks.

God of the nations, you have blessed our land with prosperity, and power, and liberty. May our prosperity be an occasion for generosity; our power, an occasion for responsibility; and our liberty an occasion for self-discipline in holy exercises and good works. Open our ears to the warning that all good gifts turn to ashes when they are hoarded. Let our blessings bless the world by the grace that is in us. As we pray for our country we pray that minority groups may be fairly treated and that there will be peaceful interaction among all peoples in this great land of ours.

And now may the memory of your goodness fill our hearts with joy and gratitude, and may our lives be an acceptable expression of our thankfulness now and in all the days to come; we pray in the name and in the spirit of Christ our Lord. Amen.

Benediction

May each of your days be a Thanksgiving Day — empty of complaints, filled with gratitude, punctuated by acts of sharing, and characterized with a smile. Now may the blessing of God the Father, Son, and Holy Spirit go with you. Amen.